THE MAESTRO

The Life of
Arturo Toscanini

BY

HOWARD TAUBMAN

SIMON AND SCHUSTER
New York

CONTENTS

v

Contents

PART TWO

FOREWORD

This is not an authorized biography. I do not believe that Arturo Toscanini would ever give aid or comfort, let alone his official blessing, to any writer seeking to do the story of his life.

Some time ago he discovered that his son, Walter, was assembling all the available data about him—and certainly this was properly prudent behavior for a man who appreciated his father's character and achievements. The maestro took his son by the shoulders, looked gravely into his eyes, and said, "Walter, if you write my life after I'm gone, it will be the greatest sorrow of my life."

If this book is a sorrow to Mr. Toscanini, I regret it, but I do not apologize. His career has been forged in the public eye and ear, and it belongs not only to him but to all of us who have been nourished by his art and have admired what he has stood for as man and artist.

For more than twenty years I have listened to him make music, have gathered stories about him, written articles about him. In recent months I have made fresh and intensive investigations. I have talked to his friends, colleagues, and family. I have also had the inestimable privilege of meetings and conversations with him.

The legend of Arturo Toscanini will grow with the years. It is perhaps right that the facts should be set down now while they can be ascertained. The invaluable testimony of many who knew him in the early days of his career is gone *beyond recall, and it would take years to retrace the decades of his activity and to hear from all who are still around to bear personal witness to his labors. I am aware that fresh details about his personality and art will continue to turn up in many places of the world where he has worked, and there is the temptation to continue hunting for them.*

I am confident, however, that the design and color of the portrait will not be changed basically by new bits of information any more than his fundamental approach to his work as a musician has changed over the years. With the maestro in his eighties and with a conducting career of more than sixty years behind him, it is safe to say that the time is not premature for a full-length biography.

H. T.

PART ONE

1

Childhood

THERE WAS nothing in the home or background of Claudio Toscanini and his wife, born Paola Montani, to suggest that any of their children would become musicians. They were poor, working people, and their parents, grandparents, and great-grandparents had been working people, laboring in small Italian towns as artisans or in the fields as farmers. If there was an outstanding talent for music in either the Toscanini or Montani line, there is no record of it.

The birth of Arturo on March 25, 1867, was an occasion for celebration only in the Toscanini home and its small circle of relatives and friends in one of the humbler sections of the town of Parma. But celebrate they undoubtedly did, for Claudio was glad to have an excuse for a party. Perhaps he thought seriously for a moment of the responsibilities of being a father and the head of a family. When two daughters, Gina and Ada—the latter, now Ada Colla, is still alive and is in her late seventies—followed, Claudio probably had passing intervals of determination to be a good provider. But luxuries in his home were unknown and food was not abundant.

One can imagine that Claudio did not brood over making do. It was not his nature to brood. He was cheerful by temperament. He took things as they came, and if the problem was hard, he had a way of ignoring it. He had served with Garibaldi in his youth, with his hair worn long and with a red bandanna tied around his throat. When he sat with his cronies in a café over a glass of wine, he probably held forth about his part in the campaigns for Italian liberation.

Claudio Toscanini was a handsome man. His son has a miniature photograph of him that must have been taken in his prime. It shows a high forehead, lively eyes, a long, fine nose, thick eyebrows, a full mustache, and flowing locks. There is a distinct resemblance to the pictures of the maestro during his middle age, and when you look at the conductor's grandson, Walfredo, the similarity of the features to those of his great-grandfather is almost uncanny.

Service with Garibaldi, though it had stemmed from a patriotic impulse, had also been a lark for Claudio. He liked movement and variety, and he was fond of a good time. Even after he settled down to raise a family and to work at his trade as a tailor in the shop that was part of his narrow, two-story, pink stucco house in Parma, his blood yearned for adventure. When he worked at designing and stitching clothes, he did so with imagination, but he was not assiduous at his trade. The family tradition has it that he was constantly taking off on new ventures, that he would leave Parma for days at a time expecting to hit it rich with the latest project and would return disappointed but not crestfallen. There were always his friends and a few drinks to make him feel optimistic again. Since his manner was dashing and his speech gay, there apparently were also women whom he found it easy and satisfying to charm.

If the failure of his ventures and the poverty of his home did not dishearten Claudio for long at any time, his good cheer did not infect his wife. Paola Toscanini was evidently a woman of strong mind and stern purpose. At times she was harsh and bitter. It was she who held the family together, dominated it, and kept the little world of relatives and neighbors from looking too deeply into the tensions and hardships of the home.

Paola was a skilled seamstress, and she saw to it that whatever commissions her husband received got done. When she could, she kept him at his work, and when he found excuses to be gone, she did it herself. At the same time she took care of her home and her children, seeing to it that they were neat and clean and pious and unashamed of their humble way of life.

The Toscaninis were often on the ragged edge financially. Their staples of food were thick soups, which were more often than not the entire meal, and occasionally there were bread and cheese. The maestro recalls that he never saw meat on the family table as a child, and there were times when he went about hungry.

Paola, a small, sturdy woman with piercing eyes, long nose, and strong chin, was fiercely proud. She wanted no pity from her relatives, and she was determined that they should have no sign of her difficulties. Little Arturo, dressed in a pressed, cleaned, if threadbare suit, would go alone to visit them in another part of town, and his mother's instructions were that he must not tell them that he had not eaten. At his aunt's house once when he was six he was invited to eat and he declined sturdily, saying he had just had a meal. His aunt, who suspected the truth, kept prodding him, but the boy was firm in his refusal. The lad, small, dark-haired, handsome, and intense, sat on the edge of a chair and watched the table being set, and finally the smell of sausages heaped high on a plate became too much for him. He confessed that he was hungry and sat down to eat. When he returned home, his mother asked him whether he had eaten at his aunt's, and the serious little boy admitted that he had. His mother whipped him.

It would be idle to speculate now whether Paola's treatment of her little boy stemmed from a cold attitude toward him or from her own troubles. Undoubtedly her life was hard, and she worked endlessly on household and tailoring chores from dawn till late in the night. She did what she had to do for her children, but apparently she had no time to spare for the normal, little tendernesses and affections. The maestro, years later, remarked that he could scarcely remember being kissed by his mother.

The father, for all his gaiety and insouciance, seemed to behave under self-conscious restraint at home. Probably he was not much different from other working fathers of his place and generation, but he did not spend much time with his son. Since the boy began to show signs of formidable talent even before he reached his teens, the father seemed to shy away from him completely. Perhaps he was intimidated by his own son.

When Arturo was graduated from the Parma Conservatory at the age of eighteen, he assumed the role of head of the family almost automatically. Claudio apparently abdicated without any opposition a family position he had occupied only in appearance. The relationship of father and son, as it had developed while the boy grew up, may be gauged from an incident that occurred when Arturo was eighteen. He was sitting up late, studying a score by a weak light in the kitchen, when his father returned home from an evening with his cronies. The older man was tipsy, and the son reprimanded him. The father burst into tears.

But all was not gloomy in the Toscanini household. There were intervals when, if things did not go brilliantly for the family, there were warmth and rapport. There were times when father and mother sat together plying needle and thread, with their children near by to help as they might. The boy thought then that he would like to grow up a master of the craft of drawing the patterns on the cloth to be cut. Occasionally the father would read aloud to the family, and the children would listen intently to the adventures of Jean Valjean in *Les Misérables,* shedding a tear over his sorrows, or to the swashbuckling action of *The Count of Monte Cristo,* their eyes shining as bravery won the day.

Little Arturo developed a passionate taste for these yarns.

As soon as he was old enough to read, he tried to borrow books. He would wander down the dusty streets of Parma and hang around the newspaper kiosks, where the periodicals with the latest romances lay open on the counter. He would stand at the kiosk reading the open pages, and if the story continued on pages still uncut, he would burrow his head under the pages like a mole and continue with his reading. He must have been a nuisance to the vendors, and perhaps he was cuffed from time to time for his pains. He was not discouraged for long. He returned and managed to get through enough of each installment to be able to follow the trials and triumphs of his heroes. It may be that in this way he began the injury to his eyes that led to extreme myopia and that was to plague him all his days.

His fondness for the tales of high adventure was responsible for the only theft of his life. He pilfered two lire from his father and purchased one of the paper-bound romances. He remembers lying in his bed one night when his father came home. He heard his father charge angrily and dramatically that his own flesh and blood had robbed him. The boy shivered and said nothing. His parents never found out—or never let on that they knew—that he had been the culprit, but the maestro later spoke of this bit of petty larceny as though it lay heavily on his conscience.

Possibly the happiest moments for the lad occurred when there were little gatherings and celebrations in the home. His father and friends would sit in the kitchen, sipping a glass of wine and singing. They would sing folksongs and arias and choruses from the popular operas. They had learned these tunes during the seasons at the Parma theater, where they would sit in the gallery with napkins tucked into their collars while they munched a slice of bread and hummed along with the singers. In the Toscanini home Arturo stood in a corner near the stove and listened, his eyes shining.

He did not join in the singing. A child was brought up to

know his place among his elders. Possibly his voice, which had a hoarseness and cracked texture that has stayed with him through life, made him self-conscious. Even though there was no sign of illness, he seemed always to have a cough. For a time his family feared that he would come down with tuberculosis. The maestro recalls that when he met Giuseppe Verdi in the latter's old age, the venerable composer was solicitous about his cough, advising him to drink sugared water as a remedy. The sweetened water did not help, nor did the doctors he went to see, and in recent years he has chuckled over the fact that he has survived all the physicians who sought to cure the cough, which is still with him.

It is certain, in view of what happened later, that even as an infant Arturo must have been inordinately sensitive to music. If his parents had had the time or experience to observe him closely, they might have noted the signs. There was no musical instrument in the home, and there was no money for even a musical toy. There were, in fact, no toys except what the boy improvised with bits of wood and cloth he might find around the house.

I recall chatting with his son, Walter, in the maestro's presence some time ago, and Walter, telling of his own youth, observed that he had had only a lira and a half a week as an allowance and that he had been obliged to use considerable ingenuity to make it serve his minimum needs. After a while the maestro said in his husky voice, "You were lucky, Walter; I had nothing."

There were no pet animals in the small house in Parma, presumably because animals need feeding, too. To this day the maestro keeps aloof from cats and dogs and other animals, and if they approach him too closely he shoos them away.

The affection that the boy did not get and was not encouraged to show at home found a hesitant outlet now and then. He remembers that when he was about five and attending a kindergarten, he saw a lovely little girl and, on

8

impulse, he went and rested his head beside hers. A little later, he recalls, he was filled with a feeling of tenderness toward a little ballerina, and he went to her and kissed her. It may be added parenthetically that he never lost his eye for feminine beauty. As an intimate of his remarked recently, "What a lifetime of susceptibility! It began at five and is still going strong seventy-eight years later."

The parents, though they had no idea that Arturo had special gifts, were pleased that he was attentive and obedient and that he learned to read early and soon devoured books. The lad's teachers in the kindergarten and in the first grade of elementary school did not regard him as anything out of the ordinary. It is true that he shone at solfeggio, which was taught in Italy from the first grade, but no one thought much of that until he came under the scrutiny of Signora Vernoni, his teacher in the second grade. She noticed that he had an astonishing facility for memorizing poems after reading them once. He visited her house once and went immediately to the piano. Without having touched a keyboard before, he carefully picked out some of the tunes from the operas he had heard Claudio and his friends sing of a festive evening in the kitchen.

Signora Vernoni, a kind-hearted and responsive woman, encouraged the boy to come to her home again. She gave him some rudimentary instruction on the piano, but he was content merely to be allowed to sit before the instrument and to let his fingers trace out the tones that pleased him.

At the end of the school year, when Arturo was nine, Signora Vernoni visited his parents and recommended that they consider enrolling him in the Parma Conservatory. Not only did he seem suited for musical studies, she said, but there was the possibility of winning a scholarship, which would relieve the hard-pressed family of paying tuition fees. It turned out that all the scholarships for the coming semester had been allotted to students who had the support of important citizens of

Parma. The Toscaninis had no such connections, and they had to strain to meet the modest costs for the first two years of his attendance at the Conservatory. Thereafter, he won a free course of studies on his merits as a student.

Since Signora Vernoni's piano lessons were not sufficient preparation to permit Arturo's passing the entrance examinations, he studied for a short while with a man named Bonini, who was a tuba player and who had a passing acquaintance with the piano. It may be guessed that the lad's native instincts for music helped him to make speedier progress than Bonini could have expected.

At nine, Arturo went off to begin his serious studies to become a musician at the Parma Conservatory. From comments he has dropped in recent years, it may be assumed that he was not too unhappy to leave the parental home for the Conservatory, where he was to board. And it may be that his parents had less than profound regrets that he was going. The maestro's own children have suspected that his mother resented his success later in life, especially since her daughters did not achieve the kind of fulfillment and happiness she hoped for them. On the other hand, after Paola died a batch of yellowed, dated clippings reporting her son's successes were found among her belongings. Obviously she took some pride in his career, but she did not spoil him by telling him so. Toscanini's daughters have confided that they found their grandmother, when they visited her in her old age, to be a difficult and bitter woman. As he grows older, they say, he looks more and more as she did in her eighties. Like him now, she slept and ate little. Unlike him, she was querulous and full of complaints.

Whether the boy, Arturo, had formulated any thought in his own mind that his mother held some private resentment against him it is impossible to say. But it is a fact that several years ago he observed to a member of his family, "To this day I wonder whether my mother ever loved me."

2

Conservatory

FROM the early fall of 1876 until July 14, 1885—that is, from the age of nine to the age of eighteen—Arturo Toscanini was a student at the Royal School of Music in Parma. In these nine years of formal education he absorbed more—of music and other things—than most others would in almost twice that time. He was glad to be at the Conservatory. He was happy to be immersed in music. He had his share of troubles and frustrations, but his years at the Conservatory, it would seem, were not merely a time for study but a way of life.

When you see the word "conservatory," you think of a gracious institution devoted to the finer things. That is how such an institution in the middle of the twentieth century would look to us. But the Parma Conservatory three-quarters of a century ago, like schools of music in other parts of Italy and Europe at the time, was more like a military school. The students wore uniforms; they lived in plain quarters; they were expected to rise and turn in at a given hour, as you would in barracks. The school was surrounded by a stone wall, and the scholars—one is tempted to say the inmates, in the perspective of our own standards—were granted the privilege of being led through the town for a walk once every two weeks.

The regimen was almost monastic. The working day was hard and long, and the food was simple to the point of plainness. This was no hardship for Arturo. In fact, he fared better than he had at home, for the food was regular and dependable.

Fish was one of the standard items on the table, and it was served up in a lot of variants. Later on Toscanini had a violent distaste for fish in any form. His wife once served some *canapés* of fish without telling him their origin. He took a bite and spat it out. On very rare occasions he ate fish provided it were fixed not to have a fishy smell.

At the Conservatory there was meat once every week or two. Each student received coupons that were to be turned in for the meat ration. Young Toscanini had not learned the habit of eating meat as a child, and he found that he could do better than turn in his coupons for portions of meat. His fellow-students, who felt put upon with such scanty meat rations, were eager to lay their hands on additional coupons, and Arturo made a regular thing of selling his to the highest bidder. With the money he would buy scores he could not obtain in the school library; for scores he had an insatiable appetite.

Other boys might gripe about diet, discipline, and masters, but not Arturo. It may be that he found life at the Conservatory more congenial than at home. He certainly cared more for music than anything else he might be doing, and he worked with diligence and intensity.

Sunday was visiting day, and the courtyard and public rooms buzzed with the conversation of family and friends come to see the students. Apparently Arturo had visitors on very rare occasions. In later years he said that he could not remember a single visit from his mother. Outwardly he wore an appearance of indifference, but one can imagine that the sight of other happy reunions must have pained the boy.

There were extended summer holidays at the school, and, like the other students, he packed a few belongings and went home. But one summer he asked for permission to remain at the school. It was granted, and he stayed there, studying and practicing, virtually alone save for the concierge and one or two others of the maintenance staff.

The school, which had been founded by Marie-Louise, was

French in its orientation, although Italian masters gave the curriculum the color of their own tastes. Besides his studies in music, Arturo worked at history, literature, and mathematics. Except for mathematics he was outstanding in all his subjects. It gave him trouble and, as he said many decades later, he still had a weak head for it.

There was no instruction in foreign languages. On his own he began to pick up a smattering of French, just as later on he taught himself English and German. Before coming to the Metropolitan Opera in 1908, he saw to it that he knew English well, but when he got to the United States he was diffident about using it. He did not trust himself to address his associates in English until he returned to the United States in the twenties to conduct the New York Philharmonic Orchestra. However, he had learned long ago to read it fluently. When he was mastering German and English, he translated from one to the other; his daughter Wally has kept a translation into English that he made of Goethe's *Mignon*.

In music he studied solfeggio with Griffini for the first two years and then with Eraclio Cerbella, who became his chorus master later. In composition he worked under Giusto Dacci; and he was assigned the cello as his instrument under the tutelage of Severino Leandro Carini.

His preference even then was for the piano, but you did not choose your instrument at the Parma Conservatory in those days. You were told what to do and you did it—or else. Arturo did not care particularly for the cello. But since the alternative was not remaining at the Conservatory at all, he devoted himself to that instrument.

He was drawn irresistibly, however, to the piano. Whenever he got a chance, he would seek out an unused piano in a remote corner of the school and play on it as long as he dared. In this way he mastered the instrument on his own. If you ask those who have heard him play the piano a great deal whether he plays it exceptionally, they will reply that he plays it with character and assurance, not perhaps with the perfect marksmanship of a virtuoso but with the marvelous grasp of tempo and rhythm of a first-rate musician who knows his own mind musically.

It was not always safe for him to steal a few hours at the piano. Once he found an unoccupied piano cell, as the practice room might be called, and began to play. He was unaware that a conference of masters was being held in an adjoining room. The headmaster heard the sound of the piano; it interfered with his remarks. He sent someone to see who was playing. Arturo was discovered at his illicit activity. He was summoned into the conference chamber, and the headmaster bawled him out. He reminded Arturo that he had no business playing the piano, that the cello was his instrument and that it would not go well with him if he were caught sneaking time with the piano again.

The boy took the reprimand without a word, but he could not have been too contrite. Apparently he persisted in his efforts to play the piano when he could. In time the school officials bowed their heads to his tenacity, and when he was graduated from the Conservatory he won honors not only in cello and composition but also in piano.

In the course of his years at the Conservatory he was punished for becoming involved in another extracurricular musical activity, since all such activity was against the rigid rules. Some of his schoolfellows joined in a little orchestra which played secretly under Arturo's direction. When the transgressors were found out, they were penalized with the loss of some of the few privileges they had. One of the penalties was being put on a diet of bread and water.

Arturo addressed himself to his assignments with concentration and energy, and since his mind absorbed musical knowledge with remarkable speed, he was usually done with the fixed tasks way ahead of schedule. He used the free time to read through scores. He was probably the most frequent visitor in the Conservatory's library, borrowing its scores for private perusal. If his comrades had music he did not know, he borrowed it. And when library and friends did not have music he was interested in, he would save his centesimi until he had enough to acquire a desired piece.

He not only read through scores on his own but found time to copy and transcribe passages from operas, sonatas, and symphonies that appealed to him. He liked to make arrangements for the secret little orchestra he and his friends had.

His acceptance by his comrades in such a leading role was obviously an admission on their part that he was one of the most gifted students in the school. They had not taken to him so readily at the start. His assiduity as a student had marked him out as a grind, and they poked fun at him. They dubbed him "*il genietto* [the little genius]," which infuriated him.

There is a story of one occasion when the students played a program for parents and friends. Arturo was one of the performers on the cello. He was sulky to begin with about being shown off, and as he played he heard someone whisper the cursed nickname. When he finished, he dashed away. There were applause and shouts, "Bravo! Come out, Toscanini!" But the little porcupine was in hiding.

His schoolmates had another name for him which he recalls with amusement. His eyes today can take on a steely stare, and apparently they could even when he was young. I remember coming on him recently as he stood staring in this way, his back straight, one eyebrow arched. "You look formidable," I said.

"It is my Napoleon look," he replied with a smile. "They called me Napoleon at school."

He liked to study, except when he was playing the cello, standing up. "I was born standing up, and I worked that way at the Conservatory," he said to me. Then he went to a table and stood over it, scribbling with an imaginary pen. "That is how I did my work as a boy," he observed.

15

His progress with the cello was so marked that by the time he was thirteen he got a job playing in the orchestra of the Parma theater during the seasons of opera at Carnival time, which falls at the Easter period. Until his graduation from the Conservatory, he played regularly during the Parma season. His pay at first was a lira and a half a performance; at the end he was earning two lire a show. He remembers that he saved his earnings and had a sum of two hundred and fifty lire when he was eighteen. Probably he was mindful of the fact that he would need to help his family when he was through at school, and possibly he felt that he might not find work when he got out and did not wish to be a burden on his parents.

He played through about thirty different operas in the Parma theater during his student years and obtained the kind of familiarity with these pieces that you can get only by playing them before a live audience. He recalls that his first Parma theater opera was Meyerbeer's *L'Africaine* and the conductor was one of his teachers. The operas were mostly standard Italian repertory pieces, with which he was familiar from private study. But it was exciting to have a part in performing them, and it was even more exciting to work on an unfamiliar piece like a Halévy opera that is forgotten today. He was responsive to every impression.

He was more than a cellist in an orchestra. Once a first violinist stumbled through a passage, and Arturo helped out by playing it on the high positions of his cello. This infuriated the conductor, who reprimanded him. Probably the young musician could not resist making certain that the passage would go properly. He listened carefully to the singers and watched the conductors intently. He recalls that the brother of Luigi Mancinelli, who was one of Italy's leading conductors, was in charge for a time. "Not a bad opera conductor," he says. And he remembers that in 1883 Cleofonte Campanini made his formal debut as a conductor in the Parma Opera.

Campanini, whose elder brother, Italo, was a famous tenor and sang *Faust* at the opening of the new Metropolitan Opera House in that very year of 1883, was also a native of Parma. Seven years older than Toscanini, he was a student at the Parma Conservatory when Arturo arrived, and he conducted performances of the school orchestra in which young Toscanini played. Later on in New York these two were to be treated as rivals, since Campanini was the conductor at Oscar Hammerstein's competing Manhattan Opera House when Toscanini came to the Metropolitan.

Toscanini speaks objectively of Campanini's gifts as a conductor. Campanini was poorly trained as a musician; he had difficulty reading a full orchestral score and conducted from a piano score which had the necessary cues penciled in. But he had the thing needful for a conductor, Toscanini recalls. He could lead, and he could fire up an orchestra and a cast. It is a pity, Toscanini adds sadly, that he did not have all the technical equipment of a good musician, for he might have been an outstanding conductor.

With Campanini as conductor, Toscanini made his first appearance as a performer in a city other than Parma the year before his graduation. Playing in the Municipal Orchestra of the city of Parma, he took part in a series of concerts at Turin during an exposition.

For his composition classes, young Toscanini composed some music. These were an Andante in E-flat and a Scherzo in G minor, both for orchestra, which he himself conducted with the school orchestra. These pieces, and an Overture in G for orchestra, as well as two works for voice and piano—"Il Pescatore (Ballatella)" and "Pagina d'album"—were written between 1882 and 1885. They were never published, but they have been kept proudly in the archives of the Conservatory. Five other pieces were published by Giudici and Strada of Turin in 1884: "Berceuse," for piano; "Il Canto di Mignon," for voice and piano, with words by Antonio Ghislanzoni, who wrote the librettos for some sixty operas, the most notable one being *Aïda*; "Desolazione," for voice and piano; "Sono Gelosa," for voice and piano, with words by Rocco Pagliara; and "V'Amo," for voice and piano, set to a poem by Heine. Two pieces were published by Giovannina Lucca of Milan in 1884 — "Nevrosi," for voice and piano, with words by Pagliara, and "Autùnno (Foglio d'album)," for voice and piano, with words by Felice Cavallotti.

This composition output is listed for the record, not as an index of achievement. Toscanini does not discuss his own music, and if he did it would probably be as the effort of a well-meaning student. Whether the music shows talent, in fact, I do not know; I have not seen or heard it. In any case, Toscanini's standards are so exacting that he would be embarrassed to have any of the pieces at large. He has specifically forbidden their being made available now.

He thought well of his own music then, although his absorption in the works of so many great composers of the past was beginning to provide him with a sense of perspective. He has not told us how he felt when Mme. Borghi, in whose honor a performance of *Carmen* was being presented in Turin in March, 1889, with Toscanini conducting, stepped out on the stage during an intermission and sang his romanza, "Sono Gelosa." A local newspaper said that it was a graceful thing which he had written for her (he hadn't) and that both she and he were applauded. He probably felt thoroughly uncomfortable through the whole thing, including the applause. It is noteworthy that his music has had no other public performances so far as the records show.

The years at the Conservatory were a time of discovery and adventure in music for the avid young student. He became acquainted with a wealth of music through reading it, playing it on the piano or the cello, with the school orchestra and with chamber-music groups that the students formed among themselves. With the orchestra he read through scores of Cherubini, Paer, Rossini. As a member of a string quartet he played a great deal of Mendelssohn, and was fonder of his chamber music at the time than of Beethoven's. He discovered Wagner. When he was thirteen, he heard at a Parma concert the Overture to *Tannhäuser* for the first time. It bewildered him. His teacher brought him one of the cello parts and made him study it. Some of the passages were difficult for him.

In 1884, Parma was the first town to offer *Lohengrin* after its success in Bologna and its failure in Milan. Toscanini played in the orchestra, and was so moved that he wept. A few years later he jotted down some penciled notes recalling this experience. "I had then," he wrote, "the first true, great, sublime revelation of Wagner's genius. At the first rehearsal and from the very beginning the Prelude gave me magic supernatural impressions, with its divine harmonies, which revealed to me an entire new world, a world that no one dreamed existed, before it was discovered by the supernatural mind of Wagner."

It is worth repeating what a contemporary thought of him as a student. According to an article by Alfredo Segre in the *Musical Quarterly* of April, 1947, the proctor of the Conservatory, who was still living in Parma in 1930, provided the following description: "Toscanini was one of the most quiet students, very reserved, not very fond of amusements. He loved his art as an ardent lover. Very often he refused to go for the biweekly walk through the town and begged me to lock him up in his little room, where he would play and study for hours."

Time had undoubtedly mellowed the proctor's memory, or perhaps he chose to remember only what he thought were the good things. Toscanini himself has indicated that there were occasions when he was anything but a model student. The rebelliousness in his nature would come to the fore, and he would find himself embroiled in a scene.

One day, when he was seventeen, the students returned

from one of their regular visits to church, and were ordered to go to their rooms to practice. As he recalled it later, Toscanini had no idea of what got into him that day. Suddenly he felt that he was not in the mood to practice and did not wish to be ordered to do so. He said so, loudly and firmly. The school official was amazed. He threatened dire punishment, but nothing would move the young fellow. He was charged with an act of insubordination. The thing became a scandal. There were even suggestions that he would be expelled from school. In the end Arturo's father was summoned, and only after he had pleaded with the authorities did they consent to let the matter pass, provided there were no further demonstrations of temper.

Another time young Arturo took a stand that must have horrified his cello teacher, the good Professor Carini. It was a stand that cast a shadow of events to come. For several months Toscanini had studied and practiced a sonata by Boccherini, which was to be his examination piece at the end of the year. A couple of days before the examination, he decided that he did not understand the music sufficiently. He could play the notes all right, and he had tried hard to probe into their meaning. But what seemed to him to be the essence of the music, which he regarded as beautiful, escaped him. He calmly told his teacher that he could not play the Boccherini at the examination. The teacher protested that he was in peril of failing, since he had not prepared anything else. What was more, the teacher went on, he played the Boccherini well enough to get by. Toscanini was obdurate. He did not understand the music, he would not play it under any circumstances, he would rather be failed. What alternative had he to suggest, the bewildered teacher demanded. Well, Arturo said, he could play a certain concerto by a Russian composer that was all technique and that he felt comfortable with. But he hadn't practiced it in months, the teacher answered. He would have it prepared, the young fellow said. He kept his word; he passed the examination in fine shape.

By the time he was ready to be graduated, Toscanini had given his teachers reason to believe that they had had a determined character on their hands. It may be that some had respect rather than affection for him. Surely they admired his attainments. He was the best sight reader in the school, and he could play from memory more extensively and more accurately than any other student. When he received his diploma his rating was 160 out of a possible 160 in cello, 50 out of a possible 50 in piano, and 50 out of a possible 50 in composition.

Loaded with highest honors, Arturo Toscanini left the Conservatory. But it is likely that he did not go forth joyously. He knew that he had to work. He had to support himself and to help his family. He was as serious and determined as if he had swallowed every word of a grim baccalaureate sermon.

3

Start as a Conductor

IT HAS become one of the standard Toscanini myths that, with no preparation whatever, he became a conductor at the age of nineteen and that thereafter he remained a conductor all his life. It is true that he became a conductor at nineteen as a result of a crisis and that thereafter he spent most of his life conducting, but it is not true that there was no preparation. The myth has enough basis in fact to pass muster, but the truth is more impressive.

The truth is that in his work at the Parma Conservatory young Arturo had done a great deal to prepare himself for conducting. It is altogether likely that he did not envisage a career as a maestro so soon after graduation, and possibly there never entered his mind even the vagrant notion that he might turn out to be a conductor. But there is little doubt that his studies, fixed and extracurricular, were the essential preliminaries for such a future.

As we have seen, he was not content to learn the cello alone, and his attraction to the piano did not stem from any desire to be a pianist pure and simple. His passion was for music in all its manifestations. Instinctively and consciously he sought to go to the root of the matter. He studied scores in their totality. If it was a piano piece he was working on, it was not to master its technique but to learn the secrets of its structure and its heartbeat. If it was a quartet, he was not concerned with the cello alone but with all four instruments and with the composer's conception as a whole. If it was an orchestral piece, he made it his business to study the entire score, to analyze how it was put together and to imagine how it should sound. It is probable that he reflected on such matters as tempo, rhythm, and balance of the choirs. He had a natural tendency to think of music in the large, which is the mark not only of a conductor but of any true musician.

There was something else in his student days that heralded the conductor. Despite the fact that this grave, determined young fellow, with the slight figure that reached just over five feet, the cold, piercing blue-gray eyes, forbidding, bushy eyebrows, and dark, thick hair covering the large head, was sometimes a source of amusement to his fellows, they looked to him as a leader in matters musical. In a school that had a number of gifted students, he stood out for his zeal, intensity, and knowledge. When the boys had their discussions, they listened to him with respect, even if they teased him at times. When he conducted the school orchestra, they realized that he knew what he wanted and that he had prepared himself for the assignment with care and thoughtfulness. It is also likely that some of his contemporaries came to him for advice and coaching.

His accomplishments as a versatile and well-versed musician were known and appreciated when he left the Conservatory. If further evidence were needed, consider the first job he got. He was offered a post as cellist and assistant chorus master with a company recruited by the impresario Claudio Rossi for a season in São Paulo and Rio de Janeiro in Brazil. He was not treated like an ordinary instrumentalist, as the rank and file of an orchestra would be. In the course of the ocean trip to South America he was drafted to coach some of the singers of the company in their parts for several operas. While the repertory was familiar and standard, it was clear that this young man of nineteen knew it thoroughly. The singers with whom he worked saw immediately that he had a rare grasp of the operas and a capacity to teach.

The company that Rossi led to Brazil was not made up of beginners and unknowns. The principal singers were well established in Italy; they included Madina Bulicioff, soprano; Medea Mei, contralto; Nicola Figner, tenor; and Gaetano Roveri, bass. The conductor was Leopoldo Miguez, a native of Brazil. The assistant conductor was Carlo Superti, and the chorus master Aristide Venturi.

The company set out from Italy early in 1886. For Arturo it was not only his first trip away from Italy but his first any distance from Parma. As a student he did not have the means to venture far beyond the region of the Po, even though he had a strong compulsion to get out into the world to see and hear how other musicians did their work. Since he had been stirred by the greatness of Wagner, he must have had an urge to go to Bayreuth at a time when the *avant-garde* among Italian musicians—those who could afford it—began their pilgrimages to the theater that the composer founded. He must have known, too, that Wagner had visited in Italy before his death, and perhaps he had a wish to go to Venice in those months in 1882 when the titan was resting there. I have heard the maestro wish wistfully that he had been born earlier so that he might have had the opportunity to discuss with Wagner some of the things in his scores that he had studied and pondered over the years.

In any event, though the nineteen-year-old Toscanini worked aboard ship, the trip must have been a grand adventure as every trip he has taken since has been a source of excitement and exploration to him. The company went to São Paulo and gave performances for two months. They were evidently far from the best performances in the world. The singers found Miguez a difficult and inept conductor to work with, and they did not disguise their feelings. The morale of the troupe, when it reached Rio in June, was poor. After a performance of *Faust*, which got its critical lumps from the Rio press, with Miguez bearing the brunt of the censure, the conductor sent an open letter to the newspapers excoriating the singers. He declared that the singers were disloyal and uncooperative, that they were to blame for shoddy performances, and that he had decided not to conduct any further performances.

One can imagine what a tumult of discussion and wrangling such a public announcement would release today, and it was a sensation in Brazil then. Since Miguez was a home-town boy in Rio and the company was made up of foreigners, feeling ran high. At the next performance, which was scheduled for June 25th with *Aïda* as the opera, Superti entered the pit and mounted the podium to take over the direction. He was greeted by a volley of protests and invectives. The audience hissed, whistled, and shouted imprecations. Rossi emerged before the curtain in an effort to explain and to mollify the crowd. He was hooted off without being able to make himself heard.

The principal singers and members of the chorus, all from Italy, gathered around the impresario backstage, jabbering suggestions of how to get out of the dilemma. Some of the orchestra players slipped out of the pit to add their voices to the hubbub. Out in the audience the mob was still howling for blood. Someone proposed that Venturi should try to lead, and the chorus master agreed to try.

As Venturi emerged in the pit to make his way to the podium, a slight figure in an ill-fitting dress suit, carrying a cello, was trying to glide to his place without being caught by anyone in authority. It was Toscanini, who was in the theater that night only because of a last-minute change of mind. His original intention had been to stay away. Even then his spirit rebelled at being involved, however obscurely, in a situation that promised to be unpleasant, and when it came time to go to the theater he did not move. But even then he was also torn by a conflicting thought—that he had obligated himself to play with this company and that he ought to live up to his contract. As he hurried to the theater he was irked with himself. He was late, and he feared he would be fined, but he was much more irritated by the notion that he must play when he had no stomach for playing.

The uproar in the house covered his arrival. It also chilled him. As Venturi took his place and lifted his baton, the audience let the replacement have it more savagely than it had reacted to Superti. The theater rocked as though it had been attacked by a cyclone. The outburst of screams and imprecations did not subside until poor Venturi, shaking his head sadly, left the podium, and even then there was an angry buzzing in the auditorium. The crowd had had its second pound of flesh and was sitting back now waiting for the fun to develop.

Backstage there was another agitated conference. This time the group around the impresario was larger, with more of the orchestra players deserting their places to join in the discussion. A note of hysteria was spreading among the company. Some of the singers wept, and their make-up became streaked and ludicrous. Toscanini was backstage, and one can be sure that his gorge was rising, in anger not only at the demonstration out front but also at himself for having come to the theater at all. Perhaps he remembered that he had not yet collected his salary for the past week as some of the choristers wailed that this would be the end of the tour and that it would mean their being stranded in this barbaric country.

At this moment one of the singers glanced at Toscanini and shouted that he could save them, that he knew the entire opera by heart. The whole company rushed to him and formed a shouting, imploring, gesticulating knot around him. They begged him to try his luck. They told him that he was their last chance and they assured him, with more confidence than perhaps they felt, that he could do it.

Toscanini agreed to try. Being a fighter by nature, he took up the baton as one might a gauntlet. But he took it up in no spirit of foolhardiness. He was confident of his knowledge of *Aïda*, and he must have calculated deliberately, if with lightning speed, that he was equal to the job of getting through the performance.

The orchestra players resumed their places, and a nervous, frightened cast braced itself to try again. The short, slight youngster of nineteen, looking a little like a child playing at being a maestro in the dress suit that was some sizes too big for him, rushed out through the pit to the podium. The audience was beginning to make motions at leaving the theater, and it may be that the troublemakers were not quite on the alert for this latest cue to set up a furor.

Toscanini did not give them a chance to get started. As soon as he lifted his stick, he gave the first downbeat and the introduction to *Aïda* began to sound. Caught unawares, perhaps, the audience listened. Possibly the ringleaders of the agitation were tired. As they started to make things hum, they were shushed by those in the audience who had come to see and hear opera. The music, after all, sounded fresh and alive.

It is part of the myth of Toscanini's debut that when he came out to conduct that night he ostentatiously picked up the conductor's score, closed it, and sat on it. The foundation of truth for this tale is that Toscanini conducted from memory. He did not bother with the score because he did not need it. If he closed it, it was because it was in his way. Certainly he did not sit on it because he did not sit at all. He has never conducted even a rehearsal sitting down, and on this occasion he was so tense and concentrated that he would have sat only if he had had to manipulate the cello.

The orchestra played as though its life depended on it, and

27

perhaps it did. The singers did their share in the same way. There was desperation in the affair, and it brought out a wonderful unity of spirit. A conductor with less natural gifts might have risen to the occasion, but this young man brought something extra to the task. He conducted with a cool precision that merely controlled the fire of his feeling.

The evening was a triumph. From hisses and catcalls the audience turned to applause and bravos. According to Alfredo Segre, to whose meticulous research we are indebted for getting most of the facts of this momentous debut straightened out, the Rio journal, *Paiz*, wrote, "By unanimous request, Senhor A. Toscanini, first cellist of the orchestra, jumped onto the podium and conducted marvelously the entire opera *Aïda*."

Senhor A. Toscanini, while he was satisfied with a perilous situation averted, remembered that he had made two mistakes during the performance. In later years he confessed readily that he had made them, and added that whenever he conducted *Aïda* he came to these places with a shock of recognition and with a consciousness that he must be careful.

After the performance the young man slept harder and more soundly than at any other time in his life. He had learned as a student to make more time for his studies by sleeping less than most lads his age, and all through his life he found it hard to sleep long, and dull to waste the hours in this way. He recalls that even when he was a young man, working hard, he would resist sleep. If he was with friends, he would sit up late talking. Then he would cheat the night by walking his friends home; they, in turn, would walk him home; he would walk them home once more; and they would end by watching the dawn come up. But on this night he slept long and hard. When he awoke he could not believe that what had happened the previous night was real. The aching muscles in his tired arms and shoulders, however, told him that it was so.

If the event seemed unreal the morning after, it took on a

special vividness as the years went by. At the age of eighty-three, he once said that he felt that that first *Aïda* had taken place the day before, and he added that he could even remember the smell of the theater in Rio.

After that debut Senhor A. Toscanini was installed, willy-nilly, as conductor of the Rossi troupe. He did not expect to continue at the job; he thought he had filled in for the emergency. But the company wanted him, and so did the public. He conducted eighteen more operas in the course of that season in Brazil. They included such well-established favorites as *Il Trovatore, Rigoletto, La Gioconda, La Favorita,* and *Faust.* The season closed with a special performance of *Faust,* and the young conductor received a flock of gifts from his new Brazilian admirers. A local critic wrote that he became "definitely the conductor of the orchestra, because he has given complete proof of his ability, coolness, enthusiasm, and energy."

Having got through a series of operas as a conductor, young Toscanini might have been pardoned if he had decided then and there that his path was clear. However, he did not think of himself as a conductor but as a cellist who had stepped up temporarily. He did not ask Rossi for a new contract and a higher salary, to which he was entitled, and accepted his modest pay, fixed for his role as cellist, without argument. Many years later he recalled that he received his money in gold coins, which he carried in a pouch. He evidently felt the need to see his earnings in cash for a long time to come. After his first year at the Metropolitan Opera, he remembered, he returned to Italy in the spring of 1909 carrying his earnings as he had, at nineteen, from Brazil. His son Walter, then a lad of almost eleven, found the pouch one day, thought it an amusing toy, and had a delightful time playing with the gold coins.

When he returned to Italy in the early fall of 1886, Toscanini was not greeted with the acclaim of a conquering hero.

One paper in Parma had made brief mention of his successful debut; the rest was silence. It must be remembered, however, that in those days Italy sent out its touring opera companies as often and as regularly as it exported Chianti wine. Each went out as the private enterprise of an impresario, who was in the business for the profit in it. While the tours ended in losses as frequently as in profits—since many of these companies were of poor quality—they were regarded by the Italians as a business venture. Nowadays when an opera company travels abroad, it usually has the blessing of an arm of the government, and more attention is paid to its course and its luck.

Toscanini quietly went home to Parma. He shared his earnings with his family, resumed his acquaintanceship with some of the young fellows who had been at the Conservatory with him, and devoted himself to the study of music. He worked hard on the cello and waited for something to turn up. Hearing of an opportunity in Genoa, he moved there and took up the task of coaching a number of singers.

4

Debut in Italy

IF THERE was no *réclame* at home for the young chap who had
bailed out a traveling troupe in Brazil, the artists who had
watched him deliver in Rio spread news of his accomplishments by word of mouth when they got back to Italy. Nicola
Figner, the tenor of the company, put in an enthusiastic word
for him with Giovannina Lucca, a lady who functioned as a
music publisher in Milan. She had a hand in the preparation
of an opera, *Edmea,* by the thirty-two-year-old composer Alfredo Catalani, for performance at the Teatro Carignano in
Turin. Figner had been engaged to sing in this production.
When he heard that Catalani was not satisfied with the direction of Franco Faccio, one of Italy's best-known conductors,
who had directed the opera earlier that year at La Scala in
Milan, Figner recommended Toscanini.

That Catalani should be willing to entertain the idea of an
unknown nineteen-year-old as the conductor of his opera
was an eloquent indication of his open-mindedness. That he
should be dissatisfied with the way so eminent a maestro as
Faccio, principal conductor of La Scala, had handled his
opera proved the independence of his judgment. He was, in
fact, an extraordinarily alert, thoughtful, and sensitive man.
While we may be certain that Toscanini would have received
his opportunity to conduct in due time and that he would
have gone on to his tremendous career with or without Cata-

lani, there is no doubt that the composer had a lasting influence on the young musician.

Catalani, only thirteen years older than Toscanini, had been through the operatic mill. Before *Edmea* at La Scala, two earlier operas, *Elda* and *Dejanice*, had been produced in Turin and Milan. He was a man of principles and ideals. He had a loathing for the excrescences of taste perpetrated in the opera houses to satisfy the whims of box holders, impresarios, publishers, singers, rich gentlemen attracted to ballerinas, and self-important maestros. He could probably point to incidents that had marred the production of his own operas. His views and perspectives were broader than his own interests, however, and he had a vision of the lyric theater as an art. His ideas matched those of Toscanini and undoubtedly his attitude reinforced the younger man's.

Their first meeting occurred in a hotel room in Milan. Figner had written Toscanini suggesting that he come to Milan if he wanted a chance to conduct *Edmea*. Toscanini tried to get a copy of the score in Genoa but could not find one. When he was ushered into the hotel room by Figner in Milan, he saw the score of *Edmea* on the piano rack. He promptly began to read through the piece at sight. As he played he hardly noticed that the door had opened and a stranger had slipped in.

The newcomer stood and listened with interest. Then he spoke. "Did you study it before?" he asked.

"No," said Toscanini, "this is the first time I have seen it."

The stranger was Catalani. They went through *Edmea* together, and Catalani was taken by the young man's sincerity as well as by his musical perceptions. He advised Depanis, impresario of the Teatro Carignano, to engage the young man, and Toscanini applied himself to *Edmea* with a will. He studied the score intensively and in a short time knew it by heart. He worked privately with the singers and he spared no effort with the orchestra. Those in the company who had not seen him work in Brazil and who had reservations about the wisdom of hiring a conductor who was still comparatively a babe in arms—it was not until the next year that Toscanini grew the mustache which gave him a more passable appearance of maturity—became convinced that he knew what he was up to. And the performance, on November 4, 1886, went well.

Toscanini's Italian debut was hailed by a few discerning writers. The *Gazzetta Musicale* of Milan called it a triumph and declared that "a splendid dawn had risen on the horizon of art." It said that "the chorus was irreproachable, the orchestra exceptionally attentive and well prepared." It said that Toscanini had "conducted with the sureness and energy of an experienced maestro" and it pronounced him "a reflective, studious, and intelligent young man." The *Gazzetta* of Turin was astonished by his memory, since he had conducted without score. Another Turin journal, the *Gazzetta* of Piedmont, remarked that he had "a calm security," was communicative, and had poise, concentration, and an infallible memory, but added the reservation that in some passages there "was a bit of uncertainty and lack of equilibrium."

Catalani had no such reservations. He was delighted with the young man. After the performance he wrote a letter to a friend in which he said, "There is a young conductor here called Toscanini, who is nineteen years old. I believe he is going to have an extraordinary career." That letter is now in the possession of Frances Alda, the prima donna who sang with Toscanini at the Scala in Milan and at the Metropolitan in New York. It was presented to Toscanini and he, in turn, made a gift of it to Alda for her collection of letters from composers.

The friendship between Catalani and Toscanini lasted until the former's death in 1893, when he was not yet forty. They had a high regard for each other as artists and they were fond of spending long evenings together exchanging opinions on music and other things. It was the first close, adult friendship Toscanini had. He was grateful to Catalani for putting

33

his trust in a young beginner, and he admired his character and point of view. It is perhaps not too much to say that this serious young man, not quite out of his teens, found in Catalani the warmth, wisdom, and experience he had not received from his father. Years later when Toscanini married and began to have a family, his first wish was to honor Catalani's memory. The composer's best opera was *La Wally,* and Toscanini set his heart on naming his first-born after the heroine in the name part. When his first child turned out to be a boy, he named him Walter after a secondary character in *La Wally.* His second child was a daughter and she was named Wally.

Catalani not only gave Toscanini faith in his musicianship and the warm glow of friendship, but he had the perception to realize that this youngster was mature beyond his years. He did not patronize him because of his youth; he treated him as an equal. This must have meant a great deal to the young fellow who was shy and retiring and had spent so much of his childhood and boyhood living within himself.

Toscanini repaid Catalani by constant devotion to his music. He conducted *La Wally* in a number of Italian theaters, including La Scala, and he did the piece at the Metropolitan. He had no illusions that it was a masterpiece to stand beside the great operas of Verdi, but he tried to give it life and durability. In 1892 he conducted *Loreley,* another opera by Catalani, during a season in Genoa, and the composer gave Toscanini virtual carte blanche. He told him in a note on a postcard to cut as he saw fit, adding, "With your artistic taste you can't do any way but well." He could not go over the score with Toscanini in advance of the performance and wrote to him, "Never mind, because I believe that no one else can divine and interpret me as you do. . . . I trust you for everything." After the performance of *Loreley,* Catalani wrote to Depanis, the impresario, "Toscanini has revealed himself as a first-rate conductor," and remarked, in a touching aside, "I received six curtain calls, which never happened to me before."

The success of his Italian debut with *Edmea* in 1886 did not turn the nineteen-year-old's head. He did not declare that henceforth he would be a conductor and nothing else. He got his cello and resumed practice. When he was invited to prepare the orchestra for a performance of Wagner's *The Flying Dutchman,* which another conductor was to lead in Turin that year, he agreed readily. He welcomed the chance to make a thorough study of the opera, and he did an exhaustive job of carrying out his assignment.

Nor was he too proud that very December to play the cello in an orchestra conducted by Giovanni Bolzoni, who had come out of the Parma Conservatory some time before him and who had attained renown as a conductor and composer. These concerts, which took place at the Teatro Vittorio Emmanuele in Turin, were on the slight side. They accorded well with Italian tastes in symphonic programs at the time, including excerpts from operas and short pieces that were light and popular. But one of the scores was Beethoven's Second Symphony, and Toscanini was delighted with an opportunity to get to know it better.

Still thinking of himself as a cellist, he made for Milan when he heard that Verdi's latest opera, *Otello,* was being prepared for its *première.* He applied for a job in the orchestra at La Scala and won the post of second cellist.

This was a musical opportunity he did not wish to miss, and he never forgot it. Verdi himself attended the rehearsals, although Faccio conducted the *première.* To Toscanini, as to all Italians, Verdi was the grand old man of Italian music. He had worshiped him as a student, and now to be sitting in the orchestra working at his music under his very eyes filled him with unspeakable emotion.

At one practice session Verdi came to the edge of the orchestra pit and inquired who the second cellist was. Toscanini stood up, his heart beating violently. To be addressed personally by the great maestro himself—this was more than he had expected. He was shocked to hear Verdi requesting him to play a passage a little more loudly. Toscanini had the score before him, and it was clear that the orchestra was playing much too loudly when the composer's own marks and the internal evidence of the musical phrase seemed to require a softer tone. He began to point out that he was following the score. Verdi smiled sadly and said it was true, but everyone in the cello section was playing louder and he had better go along with it.

Toscanini was young and idealistic, but his intolerance of accepting from performers anything less than what the score required had nothing to do with the intransigence of youth. He never ceased to be intolerant in such matters. He learned in time that Verdi's attitude had grown out of a long and futile struggle to get his works done as he had imagined them and not as others chose to "interpret" them and that he ended by accepting the recurring transformation of his ideas as inevitable. But Toscanini could not condone this resignation, even if it was bitter resignation.

Recently the maestro recalled how things had worked out when *Falstaff* was being rehearsed for its first performance in 1893. The eighty-year-old Verdi was in the theater. In the final act there is a difficult passage for the contrabasses. Only the first-desk man in the section had enough technique to play the passage at all. Verdi sadly consented that the others should be quiet, even though this distorted the effect of the music. To make matters worse, the first-desk bullfiddler was slightly deaf and got the rhythm wrong. Verdi accepted this, too, with resignation. At this point in his narrative Toscanini, who was then over eighty himself, pounded the table angrily and his eyes blazed. "I would have yelled!" he yelled. "I would not have let it happen." He sighed. "Poor Verdi," he murmured, and then he pounded the table again, shouting, "I have too much strength."

If the composer he adored had let him down on a vital

matter of musical rectitude at that rehearsal of *Otello* early in 1887, he was ready to forgive him for everything as the full passion and grandeur of this opera grew on him. On the night of the *première* on February 5th, he was taut with excitement. As he played, the power and compassion of the music stirred him even more deeply than at the rehearsals. He felt like shouting and singing and weeping. And when he returned home to Parma some days later, he was still radiant with the memory of *Otello* and with the actuality of the music which sang in his mind and blood stream. He arrived late and found his mother asleep. He woke her up, crying out to the bewildered woman, "*Otello* is a masterpiece. Get down on your knees, Mother, and say, '*Viva* Verdi.'" She got down on her knees. With him beside her, she repeated after him, "*Viva* Verdi!"

5

Conducting Becomes a Career

THE NAME of Arturo Toscanini, though he was only twenty, was beginning to get a little currency in Italy. Catalani and Depanis and Giovannina Lucca had connections, and they spoke well of the young man. And this was Italy, which had then, as it has now, score upon score of opera houses.

There were, of course, the famous theaters in the big cities with their traditions, their big-name artists, their fairly long seasons, their social pretensions, and their occasional artistic achievements. There was also a host of smaller communities with their own small opera houses, and each liked to have a modest season of its own. When they could raise the money, they would bring in artists of prominence; otherwise, they would do the best they could with the means they had.

This did not mean that audiences gladly suffered a hastily thrown-together assortment of old-timers who had no other place to go and youngsters who would take anything for a start. The small towns knew their operas and they knew what they liked in a singer. If they were displeased, they made life miserable for the performers. And they made the career of the impresario one of endless hazards.

It must be borne in mind that in Italy of this period the impresario was an essential part of the operatic scene. He took the risks of a season, organized the company, chose the operas, arranged for the sets, and kept the business going. If he was able and lucky, he put on a good season and possibly made a little profit. If he had an ear for a fresh and promising talent, he might sign him or her to a long contract and ride to prosperity on the strength of this alliance. But not many of these impresarios were men of taste or perception. They were in the opera game because it was a business and, occasionally, because they loved the theater. They were excoriated by press, public, and performers, and some deserved to be because their motives were shady and their ways tricky. The Italian public endured them as a necessary evil, for that was the way in which opera got put on. It was not until 1898 that a major opera house like La Scala turned its back on the old system. We shall come to that later.

The main point is that these impresarios, whatever their capacities, had to be hospitable to new talent which would give them a chance to freshen their wares. Such new talent, let it not be forgotten, could probably be had at very modest fees. It can readily be understood, therefore, that word of the appearance of a young conductor named Toscanini had reached the ears of a few impresarios after his success with *Edmea*. Soon after the end of his engagement with the Scala orchestra, the young conductor was put to work conducting in the provinces.

It may be that Toscanini had the ability from the start to take his place as a conductor in the principal opera houses, and it has been suggested that it was an inordinate waste of talent to have him rush from engagement to engagement and from theater to theater. But tradition decreed that a young man had to win his spurs in the accustomed way, and even for Toscanini it was an invaluable experience. He had to conduct operas with little rehearsal. He had to work with singers who could not meet his standards and whom he had to force, through the power of his will and his indefatigable labors with them, to do better than they knew how. He had to cope with difficult audiences. He had to master an ever-enlarging repertory. He had to drive himself endlessly. He became a man of the theater to his finger tips, but from the start he could not abide slovenliness and irresponsibility.

I once heard him rail at Rossini, whom he admired for the sheer effervescence of his gifts as a composer, for letting singers take liberties with his music. And another time I heard him groan as he recalled the toil of his youth. "It was hard, hard work," he said. "You cannot imagine what it means to conduct opera with poor singers, poor choristers, poor orchestra players."

If hard work was to help Toscanini become Toscanini, he got it in abundance. Engaged to conduct a season at Casale Monferrato, a small town between Milan and Turin, he found himself up to his neck in problems and hazards. He was obliged to put on *L'Africaine* after only four rehearsals, which, considering that he was new at conducting, was no mean assignment. The local paper said that "the orchestra performed miracles." He has remembered this season longest for what happened during a performance of *La Gioconda*.

During the third act, the audience set up a clamor for a repeat. It was early in the game for young Toscanini; he was to be involved in any number of battles over the hated encore, and it was to be years before he could take the inflexible stand that he would not grant one under any circumstances. But here he was at twenty, in his second engagement as a conductor in Italy, flatly refusing to agree to a repeat. The audience howled in rage. A man in military uniform, with a penetrating voice, shouted a stream of abuse, ending with, "You are a fresh young maestro." Toscanini turned around and shouted back, "You are wrong, you dog!" The young maestro won the argument. He waited the audience out and then finished the performance without giving the encore. After the show there was a gentleman waiting for him in his dressing room. He was an emissary from the military man with whom Toscanini had traded insults, and he had come, in behalf of his principal, to challenge the young conductor to a duel with weapons of his own choosing. The only weapons with which Toscanini might have had a chance were the bow and baton, and it was fortunate that the whole thing was laughed off and forgotten.

Before 1887 was over Toscanini had conducted *Carmen* in Verona, and in January, 1888, he did Donizetti's *Lucrezia Borgia*. The singer in the title role was a homely creature, and the Verona audience, which had its own idea of what the glamorous Borgia should look like, cried out insulting remarks at the poor woman and hissed her so insistently that she ran off the stage. Toscanini slammed down his baton and walked out of the pit. The performance was not finished, but this time he was not held responsible. He could not have been in sympathy with the audience's behavior, and yet he must have had a touch of respect for it because it must have gone against his grain to offer so incredible a Lucrezia Borgia. In any event, he remained in Verona to fulfill his engagement, and two weeks later he conducted a production of *Mignon* that stood the Verona public on its ear. "Under his magic baton," it was written, "the orchestra was marvelous."

After a short stay in Macerata, in central Italy, he was summoned, in the fall of 1888, to Milan to conduct for the first time at the Teatro dal Verme. A writer in the *Gazzetta Musicale* of Milan said, "Toscanini, the real helm of a boat so happily brought to port, has achieved a perfection of execution, and I wish many composers might have such an interpreter." But there was a dissenting voice. Amintore Galli, a critic of established position, had this to say of the twenty-one-year-old conductor on another occasion: "The distinguished maestro Toscanini should not give us a mere rendition of our masterpieces; he should try to master the most spiritual part of art and to translate it with the intelligence and love of a true musician. To achieve all this it is not enough to know the score by heart and conduct without using it, but it is necessary to study the spirit of a composer and the tradition of the various interpretations."

From Milan the busy young maestro went to Novara, to Turin (the Teatro Carignano), then to Genoa (the Politeama). In Genoa, when he conducted Cagnoni's *Francesca da Rimini,* Toscanini met Giulio Gatti-Casazza, with whom he was to be associated at La Scala and the Metropolitan Opera. Cagnoni happened to be a friend of Gatti's family, and at the end of the performance Gatti waited outside the theater to pay his respects to the composer. Cagnoni came out with Toscanini, and Gatti recalled in his memoirs that the young conductor was suffering from a nosebleed and could hardly talk. It is amusing to note that Gatti was surprised to find that "Toscanini was really a handsome young fellow, very elegant and affable indeed." He had heard, Gatti remembered, that Toscanini "was an extremely severe person with an inexpansive personality."

The fiery little maestro's reputation was spreading through Italy. This reputation was based not only on what audiences could see and hear of his performances but on the gossip about what went on at his rehearsals. The gossip was, of course, founded on fact, but this did not diminish the demand for his services.

In October and November, 1889, he was in Voghera, which lies between Milan and Genoa. One who was present at rehearsals, according to Alfredo Segre, reported that "the orchestra played very well, even though its members often had to bite their tongues, for the hand guiding them was an iron hand which knew how to pull the reins resolutely, no matter how painful the result might be."

Despite his youth and lack of height, Toscanini now cut an impressive figure. On his bushy head of hair sat a smart hat of a shape the maestro has worn all through his life, with the crown low and bisected lengthwise and the wide brim sloping upward like the sides of a boat. His suit of clothes was of good material and carefully tailored. Across his vest, which had fashionable lapels, he wore a heavy gold chain. He had on a wing collar and a silk bow tie. By now he was wearing a mustache, which was dark and thick. With his cold, clear eyes and classic Italian face, he was a handsome, elegant young fellow.

There was no end to the offers the young conductor was receiving. He began to make clear stipulations to the impresarios about singers, number of choristers and orchestra players, and duration of rehearsals. If they agreed to his terms, he insisted that they live up to them. In March, 1890, at the Politeama in Genoa, he had a grievance and went looking for the impresario, who was new to him. In the lobby he found a man sweeping the floor and asked to be directed to the impresario. The man paused and said, "I am Chiarella, the impresario." The twenty-three-year-old maestro, apparently accustomed to the strange ways of impresarios, acted as if finding one sweeping lobbies were the most natural thing in the world. Anyhow, he had something on his mind. "I am Toscanini. I am conducting here. I find twenty-four choristers. I need forty-eight."

"Twenty-four is all I have," the impresario replied, and resumed his sweeping.

Toscanini followed him down the lobby as he swept, and an argument raged.

"Thirty is my limit," Chiarella finally said.

"Then I'll go back to Milan." Toscanini headed for the exit. Chiarella shook his head sadly, as if the ways of maestros were more than a poor impresario could fathom. But he called to Toscanini as he reached the door. "All right," he said, "forty-eight," and he finished sweeping the lobby.

Chiarella's troubles were not over. Toscanini was not satisfied with the orchestra. This time it was not a matter of quantity but of quality. Upon his insistence, the personnel was changed drastically. Chiarella had to do a lot of explaining to the men who were dismissed, and he had to dig deeply into his purse to pay for better players. There is no record of how he felt about this experience with Toscanini, but it was agreed by contemporaries that the Politeama had an unforgettable series of performances of *Mignon*.

When Toscanini went to Turin for a brief season at the Carignano, *Mignon* was asked for. He obliged by preparing and conducting it in addition to *Carmen*.

Where to next? The secondary theaters beckoned on all sides, but the principal opera houses were not pressing for his services. They wanted the big names, and Italy had its share of eminent maestros, men like Faccio, Luigi Mancinelli, Leopoldo Mugnone, and Edoardo Mascheroni. Italy, like other countries then and now, was inclined to be more impressed when one of its own conductors had engagements abroad and came home with the imprimatur of a foreign success.

To anyone who knew Toscanini it would be unlikely that an engagement as second conductor at the Liceo in Barcelona was something he accepted because he wanted foreign window dressing. He wanted a change of scenery; he was delighted to visit another country, and he had an urge to see Spain. Furthermore, the principal conductor at the Liceo was the famous Mascheroni, and the young conductor looked forward to a season of collaboration with the distinguished maestro.

It must have been a disillusioning encounter for Toscanini. Evidently Mascheroni was not overjoyed with the choice of the second conductor. He had heard of Toscanini's growing fame and did not relish having him as an associate. Of course, he did not say so. Outwardly his manner was cordial. He contrived with what must have appeared to him to be diabolical cleverness to stick Toscanini with a back-breaking assignment. He gave the young conductor a revival of Bellini's *I Capuletti ed i Montecchi* to mount, and he told him about it at the last moment. This opera requires singers of experience, brilliant vocal technique, and exceptional voices. Toscanini did not have time to assemble a cast that would suit it best; he had to take what was available. Unquestionably this was what Mascheroni had planned, and undoubtedly he looked forward to a failure. But he had underestimated Toscanini. Working with such talent as he had at his disposal, the young conductor put together a production that scored one of the big successes of the season. Mascheroni was equal to this occasion. He got the impresario to withdraw the revival after it had had three performances.

Back in Italy in 1891, Toscanini returned to the circuit of the secondary theaters. In Turin he met the impresario Carlo Piontelli. Among the tribe of impresarios, this man was unique. Giulio Gatti-Casazza, who knew most of them well, wrote in his memoirs, "Personally, I knew only one fortunate impresario. He was Piontelli, an expert in his field, who deserved good fortune. He was the first man to take particular care in the organization of the choral and orchestral ensembles. He risked engaging young artists without renown for large theaters. He had under his wing, for some years, Arturo Toscanini, and was the first to present him in a large theater before Toscanini had reached the age of twenty-five."

Piontelli engaged Toscanini in the fall of 1891 for the winter season at Genoa's principal opera house—the Carlo Felice. He recognized the young maestro's gifts, and he liked to have fine productions presented under his management. He was not chary about spending money, and he gave Toscanini a free hand, though he knew that the latter was exacting.

How exacting he could, indeed, be Piontelli was to find out during the years of their collaboration. Piontelli acceded to virtually all his demands with style. He gave Toscanini more than what he demanded for artistic purposes; he gave him affection and loyal friendship. Toscanini later said, "The old man was like a father to me."

Piontelli, however, was to learn in 1896 how tough Toscanini had grown. At that time he gave the young conductor a chance to conduct a symphonic orchestra at the Regio in Turin. Toscanini had wished to direct symphonic music for some time, but was considered too young for such an honor. After all, the impressive maestros who received this accolade were men of years and experience and nearly always wore long beards. Toscanini had only a mustache. But by this time he had conducted the first Italian performance of *Die Götterdämmerung* and the world *première* of *La Bohème. Allora,* the Italians said with outspread hands, perhaps he was ripe for a concert.

More than fifty years later Toscanini remembered the program he had arranged for this momentous event. Schubert's C major Symphony was the principal piece, and it was companioned by Brahms' "Tragic" Overture, Tchaikovsky's "Nutcracker" Suite, and "The Entrance of the Gods into Valhalla, from Wagner's *Das Rheingold.* Toscanini rehearsed the orchestra once in the pit, and then told Piontelli that he wanted two rehearsals on the stage, where the orchestra would be playing on the night of the concert. He wished to adjust to the acoustics as they would prevail at the concert.

Piontelli promised the two rehearsals, but found it awkward to have the sets moved from the stage until Sunday morning On Sunday afternoon, on the day of the concert, Toscanini got his stage rehearsal. When it was over he went to Piontelli and said, "I need one more stage rehearsal."

"There is no time," Piontelli protested.

"Then postpone the concert to next Sunday," Toscanini said.

"Impossible."

"Why impossible?"

"Because the tickets are sold," Piontelli observed patiently, "and it is too late to inform the public."

Toscanini was inflexible. "I won't conduct without another rehearsal."

"But I heard the rehearsal just now," Piontelli insisted. "It was beautiful."

"For you, not for me."

Apparently Piontelli did not know his man even then. The two dined together, and after the repast Toscanini got up and said, "Now I go to bed."

Piontelli thought it was a joke. The orchestra was on the stage. The concertmaster, Enrico Polo, who had been a fellow-student of Toscanini's at the Parma Conservatory and was to become his brother-in-law, came out and gave the signal to tune up. The audience was in the theater. But there was no Toscanini. An emissary rushed to his hotel and found him reading in bed. Piontelli himself hurried to his room to plead with him. Toscanini would not budge. The impresario went back to the theater, announced that the maestro was sick, and refunded the money for the tickets as the indignant customers heaped irritated comments on his head.

A week later—the date was March 20, 1896—Toscanini conducted the concert with the program as originally announced. Before he did he got the rehearsals he wanted, and his work was acclaimed.

He recalled the story with the satisfaction of a man who had acted according to the dictates of his conscience. I asked him whether he knew how Piontelli had got out of the dilemma and what he had told the public.

"No," he said, with a reflective and contented look in his eyes. "I don't know and don't care. I stay in bed."

6

On His Way

WITH the opening of the season at the Carlo Felice in Genoa after Christmas in 1891, Arturo Toscanini stepped up into the big leagues of Italian opera activity. It was not yet La Scala, the most famous opera house in Italy; that was seven years off. But he would not reach his twenty-fifth birthday until the following March, and he had come faster than probably any other conductor in Italian experience.

To anyone who has known Toscanini through the years, it would be obvious that he did not become puffed up with the importance of his new duties or with the speed of his ascent. He came to the fresh task with the consciousness that it imposed heavier responsibilities on him, and he had the will and energy to face up to any problem, no matter how difficult.

The first was to overhaul the orchestra of the Carlo Felice. There were many old-timers in the ranks, men who held their posts by virtue of having been in them for many years. Toscanini did not like to discharge them, but he could not give the kind of opera he wished if they remained. He replaced them with younger men who were better musicians. The bitterness of those who were dropped was understandable, and if they spread their hatred for the presumptuous young maestro among their friends and the public of the theater, that, too, was to be expected.

Let no one underestimate Toscanini's awareness of these currents in a theater and a community. He understood the

resentments that would be leveled at him, but he did what
he felt he had to do. When he came to La Scala later, he fired
more than forty *comprimari*—singers of secondary roles—and
found himself embroiled in a scandal. He expected it and
accepted it as one of the calculated risks of his work.

The opening opera at the Carlo Felice was Meyerbeer's
Le Prophète, and it was not an auspicious start. Like all of
Meyerbeer's full-panoplied operas, it must have exceptional
singers, and Toscanini did not have the sort of casts with
which the Metropolitan Opera dressed up the piece before
and after his time there—in 1899 Lilli Lehmann, Marie Brema,
Jean and Edouard de Reszke, and Pol Plançon, and in 1918
Claudia Muzio, Margarete Matzenauer, Enrico Caruso,
Adamo Didur, and José Mardones. Those who were after the
new maestro's scalp contended that, for egotistic reasons, he
had distorted the opera. His admirers replied that he could
not turn second-rate singers into great artists but that the
orchestra had played brilliantly. The production was declared
a fiasco on the one hand, and passable on the other. Toscanini
could not have been happy with it. Thanks to the dissension
and discussion, the public came to see for itself, and the
piece ran for thirteen performances. Piontelli deserved some
credit for keeping it on the boards despite the clamor against
it.

Thereafter, things went better, but Catalani's *Loreley*,
which was a labor of love for Toscanini, reawakened the contentions. Partisan feeling, pro and contra Toscanini, ran high.
The *Gazzetta Musicale* went to the length of printing the
views of both sides in the same issue. One writer said, "All
our admiration goes to the artistic conscience, the supreme
ability and intelligence shown by Maestro Toscanini, who,
conducting *Loreley*, interpreted it according to the composer's
intentions and admirably mastered the orchestra." From the
opposing camp came this view: "The execution has been de-
ficient, and this proves once again that the success was not

due to the conductor's ability but entirely to the value of the score."

The big league of opera was rough on the performer. There were more experts, official and self-appointed, to watch and comment. If Toscanini knew about the heated turmoil that raged about his name—and the chances are strong that he did—he gave little sign of it. He did his duty as a musician as he saw it. Let the disputations seethe where they might.

In May he moved to Milan for a spring season at the Teatro dal Verme, where he conducted the world *première* of Leoncavallo's *Pagliacci*. He had been recommended for this assignment by Victor Maurel, the illustrious baritone who had sung Iago in the first *Otello* and was shortly to do the first Falstaff. Maurel, in turn, had been told about the young conductor by none other than Verdi, who, though then almost eighty, kept a sharp lookout on the Italian musical scene. *Pagliacci* was a tremendous success. The public cheered Toscanini endlessly in addition to Leoncavallo, Maurel, and the others, and the press proclaimed him a "superb conductor."

There was scarcely time for rest or study for the young maestro. He had become an ardent mountain climber and had formed the habit of going off in the summer for a holiday in the Tyrol and the Alps, where he went after the highest and most difficult peaks. He scaled Mont Blanc, and once in the course of such an excursion almost lost his life. He slipped and caught onto a rope at the last moment. Fortunately, his arms, powerfully developed from the exercise of conducting, had the strength to hold on until he could be pulled to safety.

He found time for a brief vacation in the summer of 1892, and then plunged into unremitting activity. In September he journeyed to Lucca, a town near Pisa, which, apparently undisturbed by the centuries, had not lost its simple, distinctive, almost naïve medieval quality. He went at the invitation of Catalani, who had been born and had lived there, to conduct *La Wally*. The composer was ailing, and Toscanini was touched. He could not do anything to heal the dying man, but he could conduct his opera with burning intensity. He would have conducted it with feeling in any event, but this time there was an intensification of emotion. This was an offering to a friend.

He was then summoned to the Carlo Felice in Genoa to help out in an emergency. In October, on the four hundredth anniversary of the discovery of America by Cristoforo Colombo, native of Genoa, the theater put on the *première* of a new opera by Alberto Franchetti. The opera, called *Cristoforo Colombo,* was conducted by Luigi Mancinelli, but after two performances he left to fill a contract in Spain. At least that was the official explanation, but Mancinelli had apparently quarreled with Franchetti. It is amusing to recall that Toscanini, who respected the older conductor, had occasion to chat with him and to reproach him for his impetuosity.

Toscanini was asked whether he could take over, and as a gesture of good will he was offered a full dress rehearsal before the third performance. He sat through the second performance, which Mancinelli conducted, and then said calmly that a fresh rehearsal would not be necessary. He took the score to his room and sat up most of the night studying it. The next evening he conducted from memory. Composer, singers, orchestra, chorus, and impresario were amazed; even collaborators of old who appreciated Toscanini's unusual memory were awed. But it was the quality of the performance, not the feat of memorizing, that merited the admiration. At the final performance Verdi sat in one of the boxes and joined in the applause.

In November, Toscanini moved to Rome for his first appearance in the capital. The big event was to be a new opera by Mascagni, *I Rantzau,* which had just been premièred in Florence. Instead of Toscanini, Mascagni conducted, arriving unexpectedly in Rome just before the performance. The fact that the composer of an opera chose to be his own con-

ductor at a first time in Rome did not strike Toscanini as
unreasonable, though he had been given to understand that
he would do the opera. But his sense of justice was outraged
when a journalist reported that he had cheerfully turned over
the assignment to Mascagni. Nothing of the sort! Toscanini
took pains, in an open letter, to set the facts right.

"An article that has appeared in the paper *Fanfulla*," he
wrote, "gives the impression that I have spontaneously renounced the honor of conducting *Rantzau* in favor of Mascagni. This is not true. Far from renouncing the honor, I
would have been very proud to have it, and I felt that I was
able to carry out the task and that I was worthy of it, even
if I would have had such a limited amount of time. But
Mascagni wanted to have the honor of the first three performances himself."

Mascagni had the honor of all the performances. Toscanini
left Rome in a huff. He went to Sicily, where he conducted
at the Politeama Garibaldi in Palermo.

That winter season of 1892-93 turned out to be one that a
musician with less than Toscanini's remarkable memory
would have remembered in detail. At times he must have felt
that he was more like a gladiator with a pack of wild beasts
to confront and tame than a conductor. In some five years
of working in various towns and theaters, the young conductor
had had a generous exposure to the volatility and demonstra-
tiveness of Italian audiences, and he had not forgotten the
turbulence of that gathering in Rio the first time he directed
an opera. But the Sicilians were something new under the
sun.

Many years later Toscanini found it possible to talk of
the deep impression the Sicilian countryside and the remnants
of its ancient civilization and culture had made upon him.
"More than Rome," he said, "Sicily made me feel as if I were
in another world." He evidently found the time and peace

of mind to explore and appreciate the island, but there must have been moments when he could think only of getting out of the place for good.

To begin with, the season opened on Christmas Eve. Whether it was the impresario's or Toscanini's notion to pick this date is of no importance now, but whoever was responsible knew nothing about the habits of Palermo's people. It was their custom to spend the evening of December 24th playing *tombola,* a Sicilian version of lotto, very much like the game of bingo in the United States. After they had had their fill of *tombola,* they liked to go to church for Mass. This arrangement left no room for the opera, and it made no difference to the local public that the opening piece was *Pagliacci,* which, you would think, could not fail of its effect anywhere.

The audience was not large that evening. Most of the regular operagoers held fast to their tradition of *tombola* and Mass, and those who came were determined to teach the company a lesson. The hissing began as Tonio pulled aside the curtains and stepped out to sing the Prologue, and it continued at the end of one of the most sure-fire arias in the operatic catalogue. It mounted in fervor as the evening wore on. No one was spared. Singers, chorus, orchestra, and conductor received their meed of unflattering attention.

If the company had decided there and then to pack up and leave, it could not have been blamed. Once the *faux pas* it had made had been explained and apologies had been expressed, an uneasy peace settled on the season. It lasted only until *Cavalleria Rusticana* was put on. Here was a story of Sicily, reflecting in its passions and violence the mood of the country. A Palermo audience, you would guess, would respond favorably to this opera, and that is why the impresario had billed it. Probably it would have gone well if the conductor had acceded to the wishes of the leaders of the Maffia, a secret society which flouted the law and its guardians and which resorted often to violence and crime to carry out its ideas.

The Maffia, then a dominant power in Sicily, was used to having its own way. Its wishes were commands to government officials, businessmen, farmers, teachers, and even clerics. It was certainly accustomed to getting what it wanted in the opera house. If it found an aria to its liking, it expected to have it repeated. If one of the leaders of the Maffia took a shine to a ballerina, he had but to signify the tenderness of his emotion and the girl was encouraged to do her dance a second time.

But Toscanini was not the man to compromise with outside forces when it came to running an opera performance. He probably knew about the Maffia's reputation for violence, but he would not be intimidated. With unrelenting determination he conducted *Cavalleria Rusticana,* indifferent to the wishes of the Maffia. Though the impresario pleaded that he give in a little, there were no encores.

After the first performance, the audience was heatedly indignant. After the second it was whipped up into a fury, and when it left the theater it paraded through the streets of Palermo in a demonstration of hostility for the company and its impresario and conductor. The marchers shouted threats, and it looked as though the resentment would turn into a personal attack on members of the hated company.

Toscanini gave no sign of fear of bodily injury. He was a fighter. He would not back down and he would not walk out, not when they were trying to force him. At the next performance, the crowd was gathered for the kill. Its mood was part ugly and part stirred up with the promise of blood. As the young maestro made his way through the pit to the podium, it set up a menacing clamor. Toscanini marched ahead unafraid and plunged into his work as if the hissing and shouting did not exist. His courageous leadership rallied

the fearful company, and accomplished something more important—it won the admiration of the leader of the local
Maffia, who evidently had sporting instincts.

This worthy gave the order to call off the demonstration.
The young fellow in the pit was an antagonist to be respected.
It would be an honor to have him in the top councils of the
Maffia. Since he was a foreigner—Italians from the mainland
are still looked upon as outlanders by many Sicilians—and a
musician, let him do his duty in his own way.

The audience was perhaps slow to get the idea that the
Maffia had changed its position, that from now on the policy
would be protection for the young maestro rather than opposition. Those who carried on against Toscanini were quickly
informed by the bully boys of the Maffia to lay off. By the
time the performance came to an end, the company had not
only an attentive but an enthusiastic audience—and on Toscanini's terms.

Succeeding productions were put on without incident. But
on March 19th, when a performance of *The Barber of Seville*
was booked, there was another crisis, and this time Toscanini
blew up. With the start of the Overture the audience began
to yelp for something. The conductor did not know what it
was shouting about. He tried to keep on conducting on the
assumption that the tumult would let up as it had on
previous occasions. There was no pause in the outburst. Toscanini turned around, flung his baton into the audience, and
walked out.

He did not learn what had brought on this demonstration
until many years later when he happened to encounter an
old man from Palermo who had been in the theater that
evening. It seemed that the Sicilians, conscious of the fact
that March 19th was Saint Giuseppe's day, wanted Garibaldi,
their latter-day hero who carried this first name, honored
with the playing of the "Hymn of Garibaldi." It is possible
that Toscanini would have been glad to join in paying his

respects to Garibaldi, a man whom he admired, but how was he to know what the racket was all about?

Toscanini's outburst of temper in the theater did not alienate the crowd permanently. He was prevailed upon to return to the podium on another night.

After that season in Sicily, Toscanini did not work for almost a year. The experience in Palermo was not responsible for his inactivity, although it would have justified a desire to be away from the wars of Italy's opera houses for a time. The young maestro was stung by what looked to him like a shady deal. The contract he had expected to sign did not make clear the name of the theater he was headed for. He had a suspicion that he was to be used in machinations against another conductor, and he would not be part of such knavery, despite the fact that the promised fee was high. He rejected the contract, and by the time word got about that he was free, nearly all the theaters had made arrangements for the following season.

It is probable, too, that Toscanini was fed up with the ways of Italian opera houses. Some twenty-five years later, in a similar spirit of bitterness and fury, he turned his back on all of them and simply quit conducting. In 1893 he gloomily withdrew from public life. He kept away from many of his friends and associates. Like a hurt animal, he holed up. He read, studied music, and took out his cello and resumed practicing, just as he had in his student days. He muttered to those who dared to ask him about his plans, as he did in his fifties, "I can always earn a living by playing the cello."

7

Back to the Wars

TOSCANINI did not have to turn to the cello for a livelihood. When his black mood began to dissolve and he resumed taking notice of the Italian musical world, he found that he had not been forgotten in the months of retirement and that offers to conduct were still being made. He accepted an engagement at the Regio Teatro Nuovo in Pisa, and in March, 1894, plunged back into public activity.

He took his cello along with him. He could not have doubted his capacity to take up where he had left off as a conductor. Perhaps he had found renewed pleasures in working with the stringed instrument and proposed to keep up with it. He managed to find time to play it, too. Once he had the operas prepared and on the stage, he found, according to his own words years later, that time hung heavy on his hands. He induced three members of the orchestra to join him in afternoons of quartet playing. He had not played chamber music since his student days, and he suggested that they try some Mendelssohn pieces he had been fond of as a boy. But this music, he recalled later, struck him as oddly ungratifying; it did not give him the satisfaction of ten years before. The group tackled a Beethoven quartet. This was it; this gave him a tremendous lift. In recent years he has spoken of the last, great quartets of Beethoven, which he studies endlessly, as his bible.

The hours had not hung heavily on his hands when he had

arrived in Pisa. He had begun by cleaning out the orchestra and had followed with a thorough job of overhauling the chorus and the roster of singers. As usual, he created resentments and made enemies. But the productions of *Otello* and Puccini's *Manon Lescaut,* which the composer attended, proved to be worth the trouble he had taken with them.

The public found them good, but this did not mean that the season was without its crisis. One evening, during a repetition of *Otello,* a bomb was tossed backstage. It was not much of a bomb, but even a small, homemade affair can pop off with a big noise. When this one exploded, it smashed window panes and lamps, and the audience became terrified. As some people started up the aisles toward the exits, there was a panicky outburst of pushing and screaming. Toscanini acted quickly and coolly. He ordered the orchestra to strike up the "Garibaldi Hymn." The audience came to attention slowly. Toscanini and the orchestra followed with the "Marcia Reale," the national anthem. The audience, on its feet, remained in its places, and its unease subsided. By now the acrid fumes had drifted out of the shattered windows, and the feeling of mob fright was gone. People chattered more calmly, and when they saw that the maestro remained at his place waiting for them to get back to their seats, they drifted back. The performance went on. The thrower of the bomb was not apprehended, but it was agreed on all sides that one of the dismissed performers had been responsible.

In the ensuing months and years, Toscanini could not have found much time for the cello or chamber music. Once back in the swing of Italy's widespread opera circuit, he kept going steadily. In Ravenna, in May, a journalist predicted that he was destined for La Scala. In October he resumed his association with Piontelli and under his aegis conducted *Falstaff* and *Cristoforo Colombo* in Treviso, with Franchetti on hand to embrace him on stage. Perhaps the composer thought that he was flattering him in his way, or it may have been an impulsive gesture. Years later Toscanini, older but still in some respects a porcupine, spoke without enthusiasm of Franchetti. "He was a gray man," he said, and he probably still recalled with distaste the public display of affection.

In Treviso, Toscanini, who was always game to try something new, undertook to learn to ride a bicycle, which was then coming into fashion. It was one of the high-saddled type with a large rear wheel. Toscanini took a bad tumble and almost injured himself severely. He did not bother with bicycle-riding again, but he observed one day recently to his son, "By the time you were riding bicycles, you had a sensible size."

In November, Toscanini was at the Teatro Communale in Bologna, where he conducted the world *première* of *Savitri* by a composer whose name you will have trouble finding in the modern musical dictionaries, Natale Canti. Toscanini was to spend endless hours and energies over the years preparing and conducting new operas, all by Italians. With the exception of *Pagliacci* and Puccini's *La Bohème,* these operas have had little currency. A few managed to survive for a while in Italy, where they are revived from time to time. The others are remembered only by a few students of musical history—and by Toscanini. He mastered them all by heart, and years later he could still dredge up out of his memory passages from the unfortunate works. He would recall them with no pride or pleasure but with a grim satisfaction that they had been his contribution to the music of his own time.

In December, Toscanini arrived in Genoa to take charge of the winter season at the Teatro Carlo Felice. In the course of fifty-eight days he conducted a total of sixty-four performances of seven operas. So many performances in so concentrated a period constituted an exhausting job, but one must go behind the performances to grasp the full measure of the task that this indefatigable little man performed. For the principal burden was not in conducting the performances; it lay in the preparatory labors.

Toscanini had several assistants to help prepare the singers and the chorus, but it was his procedure then, as it remained through the years, to take the full responsibility himself. He drove himself to find time to work personally with every element. And he did not accept singing and playing that was almost always correct; it had to be correct all the time, and it had to live up to his conception of the spirit of the piece.

He worked on *Falstaff* with scrupulous care. At one point a difference of opinion broke out between him and Antonio Pini-Corsi, the singer who was the Ford. Pini-Corsi sang a phrase in the second act more slowly than the markings in the score warranted. Toscanini called him to order, but Pini-Corsi, who had been chosen by Verdi for this role for the opera's *première* at La Scala in February, 1893, and who later sang at the Metropolitan in the period when the maestro was there, replied that his tempo was what the composer had required. Toscanini doubted that Verdi would write one tempo indication in the score and permit another in performance. He insisted that the tempo must be taken as written. Every time they came to this passage during the rehearsals, the argument cropped up. Pini-Corsi would protest that he ought to know what he was doing; Toscanini would reply that he had no choice but to follow the score. It may be imagined that some of the other singers, all kept to strict account by the conductor, listened to the discussions with lively interest and that most of them secretly sympathized with the stubborn Pini-Corsi.

Piontelli, an old hand at the business, must have wondered whether the bickering would end in a blow-up, and he decided to get the matter settled once and for all. Knowing that Verdi had arrived in Genoa, where he usually wintered, he arranged to take the company to visit him and to pay its respects. He hoped, of course, that the troublesome question would be put to the old master.

The company entered the large apartment on an upper floor of the Palazzo Doria, overlooking the Piazza Principe and the port on one side and the Ligurian hills on the other. The eighty-one-year-old composer and his wife, Giuseppina, entertained the party graciously, but no one mentioned the dispute. Toscanini was consumed with eagerness to raise the question, but he could not bring himself to broach a serious matter when everything was going so pleasantly and smoothly. The guests were about to leave, and Toscanini himself was at the door, when he turned back and blurted out the thing uppermost in his mind. Pini-Corsi came forward to give his version. The other members of the company clustered about the composer. The old man listened and smiled sadly. Toscanini, he said, was right; Pini-Corsi had forgotten the tempo he had taken at the first performance.

Then Verdi recalled how he had brought *Don Carlos* to the stage of the Paris Opéra in 1867, how he had spent weeks working painstakingly with each singer and with chorus and orchestra, and how, as a result of this patient effort, he had arrived at a performance that satisfied him. Then he had left Paris and had been gone for a month. When he had returned and listened to *Don Carlos* he could not believe his ears. Not a single tempo remained as he had written or taught it. "I had to start over again from the beginning," he ended.

As Toscanini listened to the old man, he recalled his own impatience with the master's acceptance of details of performance that differed from the score's indications at the *première* of *Otello*. At last he understood Verdi's resignation.

From Genoa, Toscanini went directly to Pisa. He had to make more changes in the company, particularly in the orchestra. For *Falstaff* requires not only singers who can adapt themselves to a well-knit ensemble with the sensitivity of good musicians; it must have an orchestra that can play with

61

delicacy and flexibility. Toscanini would not tolerate anything less than such an orchestra, and he was summary with those who were not up to the task. The result was a glowing performance, and the Pisa reviewers remarked that they were unused to such playing in the orchestra.

Someone in Pisa took the trouble of telling Toscanini just what he thought of him. If it was not a dismissed musician, or the close friend or relative of one, it was some equally disaffected soul who sent Toscanini an anonymous letter, not the first or last that the conductor received in his career but one of the most heart-felt in its attempts to be objective. Alfredo Segre dug it up, and here it is in part:

You are too proud and you have hurt us; and therefore for us your orchestra does not exist. If another conductor who enjoys our favor were in your place, you would hear tremendous applause. . . . To tell the truth, you are a nice young man, full of intelligence, and you will become great; but all intelligence disappears in one who is impolite toward the audience. You are a misanthrope; you don't want to be introduced to students or important men. . . . We have rendered great honors to conductors such as Mugnone, Mancinelli, Catalanotti, Mascagni, and Mascheroni, because they are kind and polite, and you would have enjoyed our favors had you not such a horrible character. . . . We warn you that the audience will ask for several encores and you had better execute them without being begged to. . . .

From Pisa he moved to Venice, where he conducted both at the Teatro Malibran and at that little jewel of an opera house La Fenice. The royal family acknowledged his growing importance as a maestro by attending a concert at which he directed, curiously enough, three different overtures—those to Verdi's *Sicilian Vespers*, Rossini's *William Tell*, and Wagner's *Tannhäuser*.

In his years as a symphonic conductor he played these pieces often, but usually only one on a program. It did not seem odd in the nineties, particularly in Italy, where symphonic programs were rare, to have three overtures in one evening. Toscanini himself thought nothing of it, but in 1950 I heard him berate himself for his thoughtlessness in conducting the Overture to *William Tell* and the Prelude to *Die Meistersinger* on one program in the course of his American tour with the N.B.C. Symphony Orchestra.

As in later years, he found the preparation of the overtures taxing work, and orchestras have since found that he will often devote as much time and attention to a familiar overture as to a major symphony. He became convinced that an orchestra's approach to such a piece was that it was easy, and once an orchestra thinks a piece is easy it relaxes. Toscanini grows wild at the condescension implied in this attitude. Even before he begins rehearsing a so-called "easy" overture he is alert for the slightest slackening of zeal. A violinist who played in orchestras with Toscanini for twenty years observed recently, "I can tell in advance when we are going to have trouble at rehearsal. When I see a little Rossini overture on the program, I know there will be the devil to pay. He cannot believe that we will take it as seriously as he wants us to, and he is always ready to jump on us. To be honest, we almost never are as serious about it as we get to be before he is through with us."

In June, Toscanini was in Trento, and in October in Treviso. He had no engagements for the summer, but one can imagine that he spent many hours in July and August not vacationing from music but concentrating on study. For he had committed himself to appear at the Teatro Regio in Turin during the winter season, and the bait the impresario had used to obtain his services was an offer to present the first Italian production of *Die Götterdämmerung*.

8

Premières

A GUSHING LADY met Toscanini at a dinner party in New York during his period with the Metropolitan Opera just after he had finished conducting the final music drama of Wagner's *Ring*.

"It must be exciting," she said breathlessly, "to conduct *Die Götterdämmerung*."

He recalled her words much later with indignation. "*È stupida*," he said with a snort. "My cheeks are hollow and I can hardly breathe, and she talks like a picnic."

The big Wagner works have always been an especially arduous and exacting labor for him. Of *Die Meistersinger*, he once said, "By the time I get into the third act, I feel as if the performance began the previous day."

Naturally, he would not have undertaken to conduct these scores if they had been merely a chore. His admiration—one might say adoration—of Wagner did not diminish with the years, and he drew tremendous satisfaction from preparing and performing his works as he thought they should be done. Of course, it was grueling labor, but those who watched him prepare a Wagner music drama said that he seemed to thrive on it. When he was doing *Die Meistersinger* at Salzburg, Toscanini had a pianist who was in his twenties as his assistant. At the end of a rehearsal, the young man looked haggard and the maestro, then almost seventy, was blooming.

One can only guess, at this distance, at the amount of time, thought, and devotion Toscanini poured into the preparation of Italy's first *Götterdämmerung*. He had not yet been at Bayreuth, and he had not seen a production of the music drama before. Nor did he have anyone who knew the score from working with the composer to consult with. He had to master it in all its detail and magnitude on his own.

He realized at the outset that the orchestra normally recruited for the Turin opera season would not suffice for this music drama, which is a vast symphonic edifice as much as, if not more than, it is a creation for the stage. He made it a condition of undertaking the task that a fine orchestra, strong in all its choirs, be assembled. Some local citizens, abetted by the press, waged a campaign to get the city to approve the formation of a permanent orchestra, which was to be available for the opera season, and the movement carried the day.

Toscanini supervised the formation of this orchestra, and once he had it properly organized he needed only ten days of rehearsals to have it ready for the performance of *Die Götterdämmerung* on December 22, 1895. He had taken longer with the singers. And while he worked, the impresario took pains to orient the operagoers of the town in the background and mysteries of Wagner's work. He had a pamphlet prepared and published which told the story of *Der Ring des Nibelungen*. It must have helped, if only by putting listeners on their guard that this work required special attention. The music drama was sung in Italian, and translations of the libretto were in the hands of the audience at performance time.

It must be remembered that Italian audiences were in the habit of following the action on the stage with librettos in hand, even for Italian operas. If the opera were thoroughly familiar, the public might do without librettos, but if it were new or rarely done, listeners came equipped to keep up with the story. Audiences in Italy would not dream of sitting through an opera without having an idea of what it was all about. Even the stagehands, when they were not busy, would be seen sitting in the wings with a libretto in hand.

The first *Götterdämmerung* in Italy was an event. Opera-goers, students of music, and critics came from all over the country to hear and see this unusual work. The cult of Wagner had begun to drift across the Alps some years before, and it was now reaching considerable intensity. Wagner himself had talked of his scores as the music of the future, and the *avant-garde* of Italian music lovers had ranged itself on his side. Though the public as a whole listened to Wagner with interest, its heart remained with Verdi and the operas of the Italian school. But there were some among the ardent advocates of the lord of Bayreuth who, in their zeal to be advanced, looked down their noses at Verdi. Toscanini was no such zealot. To him Wagner was a genius but he did not have to be worshiped to the exclusion of other and different kinds of operatic genius.

He and his company served *Die Götterdämmerung* brilliantly. The Italian audience found the music drama good, and it was unstinting in its approval of the way it had been staged and played. There was special admiration for the work of the orchestra. A writer in *La Stampa* of Turin said:

In only ten days of rehearsals, under the intelligent and skillful direction of Toscanini, there is such fusion, such accuracy of interpretation and execution, such a vital and youthful spirit, as to make this orchestra one of the best in Italy, and certainly it is an orchestra that we have not heard in Turin for many years. We must realize that the execution of *Die Götterdämmerung* is one of the largest musical tasks for any conductor and it requires, even in German theaters, months and months of preparation. Toscanini has prepared and conducted the whole opera with great love and rare artistic understanding. He was able to obtain from the orchestra every finesse of color and expression and magnificent pianissimi and crescendi. . . .

A correspondent of a New York musical journal was in the audience that night, and he sent home what was probably the first word America had in print of the young Italian conductor. This reporter said that he had not heard so perfect a performance even in Germany, and he added, with remarkable prevision, that New York would find it a source of pride if it could induce him to come and conduct there.

Toscanini, of course, had had a hand in every phase of the production of *Die Götterdämmerung*—not only music but staging, sets, costumes, and lighting. Indicative of his preoccupation with every detail was the incident that occurred in this theater the following season when he directed *Tristan und Isolde*.

Toscanini wanted the lights in the auditorium turned off. That brought on a violent disagreement between him and the audience. Obviously he wished to have the mood of the dark and mysterious night projected in the second act. But the audience raised a howl of protest. Some undoubtedly preferred to have light so that they might watch their neighbors, a few upstairs needed it so that they might see to eat their box lunches, and many were annoyed because they were unable to follow the libretto. The protest was so vociferous and prolonged that Toscanini had to stop conducting. The impresario had the lights turned on, and the conductor became furious. He ordered that they be extinguished, and when his request was not carried out, he brought down his baton on the reading lamp near him and smashed it to bits. There was a hurried consultation backstage, and finally a compromise was worked out—to have the theater in a dim half-light—and this left everyone muttering discontentedly.

On February 1, 1896, came another event that made this Turin season memorable. It was the world *première* of Puccini's *La Bohème*.

The public fell in love with *La Bohème* immediately; it

was played twenty-four times that season, and probably only the house of Ricordi, Puccini's publisher, can tell how many thousands of times it has been played the world over since. But even *Bohème* was not without its antagonisms.

A few in the audience resented the fact that singers were forbidden by Toscanini to step out of character for bows or encores. He had warned the Mimi, sung by Cesira Ferrani, that it would not go well with her if she rolled around on her bed of pain to attract attention in the fourth act when she must be dying of consumption. And some of Turin's principal critics were unflattering in their remarks about the opera. One complained because colored posters had been employed to announce the *première;* the use of color on billboards was new then and apparently this gentleman thought that this, too, was within his province.

The opposition had a deeper source. Leoncavallo, it seems, had once proposed doing an opera based on Henri Mürger's *Scènes de la Vie de Bohème,* in collaboration with Puccini, and the latter did not appear to be interested. When Leoncavallo heard that Puccini was completing an opera based on this book, the libretto by Giuseppe Giacosa and Luigi Illica, he set to work composing his own setting of *Bohème.* Behind Leoncavallo stood the publishing house of Sonzogno, major rival of Ricordi, and Sonzogno was anxious to have an opera to compete with the Puccini work. During the spring of 1897, when Toscanini was in Venice to conduct Puccini's *Bohème,* Leoncavallo's opera opened at another theater, and during the following October, when Toscanini was doing Puccini's work at the Teatro dal Verme in Milan, a production of Leoncavallo's was hastily put on at the Teatro Lirico.

The public, which has the last word in such competitions, soon made the decision. It had set its seal of affection on Puccini's version at the *première* in Turin. One can be sure that it would have made its way through the world without Toscanini to assist at its first performance. But Puccini knew how much the conductor had contributed to the *première*, and he embraced him tearfully. Those who did not hear and see Toscanini working in the pit of an opera house got some idea of the passion and tenderness he could bring to this music when they heard his broadcast version with the N.B.C. Symphony early in 1946.

In the spring of 1896, Toscanini was summoned to La Scala, not yet to conduct opera but to direct a series of four symphonic programs which, in the past, had been assigned to the most eminent conductors of the period.

It must have been a moment of emotion for him to step out on the stage of La Scala as the maestro, even if it was not to conduct opera, for which the theater had won its renown. At nineteen he had played in the pit for the *première* of *Otello*, and whenever he had been in Milan as a young man he had bought a ticket for the gallery. In later years, whenever he reminisced about theaters and concert halls in which he had worked or been a member of the audience, he spoke glowingly of the acoustics of La Scala of those days as the most memorable.

His Scala programs included music by Haydn, Tchaikovsky, Wagner, Beethoven, Grieg, Brahms, Schubert, Mancinelli, Girard, Edoardo Trucco, and Ponchielli; and Camille Saint-Saëns, who was in the audience when Toscanini directed his "Danse Macabre," rushed backstage to tell the conductor that this was the first time he had heard it played throughout in the tempos he had indicated.

In June, Toscanini resumed the opera circuit with *La Bohème* as the *pièce de résistance* in various towns. In December he was back in Turin, where he conducted two concerts at the Teatro Vittorio Emmanuele, and then had full responsibility for the heavy winter season at the Teatro Regio.

In June of 1897 he took time off from his musical rounds for a personal matter. On the 21st of that month he was married to Carla de Martini, daughter of a Milan banker. Although

The Maestro: Part One

Carla was not a musician, Toscanini had met her as a result
of music. Carla's sister, Ida, was a soprano, and she had appeared under Toscanini's direction some time before in the
town of Voghera. Carla had gone with her sister. She must
have been a curious and susceptible chaperon—a teen-age
girl, simple, fresh, and lovely. She made no pretense of knowing music, and in her shy, unaffected ways she was attractive
not only in herself but as a contrast to the sharp, demanding
women of the theater with whom Toscanini had to work constantly. His old Parma friend and concertmaster, Enrico Polo,
who played with him often, was in Voghera in the pit, too.
He fell in love with and married Ida de Martini.

Toscanini's wedding took place in Milan, and the bride's
parents signalized the occasion by a proper celebration. The
groom's parents and sisters were not present. Now thirty, he
did not see any need even to consult his father and mother
about his plans. In the years since his departure from Parma,
he had kept in touch with them and had sent them funds.
But they lived in worlds apart. Though his career was bur-
geoning and they took enormous pride in it, his parents never
came to the theater to see him conduct or hear him acclaimed.
Nor was there much contact between the elder Toscaninis
and the de Martinis. Arturo did not encourage it, although he
brought his wife and later his children to visit his parental
home. One day he discovered that his father had gone to his
father-in-law to seek a loan, and he was so ashamed and horrified that he became more determined than ever to keep his
life separate from theirs.

9

La Scala Calls

IF ANY impresario or singer imagined that marriage would turn Toscanini into a cooing dove when it came to artistic standards, he did not know his man. Nor did the maestro long leave the opera world in doubt. In September, 1897, he accepted an invitation to conduct in Bergamo, the city in which Donizetti had been born a hundred years before. *La Favorita* and *Lucia di Lammermoor* were chosen for the centenary observance, and the first of these reached the stage on schedule.

In the midst of the preparations for *Lucia,* two of the principal singers fell ill. The impresario began to look about for replacements because the date for the opening of *Lucia* was approaching. Toscanini advised postponement until the singers were recovered. The impresario replied that he could not be sure when they would be well; he had promised *Lucia* on a certain date and he proposed to keep his word. Toscanini told him that the indisposed singers were indispensable. The impresario pooh-poohed the notion that it had to be those singers and none other. Toscanini retorted that he knew the available singers and that it would have to be these. The impresario hired substitutes, anyhow, whereupon Toscanini left Bergamo and the production of *Lucia* to another maestro. *Lucia,* it might be added in passing, turned out to be a failure.

Before returning to the Teatro Regio for the winter season, Toscanini conducted opera at the Teatro dal Verme in Milan and a series of concerts in Bologna. There had been an understanding that after he concluded his winter season in Turin he would return to La Scala for the symphonic series, but in the season of 1897-98 Italy's most renowned opera house remained closed. Things had not been going well with it for some time, and the city administration had declined to make its annual grant of funds. Turin made the most of the opportunity. An International Exposition was scheduled for the summer, and Toscanini was engaged to conduct a large number of symphonic concerts. He was delighted to have an opportunity to conduct orchestral programs, especially since the Turin officials shrewdly gave him a free hand in the selection of programs.

Before plunging into these concerts, Toscanini celebrated the arrival of his first child. On March 21st, Walter was born. It was just nine months after Toscanini's marriage. He got a kick out of the perfect timing. In later years he liked to mention the date of his marriage and the date of Walter's birth and added, with sparkling eyes, "I was always in tempo."

He had a few weeks in which to relish the infant, and then he got to work on the orchestral series. And work he did. He cannot recall any period in his life when he worked harder. Between May 9th and July 14th and between August 20th and November 1st, he directed forty-three concerts with almost constant changes of program. Only a Haydn symphony and a Mozart symphony and overture were repeated. He conducted one hundred and thirty-three compositions by fifty-four different composers. Forty-eight of these pieces had not been heard in Turin before, and some were new not only to the public but to the conductor.

The programs were a calculated mixture of big, serious works and light, easily accessible pieces, since Toscanini was mindful that Exposition visitors would represent all manner of tastes. But the programs ranged over a large musical area, from the sixteenth-century masters of Italian music to living composers of many countries. Beethoven was represented by the First, Third, Fourth, Sixth, and Ninth Symphonies (only two movements) and several of the overtures; Brahms by the First and Fourth Symphonies; Schumann by the Fourth; and Schubert by the "Unfinished." There was music by Weber, Mendelssohn, Cherubini, Rossini, and Berlioz. There were, among contemporary composers, Dvořák, D'Indy, Lalo, Saint-Saëns, Massenet, Bizet, Franck, Humperdinck, Goldmark, Lassen, Grieg, Svendsen, Fuchs, Stanford, Cowen, Smetana, Rimsky-Korsakov, Ponchielli, Orefice, Bazzini, Faccio, Celega, Foroni, Catalani, Mancinelli, Franchetti, Bolzoni, Sinigaglia, Martucci, Sgambati, and Tosi. There were also important scores by Tchaikovsky and Verdi.

Toscanini directed the first Italian performance of the "Pathetic" Symphony. It seems ironic, in the light of Toscanini's later record with the symphony, to discover that he espoused it first in his own country. For many years, when he was at the peak of his fame as a symphonic conductor, he did not conduct Tchaikovsky at all. When he was with the New York Philharmonic, he was condemned for his snobbishness, since it was assumed that he looked down on the Russian as an inferior composer not worthy of his notice.

That was not and could not be his attitude. In ignoring Tchaikovsky he was being honest. He had no feeling for the music, and he would not conduct what he did not feel. But some years ago he began to conduct Tchaikovsky again—first the "Manfred" Symphony, then "Romeo and Juliet," and finally the "Pathetic." What drew him back to the "Pathetic" was partly his irritation with the tearful and distorted way in which certain conductors among his contemporaries conducted it and, more important, his reading of a new biography of the composer. He was so deeply touched by the tortured, inner life of poor Tchaikovsky, as it was revealed in Catherine Drinker Bowen's *Beloved Friend,* that he took up the score of the "Pathetic" and found that he wished to conduct it once more. "It is honest music," he said.

73

In preparing Verdi's *Pezzi Sacri* for chorus for their first performances in Italy, Toscanini was disturbed by a passage in the Te Deum. He felt that the music here required a ritard, but there was no such indication in the score. He decided to go to Genoa to consult Verdi. The night before his appointment with the old composer he could not sleep, he was so agitated at his own temerity. He kept hoping that Verdi himself would play through the music, but the composer, now fragile and weary, invited his young visitor to sit down to the piano. Toscanini was hesitant. He forced himself to play, and when he came to the troublesome passage, he gave it the ritard that it seemed to him it must have. When he was finished, Verdi patted him on the back and said, "Bravo!"

"Then the ritard here"—Toscanini pointed to the place—"did not offend you?"

"No." Verdi smiled. "It is what I want."

"But you did not indicate a ritard?"

"I was afraid to," the composer said. "If I had written it down, it would be played too slowly. A true musician would sense that there should be a ritardando."

During this symphonic season in Turin, Toscanini would sit up all night studying scores. He left nothing to chance. Whether the music was new to him, whether he had not seen it for years, or whether it was something he had played the previous year, he went over it with unrelenting thoroughness. There were times when he fell asleep score in hand. In the afternoons he would rehearse and in the evenings conduct.

One evening during a Beethoven-Wagner program, he found himself thinking of something other than the music as the orchestra got under way with the Prelude to *Die Meistersinger*. He was shocked suddenly to find that he was lost. But he kept beating time and shouted *"Da capo!"* to the orchestra. Without a pause in the music, the men returned to the beginning and went on from there.

Recalling this incident years later, the maestro observed,

"Whatever happens, I keep beating time. Something will happen."

Apparently, it does. There was another occasion when he became preoccupied as he stood on the podium, and he found, to his horror, that his stick was in an upbeat while the orchestra was on the downbeat, but the music went on as he righted himself. Another time, when he was conducting the N.B.C. Symphony, he noticed that an instrumentalist sitting near him seemed to be weaving and sawing as though he had lost control of his movements. It looked as if he might topple out of his chair. Despite his shortsightedness, Toscanini could see the fellow, and he knew that he was either sick or drunk. As the music unfolded, an official slipped out and helped the musician off the stage. Toscanini had kept on beating time, and something had happened, sure enough.

Before this Turin season of concerts was half over, Toscanini's mind was on other things. In the spring he had had his first feelers from La Scala. Would he take over the job of conductor and artistic director? He had waited a long time for such an invitation, but he did not accept without conditions. In the years preceding its closing, the theater had gone downhill, and if the shame of shutting its doors after more than a century of activity was to be redeemed, it must be done on uncompromising artistic principles.

Toscanini was dead set against the institution of the impresario. He had had his share of good, bad, and indifferent impresarios, but he did not think that even the best were the proper foundation for a major opera house. He thought that the theater should be run on a more dependable plan, that its fate should not be tied up to the good or bad luck an impresario might experience.

He was asked what he thought of the idea of having a director general installed, a man of superior background and training, who would function much as the government-appointed intendants of the German opera houses did. He replied that this was a promising approach, but whom did the Scala people have in mind? He was told that there was a young man named Giulio Gatti-Casazza who had served in a similar function for five years in Ferrara. Toscanini remembered Gatti and seemed to approve.

In July, 1898, Gatti, who had been appointed to the post, had his first meeting with La Scala's directorate, which was headed by Duke Guido Visconti di Modrone and which included Giuseppe Gallignani, head of the Milan Conservatory, and Arrigo Boito, composer and the librettist for Verdi's *Otello* and *Falstaff*. In his memoirs Gatti recalled how he outlined the parlous state of La Scala's affairs: "Theater almost abandoned, finances and subsidy far below essential demands; no scenery, chorus, ballet, school, orchestra, stage crew; everything gone and everything to be reorganized; publishers in bad humor; the press anything but friendly; no ledgers showing expenses or receipts or salaries during the previous seasons, the impresarios having left not a scrap of information behind them; and only a short time ahead of us to prepare the coming season."

It was Boito who stopped the gloomy recital with the cry that directors must perform miracles, and Duke Visconti took Gatti aside and promised financial help out of his own pocket provided artistic results were achieved. Gatti traveled with Boito to Turin for conferences with Toscanini, who knew what La Scala's situation was.

Toscanini was full of plans for the Scala season. He did not fret over the problems that lay ahead. He welcomed the chance to build afresh, and his sense of excitement conveyed itself to Gatti, who, deep in his heart, was looking forward to meeting the challenge with the same enthusiasm, even if his nature was inclined to be more somber.

Toscanini could hardly wait for the final Turin concert, so eager was he to plunge into preparations for the Scala season. The Turin impresario was host at a lavish banquet to Toscanini after the last concert. He expressed the sorrow of Turin that the conductor was leaving for La Scala, but consoled the company with the thought that at least Milan had had to come to Turin to find a real maestro.

Here is a summary of the places in Italy in which Toscanini conducted—and the operas—between his Italian debut with *Edmea* in Turin in 1886 and his arrival at La Scala in 1898:

Casale Monferrato (1887)—*L'Africaine, I Lombardi, La Gioconda*.

Verona (1887-88)—*Carmen, Lucrezia Borgia*.

Macerata (1888)—*Aïda*.

Milan, Teatro dal Verme (1888)—*La Forza del Destino*, Ponchielli's *I Promessi Sposi*, Antonio Cagnoni's *Francesca da Rimini*.

Novara (1888-89)—*Aïda, La Forza del Destino*.

Turin, Teatro Carignano (1889)—*Carmen, Edmea*.

Genoa, Politeama (1889)—*Francesca da Rimini*.

Voghera (1889)—*Aïda, La Favorita*.

Brescia (1890)—*La Gioconda*, Puccini's *Le Villi*.

Genoa, Politeama (1890)—*Mignon*.

Turin, Teatro Carignano (1890)—*Mignon, Carmen*.

Sinigaglia (1891)—*Cavalleria Rusticana*.

Turin, Teatro Carignano (1891)—*Cavalleria Rusticana, Luisa Miller*.

Genoa, Carlo Felice (1891-92)—*Le Prophète, Simon Boccanegra*, Mascagni's *L'Amico Fritz, Loreley*.

Milan, Teatro dal Verme (1892)—*Hamlet, Pagliacci* (world *première*).

Lucca (1892)—*La Wally*.

Genoa, Carlo Felice (1892)—*Cristoforo Colombo, La Wally*.

Rome, Teatro Costanzi (1892)—*Carmen, La Forza del Destino*, Gnaga's *Guglielmo Swarten* (world *première*).

Palermo (1892-93)—*Pagliacci, Loreley, Cavalleria Rusticana,*

Norma, The Flying Dutchman, The Barber of Seville, Rigoletto, La Gioconda.

Pisa (1894)—*Otello, Manon Lescaut.*

Ravenna (1894)—Massenet's *Le Roi de Lahore.*

Brescia (1894)—*Manon, I Puritani, La Traviata.*

Treviso (1894)—*Falstaff, Cristoforo Colombo.*

Bologna (1894)—*Falstaff, Cristoforo Colombo,* Natale Canti's *Savitri* (world *première*).

Genoa, Carlo Felice (1894-95)—*Falstaff, Cristoforo Colombo, Cavalleria Rusticana, L'Amico Fritz, Tannhäuser, Savitri, La Forza del Destino.*

Pisa (1895)—*Falstaff, Cristoforo Colombo.*

Venice (1895)—*Falstaff, La Forza del Destino, Cristoforo Colombo, Le Villi,* Antonio Lozzi's *Emma Liona* (world *première*).

Trento (1895)—*Cristoforo Colombo.*

Treviso (1895)—*Tannhäuser, Loreley.*

Turin, Teatro Regio (1895-96)—*Die Götterdämmerung, Falstaff, Savitri, La Bohème* (world *première*), Paer's *Le Maître de Chapelle, Emma Liona.*

Trento (1896)—*La Bohème.*

Brescia (1896)—*La Bohème.*

Venice (1896)—*La Forza del Destino, La Favorita,* Apolloni's *L'Ebreo.*

Bologna (1896)—*La Bohème, Le Villi.*

Turin, Teatro Regio (1896-97)—*Andrea Chenier, Samson et Dalila, Mefistofele, Tristan und Isolde,* Arturo Buzzi-Peccia's *Forza d'Amore* (world *première*).

Venice (1897)—*La Bohème.*

Bergamo (1897)—*La Favorita.*

Milan, Teatro dal Verme (1897)—*La Bohème, Manon Lescaut.*

Turin, Teatro Regio (1897-98)—*Die Walküre, La Bohème, Mefistofele,* Luigi Mancinelli's *Ero e Leandro,* Enrico de Leva's *Camargo* (world *première*).

10

At La Scala

WHEN he lets his mind rove over all the theaters of three continents in which he has conducted opera, Arturo Toscanini speaks with special affection of La Scala. He has warm memories of Bayreuth and Salzburg and of performances, colleagues, and incidents in other opera houses, but it is clear that La Scala is closest to his heart. And it could scarcely be otherwise to one who was born and raised in Italy and who, despite visits and residence elsewhere, is an Italian to his roots.

La Scala is Italy's most important opera house, and for many years it bulked as the most important in the world. When the theater was opened in 1778, it was the best equipped of its time, and its artistic reputation through the years matched its physical facilities. It was the theater that introduced Verdi's first opera, *Oberto, Conte di San Bonifacio,* in 1839, and his last and greatest, *Otello* and *Falstaff*. All the principal Italian singers of a century—as well as artists from other lands—strove to appear there, and so did the conductors.

Toscanini had established himself firmly in other theaters, but to arrive at La Scala was like coming home. He was to know the joy of accomplishment and the fury of frustration there. He fled the theater on several occasions, but after a few years, or a great many, he returned. Even when he condemned indifference and stupidity in its management, he remained fond of the theater. There was a time after the First

World War when, though he himself was not working much or earning much, he made a substantial anonymous gift to La Scala. During the twenties, when he assumed full direction of the theater and gave Milan unforgettable years of opera, he was granted a large bonus at the end of one season. It was well over one hundred thousand lire, but it was his due, since he was working for a modest fee. He turned the money back as a gift to La Scala, and to this day you can find the gift listed on a plaque with the donor described as anonymous.

Whatever the future might hold, Toscanini tackled his duties in 1898 not only with his usual energy but with the inarticulate major premise that now, at last, his was the opportunity to serve La Scala.

He knew—he had been to the wars—what an opera house needed: a fine orchestra; a good ballet and chorus; imaginative sets, costumes, and stage direction; and dependable singers, if they could be had. Most important, it needed a guiding hand that would make sure that a unified artistic point of view would prevail. He wanted the emphasis on the opera as a whole, not on details of performance or the whims of personalities.

Milan had a fair idea of what Toscanini would seek to do. His reputation had preceded him. The newspapers and periodicals had been mentioning his work for years, and there had been a few opportunities to view him at close range at the Teatro dal Verme. Tension was high even before Toscanini arrived in Milan in November with his wife, his baby, and the child's nurse, a young Italian girl who was to remain with the family for more than forty years. People said that Toscanini would stir things up. They said that he would respect no one in the company or in the audience. They whispered that the fashionable ladies would have to remove their plumed hats if they were to be permitted to remain in the theater. They said—most fearful thing of all—that he would come to the same end as Faccio. They recalled that nine years ago

Faccio had conducted the Italian *première* of *Die Meister-singer*, and the onerous task had driven him mad. It was true that Faccio had suddenly lost his grip during a rehearsal of *Die Meistersinger*, was taken to an insane asylum, and died there a year later. Well, Toscanini was beginning at La Scala with *Die Meistersinger*. . . .

Toscanini did not go mad, but the Scala company knew it had been put through a grinder before it got *Die Meister-singer* on. For a month before the opening Toscanini worked with the orchestra, the singers, and the chorus, and he found time to check up on the sets. Antonio Scotti had been engaged to sing Hans Sachs, and he arrived some days before the opening from a triumphant season in Chile. He had never seen the score and when he opened it in Chile, he cried, "*Dio mio*, I am finished. My career is over." His accompanist had thrown up his hands in dismay. During the twenty-eight-day voyage from Chile, Campanini, who had been the conductor there, offered to work with Scotti. When the handsome, dark-haired young baritone appeared at La Scala for his first rehearsal, Toscanini stopped him, annoyed that he was omitting part of his first-act music.

"Who made those cuts?" the conductor demanded.

"I don't know," Scotti said. "They were in my score. Maybe the publisher."

"I don't make them," Toscanini said coldly.

"But we are only a few days from the opening," Scotti protested.

"I'm sorry," Toscanini said. "I don't make them."

Neither did Scotti, and he had to hustle to memorize the restored parts.

The performance paid off for the attention and effort that had gone into it. The public liked it; most of the press, with the exception of a bleeding-heart writer who cried out that Toscanini was making intolerable and ruinous demands of the singers, hailed it, too. The *Corriere della Sera* sought to tick off a Paris rival which had written that the Opéra's production of *Die Meistersinger* was better than Vienna's, Berlin's, Munich's, London's. The reviewer in Milan's leading paper would not go so far as to claim that La Scala's *Die Meistersinger* was superior to those of the other cities; he would merely state that it surpassed Paris's.

Toscanini had reason to be gratified with this start. He had not conducted *Die Meistersinger* before, nor had he ever seen a performance of it. He had brought it fresh from the printed page to the stage. But he was to learn the very next summer that you can fail to see a thing even though you do not spare yourself in studying it. At Bayreuth in the summer of 1899, where he traveled with Gatti-Casazza, he heard *Die Meistersinger* conducted by Hans Richter. Early in the Prelude Richter made a rallentando that Toscanini did not remember having seen. As soon as he got out of the theater he rushed to examine a score. The rallentando was there.

"Sono stupido!" he shouted at himself. One felt fifty years later that he was still annoyed with himself for this oversight.

The other operas of that first Scala season were Mascagni's *Iris*, Meyerbeer's *Les Huguenots, Falstaff*, Massenet's *Le Roi de Lahore*, and Rossini's *William Tell*. After the production of *Falstaff*, which had Scotti in the title role, Verdi sent Toscanini a telegram, "Thanks, thanks, thanks." From Verdi, who was not given to flattery, this was high praise indeed.

There were plenty of dissenters, however. Some were annoyed because Toscanini would not allow Scotti to repeat *"Quand' ero paggio."* Others attacked the conductor on the ground that he was a slave to the metronome. They said that his beat was inexorable, that his rhythms were rigid, that he was an enemy of Italian song and a wrecker of the art of *bel canto*. One of Italy's greatest exponents of *bel canto*, Battistini, possibly the finest baritone the country ever produced, came to the Scala and insisted that Toscanini had brought *bel canto* back to Italy, but whatever he might say carried no weight with those who attacked Toscanini. Had not the conductor done *Die Meistersinger?* Did not his record show an earlier preoccupation with Wagner? It stood to reason, the man was at heart a *Kapellmeister,* not an Italian conductor.

Years later Toscanini touched on the curious paradox: In Italy they accused him of being a German conductor, and in Germany they said he was an Italian conductor. In the midst of battles, this pat analysis irked him; now he chuckles over it.

Toscanini gave the Milanese further reason to take pot shots at him during that first season at La Scala. A revival of Bellini's *Norma* had been promised. Gatti-Casazza described it tactfully thirty-odd years later as "a piece of bad luck" that *Norma* had to be withdrawn at the eleventh hour. It was not bad luck; it was Toscanini. He worked endlessly on *Norma.* It did not go as he wished. The role of Norma is one of the most difficult in opera; it requires a dramatic soprano with a voice that has range and power and sustained purity and, at the same time, the flexibility of a coloratura. Toscanini warned that the soprano would not do, but upon the insistence of others he kept trying. He tried through the dress rehearsal and then announced flatly that he would have no part of this *Norma.*

William Tell was chosen by Toscanini and Gatti-Casazza as the substitute opera. They had planned to do *Otello* during the season and had invited Francesco Tamagno, the tenor who had sung the title role at the opera's *première*, to return to La Scala for a revival. But Tamagno had asked for ten thousand lire a performance, a staggering figure in those days. It was suspected that he was angry at Verdi for not using his influence to get him a French decoration he wanted and had deliberately pegged his fee. Before the season was over, Tamagno got his decoration and offered to sing at La Scala.

Toscanini rushed *William Tell* through rehearsals at breakneck speed, and just when it was ready to open, Tamagno came down with a cold. He complained that his nose was stuffed, and when it was stuffed he could not sing. The performance was held up while he sat in his hotel room and sniffed watchfully. Toscanini was impatient, the public made snide quips, and La Scala was embarrassed. Each day Gatti-Casazza waited upon Tamagno for hopeful news, and finally he tried a new tactic on his stricken tenor. The public was whispering, Gatti said mournfully, that Tamagno was afraid to sing. The tenor let out a roar of anger, and suddenly, as he stopped to catch his breath, he cried, "Look, my nose is clear." *William Tell* was put on that evening. It was a production that closed Toscanini's and Gatti's first Scala season distinctly on the alkaline side. There was a deficit, but Duke Visconti, satisfied that he had got the artistic results he had hoped for, cheerfully paid it out of his own pocket.

Toscanini's labors were not over. He directed four concerts at La Scala. At the first he conducted Don Lorenzo Perosi's oratorio *La Resurrezione di Lazzaro,* Verdi's *Pezzi Sacri,* a symphony by Schumann, and a march by Schubert in a Liszt orchestration. At the next three concerts Brahms, Berlioz, Wagner, and Beethoven figured prominently, in addition to a group of Italian composers, most of them contemporaries.

After his first visit to Bayreuth, where he saw the *Ring* conducted by Wagner's son, Siegfried, *Parsifal,* directed by Franz von Fischer, and *Die Meistersinger* under Richter, Toscanini returned to Milan to prepare for his second season at La Scala. The first two productions were to be *Siegfried* and *Otello,* and he undertook the unbelievably arduous task of rehearsing them almost simultaneously. The casts for the two operas were different, and Toscanini would spend time with each group each day. He and Gatti-Casazza had agreed to open on December 26th with *Siegfried* and to follow the next night with *Otello.* To get one of them ready was a big job; to put both through their final paces in the same interval was an assignment that only a Toscanini would have dared to undertake and could have carried through. It must be remembered that this was the first *Siegfried* by an Italian company, and Toscanini did not baby himself, his company, or his public by making excessive cuts.

The old-time subscribers of La Scala did not take kindly to *Siegfried,* though they suffered through it. The experts told them that they had heard a magnificent performance. It must have been, in fact, an extraordinary one. Apparently Toscanini did not overwhelm his singers with the sonority of his orchestra. Everything, on the testimony of those who were there, was handsomely proportioned, and Giuseppe Borgatti, the tenor who became Italy's leading Wagner interpreter, handled the long and difficult role with resourcefulness. He had been at Bayreuth with Toscanini, and he had worked with a will to master the role under the conductor's tutelage.

For *Otello* there was Tamagno, and Toscanini led a taut, seething performance. The Milanese public had every reason to be pleased, but there were always elements with grievances, and they were waiting to get at Toscanini. Their chance came with *Lohengrin,* the next production.

The conductor was a happy man during the preparation of *Lohengrin.* He was rehearsing the third act with the orchestra, he remembered later, when someone rushed into the theater with a message. It was word that his second child, a daughter, had just been born. The orchestra shouted its congratulations. He sought to act as though nothing unusual had occurred and ordered the rehearsal to go on. "I didn't know what I was doing," he recalled. The cheerful faces of the men in the orchestra told him that they were tolerant of his effort to act unconcerned. Finally, he put down his baton and dashed off to see mother and child. He recounted years later how he was struck by the perfect beauty of the child's face and how he had whispered to his wife, "Carla, you must have sculpted that face with your hands." He was joyful that at last he had a daughter whom he could name Wally in honor of his departed friend, Catalani.

The memory of *Lohengrin* would be warm all his life, and things happened at the performance to keep it green in another way. The Prelude, which had hit him with such impact in his teens, made a tremendous impression on the audience, and it clamored for a repeat. Toscanini would not grant it, and the evening began with irritation on both sides. In the third act the curtain was lowered between scenes for only a few moments, as required by the composer, and again there was an outcry. La Scala audiences seemed to think that there should be an intermission here so that there might be time to chat with one's friends and to take a bit of refreshment.

It may be that the audience was restless because it found *Lohengrin* long-winded. Other audiences have felt that Wagner was too much of a good thing, and for an Italian gathering, save for the Wagnerites in it, that might well have been the case. But certainly the Scala audiences of this period could not have minded a long evening in the theater. It was traditional to follow the opera with a ballet. Imagine the durability it took to sit through *Siegfried* or *Lohengrin* and then to be game for a ballet. Toscanini thought the procedure insane, and Gatti-Casazza agreed with him. In their third year at La Scala they eliminated the ballet after a long opera, especially after Wagner's works.

Tosca, which followed Lohengrin, did not fare well in the press. Yes, *Tosca*! But this time it was Puccini who was held culpable, not Toscanini. Puccini, one writer said, had not written a single original tune in the piece. The opera had gone famously at its *première* in Rome some months before, and the public warmed to it in Milan before the evening was over. And Toscanini was indulgent about encores. He let the soprano, Ericlea Darclée, repeat *"Vissi d'arte,"* and the tenor, Borgatti, encored *"E lucevan le stelle."* The man, his enemies muttered without pleasure, was unpredictable.

To round out a season of unremitting labor, Toscanini prepared and conducted two more *premières*. One was a new opera, *Anton,* by a twenty-seven-year-old Italian composer, Cesare Galeotti. The other was Tchaikovsky's *Eugene Onegin,* which had not been done in Italy before.

Toscanini was now pleased with the way the Scala orchestra, which he had assembled and worked with for two seasons, had come along, and he was eager to show it off to other cities. Besides giving the usual four concerts at the Scala after the opera season, he took the orchestra on a tour of Piacenza, Parma, Bologna, Treviso, Udine, Trieste, Venice, and Brescia. His native town made an occasion of the visit, presenting him with a laurel wreath after the concert, and it is probable that his parents, who had shared in his fame at a distance, were there to beam and to receive the compliments of their neighbors.

It was the first of several tours he was to take with different orchestras over the years, and the reaction was much the same as it was to be later. "It is a triumphal tour," said a Milan periodical. "Toscanini is at this moment at the peak of his career." If one is to judge by his behavior on other tours, he was also having a grand time. After all, he had worked in the same theater for two seasons, with no other engagements. He was fond of traveling, and he was glad to be on the road with an ensemble he thought well of.

Clearly his duties at La Scala, strenuous though they were, did not suffice to consume all his energies. Before the next season began he prepared and conducted the world *première* of *Zaza,* a new opera by Leoncavallo. This took place at the Teatro Lirico, not at La Scala.

For the beginning of the Scala season of 1900-01, Toscanini again prepared two productions at once—*La Bohème* and *Tristan und Isolde.* The *Tristan* went well, and it was planned for the opening of the season. The gossip that seeped out of the theater built up great expectations for it. Then it could not be done as the season's starter because Borgatti, the Tristan, fell ill. Naturally, Toscanini was shouldered with much of the blame by the public, and before the curtain could be raised for the season there was fresh grumbling about him.

La Bohème had not gone so smoothly in rehearsal, but it had to serve as the opener. Toscanini had had trouble with a young fellow who was to make his debut at La Scala, a tenor named Enrico Caruso.

Caruso was then, and remained throughout his career, a nervous, sensitive artist despite his capacity for gaiety. The importance of this debut lay heavily on his mind. He reacted to every bit of gossip he heard about himself, and Milan was full of rumor mongers. He heard that he was not well, that his ability was doubted, that his fee of fifty thousand lire for three months was outrageously high, and he worried about all these tales. At his first rehearsal he sang "*Che gelida manina*" in full voice but used falsetto for the high C. Toscanini asked him whether he could give more strength to the high C, and Caruso said he could. "Let's hear it," said Toscanini. "It is too early in the morning," Caruso replied, and the conductor did not press the point.

At the third rehearsal Caruso still sang the high C softly Toscanini was evidently patient. He stopped and said he could not go on unless he heard the note full voice and suggested, in a rare, conciliatory spirit, that it might be easier for the tenor if the aria were transposed down a half tone. Caruso agreed to the change, but when he got to the B-natural, he still sang half-voice.

Toscanini was undoubtedly brooding about this tenor and his top tone. He called a special rehearsal for the morning of the very day the dress rehearsal was scheduled. Caruso was summoned to the theater at nine in the morning and told that there would be "a small rehearsal." Toscanini went through the third act, stopping often for changes and repetitions. Then he went on to the fourth act. It was followed by the first and second acts. There was no mention of lunch, and Caruso, realizing that his soup was getting cold, was furious. He sang

ILLUSTRATION SECTION

Claudio Toscanini, Arturo's father, was an imaginative, not-too-successful tailor of Parma, who had been a follower of Garibaldi. (See pages 3-5.)

Arturo Toscanini, from a photograph taken in 1870, when he was three years old.

Toscanini at the age of eight, with his Aunt Clementina and a girl who may be one of his two sisters. A year after this photograph was taken, Arturo was entered at the Conservatory of Parma. (See page 9.)

Caricature of Toscanini that appeared after his Italian debut as a conductor at the age of nineteen. "A splendid dawn has risen on the horizon of art," said one critic about *il bambino Toscanini.* (See page 33.)

At twenty-two, the young maestro had grown a mustache and was getting engagements here and there in provincial opera houses. (See page 39.)

Toscanini with Enrico Polo in 1896, when Polo was his concert-master with the orchestra at Genoa. (See page 47.) Later, Polo was to become the brother-in-law of Mme. Toscanini.

On June 21, 1897, Toscanini was married to Carla de Martini. Nine months later, to the day, Walter Toscanini was born. (See page 72.) This photograph was taken when Walter was three years old.

After Walter, came two daughters, Wally and Wanda. This photograph shows the proud father with the younger, Wanda, when she was three.

In his thirties, already established at La Scala as one of Italy's leading conductors, the maestro's face showed some of the strain involved in always maintaining the highest standards.

Brought to the Metropolitan Opera House in 1908 by Gatti-Casazza, Toscanini soon became its dominant musical figure despite frequent disagreements with both the impresario and such stars as Geraldine Farrar. (See Chapter 12.)

Caricatures by Enrico Caruso.

During World War I, Toscanini insisted on being as close to the front as possible. This photograph was taken during the Battle of Monte Santo. (See pages 142-143.)

In 1926, Toscanini was musical director at La Scala in Milan and also conducted the New York Philharmonic. This photo shows him arriving in New York for the Philharmonic season accompanied by Wally, Carla, Walter, and Wanda Toscanini.

COURTESY: N.B.C.

One more assignment undertaken by Toscanini was conducting at the Salzburg festival, where he first went in 1934. Here he is shown rehearsing with Erich Leinsdorf and Lotte Lehmann for a performance of *Fidelio*. (See Chapter 19.)

In 1937, when he was seventy, the N.B.C. Symphony was formed for Toscanini to conduct, and he has remained its principal conductor ever since. The top two pictures show him conducting during a motion picture he prepared for the OWI's war effort; the lower two are taken from his historic first appearance on television. (See Chapter 21.)

Today, Toscanini's American residence is in the Riverdale section of New York City. Here he delights in the company of his family, including his three grandchildren, Emanuele Castelbarco, Walfredo Toscanini, and Sonya Horowitz.

The maestro never gave lessons but, of course, made a very occasional exception for his beloved granddaughter Sonya.

throughout full voice and in the first-act aria reached the B-natural surely and strongly.

As he left the theater in midafternoon, he was astonished to hear an announcement that the dress rehearsal would begin at 9 P.M. He was primed to protest, even to Toscanini, but was assured that the dress rehearsal would be sung half-voice. When he arrived in the theater that evening he found that there was a sizable audience. Dress rehearsals at La Scala in those days were almost like performances, and the invited guests included important citizens of the town, opera officials, subscribers with influence, critics, members of the company who were not singing in the opera, and friends and relatives of all. Caruso found, too, that his colleagues in the cast were singing full voice, but he refused to follow their lead.

Toscanini was irked by this, and said so to Gatti-Casazza, who went backstage to talk to Caruso and to beg for more voice. Caruso said he had recently eaten and could not comply. Thoroughly upset by now, the tenor had trouble even with half-voice singing in the second act. Toscanini rapped his baton and pointed it at Caruso. "If you don't sing, I can't go on," he shouted. Caruso started to explain about his digestion. Toscanini glared at him, slammed down his baton, and walked out of the pit.

It required the intercession of Duke Visconti to get the rehearsal finished. The Duke went backstage to confer with Caruso, who was ready to return the advance he had received and leave the theater for good. The Duke got from the tenor a promise that he would sing out as best as he could, and then he conveyed the message to Toscanini. The rehearsal was resumed and ended at one in the morning.

When Caruso awoke the next day he was ill. Then he was told by Gatti that because of Borgatti's illness, *La Bohème* must open the season. The tenor protested that he was just as sick as Borgatti, but after two hours of arguments Gatti prevailed.

Caruso did not sing his best that night, and in view of the public's displeasure at having *La Bohème* instead of the promised *Tristan und Isolde,* Puccini's opera got a cold reception. Things picked up as the work was repeated, and Caruso's stock went up steadily with the tough Milanese audiences as he did himself greater justice in Mascagni's *Le Maschere,* Boito's *Mefistofele,* and Donizetti's *L'Elisir d'Amore.*

L'Elisir d'Amore was another battle for Toscanini and Gatti-Casazza, and Caruso had a big share in helping them to win it. *Le Maschere,* Mascagni's new opera which was performed for the first time simultaneously in Turin, Genoa, Venice, and Rome as well as in Milan, was a failure, and another production had to be put together quickly to replace it. *L'Elisir* was decided upon after Toscanini, who despaired of finding a *basso buffo* to do Dulcamara, agreed to try it with an old-timer named Federico Carbonetti, who spent his time singing in the secondary theaters.

Carbonetti's appearance was not auspicious. In the middle of winter he arrived in town without an overcoat and with a battered canvas valise held together by cord. He began by laughing at those who said he was old, crying out that he could travel in cold weather without an overcoat while the youngsters were too soft to emulate him. At rehearsal he cheerfully sought to induce Toscanini to let him add top notes not required by Donizetti. They are fine notes, he said genially; you should listen to them. Toscanini looked at the old chap and laughed grimly. But Carbonetti was agreeable. If the maestro did not see things his way, he would not press him.

The news that such an artist had been engaged by La Scala caused further abuse of Toscanini. The idea of doing *L'Elisir* with such a personage at the Scala, they complained; it's like turning La Scala into a provincial theater.

It turned out that Carbonetti, obeying Toscanini's instructions with good will, disarmed and amused the public, and as for Caruso, he conquered. His singing of the aria *"Una furtiva lagrima"* was perfection, on the word of Toscanini, who said many years later that the tenor never sang more beautifully. Toscanini, it should be added, felt that Caruso was going downhill in his years at the Metropolitan. He thought that the voice, which he regarded as a phenomenon of our time, was at its purest and most electrifying in that production of *L'Elisir d'Amore* at La Scala in 1901.

Caruso, for his part, was now sure of himself. In fact, that very season when he was joined by Feodor Chaliapin for the revival of *Mefistofele,* and when the Russian basso ran into difficulties with Toscanini over singing half-voice, Caruso reassured him offhandedly: "You must not worry. He knows what the rest of us can do, and your voice is new to him. Toscanini is like one of those dogs that bark and do not bite."

Chaliapin's debut at La Scala that season, his first appearance outside of Russia, gave the Milanese plenty to talk about. The news of the engagement of "this Scythian barbarian" was enough to set them off. The operatic world was outraged at the idea of hiring a foreigner when Italy had all the talent a theater could wish. Boito, the composer, who had been reluctant to sanction a revival for fear it would not go well, was disturbed. And at the first rehearsal Toscanini, who had also begun to fret under the impact of rumors about Chaliapin's lack of talent, had reason to be disturbed, too. After the rehearsal he sat down and wrote a note to Gatti-Casazza; this was something he had never done before. He asked that the evening rehearsal be called off and he demanded a conference with Gatti.

When Toscanini and Gatti met that evening, the former said that Chaliapin had hummed instead of singing out. Asked why he had not requested the Russian to sing out, Toscanini replied that he was afraid to intimidate him. He was almost afraid, he added with an embarrassed smile, to hear his voice after all the talk there had been about it.

At the rehearsal next day, Chaliapin resumed singing in a soft voice, and Toscanini, without resentment, said that he would have to sing out, and patiently explained the reasons. The Russian basso's good-humored reply was that he would be glad to. His full voice had quality and character and he knew how to use it. Toscanini was delighted. At the end of the rehearsal he told Chaliapin that they would work together and turn out something extraordinary. And they did. Even the chauvinists of the Milan public had to concede that this "barbarian" was an artist.

Toscanini later revised his opinion of Chaliapin as an artist. He remarked that the Russian began to be a law unto himself, that he exaggerated the music to please himself, and that, like so many singers before and after him, he could not keep up to a high standard. And yet when Toscanini saw Chaliapin in *Boris Godunov* in Paris some years later, he was so stirred by the magnificence and humanity of the singing and acting that he rushed backstage and kissed Chaliapin. The tall, brawny basso responded by throwing his arms around the little maestro, lifting him off the ground, and swinging him around in a crushing embrace.

The *Tristan und Isolde* of that season turned out to be all that had been expected of it. People came from all over Italy and from abroad to hear it. Was it this production that Gustav Mahler heard, which caused him to write in excitement about this Italian conductor, Toscanini, to his young friend and disciple Bruno Walter? Years later Walter told Toscanini that the first he had heard of him was from Mahler after a performance of *Tristan.*

Goldmark's *Die Königin von Saba* and a new opera by Isidore de Lara, called *Messaline,* were the other operas of the season, but the event that bulked largest in the heart and memory of Toscanini was the death, on January 27, 1901, of Giuseppe Verdi.

Toscanini had visited the maestro from time to time when-

ever there was good reason, and the venerable old master was
fond of having the young musician, whose eyes were so bright
and alert and mind so clear, come and chat with him about the
world of music. For Verdi, almost to the very end of his long
life, maintained a lively interest in all that was happening. It
is not going too far to guess that he discerned in the young
man a spirit much like his own. Verdi had confronted realities
all his life. He had seen the world clearly—without cynicism
and without illusions. Here was a young man who seemed also
to be intolerant of dishonesty and sham. Here, moreover, was
a musician who had proved his devotion by putting on the
composer's operas with fervor and perception.

During the previous season there had been the incident of
Tamagno and *Otello.* The tenor had insisted during rehearsals
that his singing of a passage in the last act was exactly as
Verdi had taught it to him. Toscanini had been at those rehearsals as a cellist, and he insisted that not only was he
following the tempo markings in the score but that he remembered them vividly from the performance. Tamagno would
not give in easily, and Toscanini had invited him to visit
Verdi for a decisive opinion. Verdi had held that Toscanini's
memory had been accurate and had congratulated the conductor, much to Tamagno's disgust, who clung tenaciously to
the belief that both had changed their minds.

Toscanini remembered Verdi on birthdays and holidays,
and for the New Year of 1901 had exchanged greetings with
him. The maestro still carries a yellowed card on which the
composer, in a shaky hand, had written best wishes for the
New Year to his young friend.

Little more than a week before Verdi's death, Toscanini
had gone to visit the old man, who was now living in Milan
and was eager to hear about Mascagni's latest opera, *Le
Maschere.* Toscanini told of the fiasco and gave some details
of the piece. Verdi seemed to be interested in the fact that
Mascagni had tried to create the role of a stammerer in music

and wanted to know how it had been done. Toscanini said that the musical line gave the impression of stammering, and Verdi scoffed at the whole idea, pointing out that stammerers as a rule are not subject to their speech impediment when they sing.

It was clear to Toscanini that the old man, despite the clarity of his mind, was fading. His vitality had been declining since the death of his beloved wife four years before, and now he seemed to cling to life by the thinnest of threads. Toscanini went back to see him a couple of days later. This time the conversation dragged painfully; it was difficult for Verdi to concentrate on it. Toscanini left with a sad heart.

On January 22nd, Verdi suffered a stroke and until his death he lay in a coma while the city and nation joined, as it were, in a sorrowing death watch. La Scala closed its doors during this interval. They were reopened on February 1st, five days after Verdi's death, for a program honoring his memory, which was conducted by Toscanini. Music—all by Verdi —from *Nabucco, I Lombardi, Rigoletto, La Traviata, The Sicilian Vespers, Un Ballo in Maschera,* and *La Forza del Destino* was played and sung, and among the soloists were Caruso and Tamagno. Giuseppe Giacosa delivered a eulogy.

On February 27th the remains of Verdi and his Giuseppina were driven through the streets of Milan from the cemetery to the chapel of the Casa di Riposo, the home for aged musicians that Verdi had founded and endowed in his will. Great throngs lined the route, and Toscanini led a chorus of more than eight hundred voices in a shattering and exalting passage, "*Va, pensiero,*" from *Nabucco.* That evening, after a performance of *L'Elisir d'Amore,* he repeated the program of the commemorative evening of February 1st.

Some who know Toscanini well say that he has sought consciously to live as Verdi did. That seems dubious, but there is no doubt that, even though Toscanini was endowed with an implacable will and incorruptible integrity, he has been influenced all his life by Verdi's career as a man and as an artist. I heard him remark once, deprecatingly, "They say that my character is like Verdi's." Deep in his heart he would wish it to be so. And it is so.

11

Departure and Return

AFTER the stirring, arduous months at La Scala, a vacation would have been in order for most people. But Toscanini headed for his first season in Buenos Aires. The long ocean voyage was a holiday to him, for traveling with him were some of the cheerful companions of La Scala, including Caruso. If Toscanini plunged into another heavy schedule of operas in the Argentine capital, perhaps that was the best vacation for him. No matter what he might say then or later about the irritation and weariness induced by struggling with singers and instrumentalists, he was happy when he was working in music.

The Buenos Aires season lasted for about three months. It paid well, since the Argentines bid high for the best artists. And the audiences resembled the Italian public. They were not content just to applaud mildly. They knew how to cheer and to hiss. Their greatest excitement was over a Caruso, but they knew how to value a Toscanini, too. In the course of that season Toscanini gave them such operas as *Tosca, Rigoletto, L'Elisir d'Amore, Iris,* and *La Traviata* as well as Wagnerian works, which were relatively unfamiliar at the time. One of the oddities of casting was the appearance of Caruso as Lohengrin a couple of times; but it was clear that Caruso, even with Toscanini to guide him, was not made for Wagner.

Toscanini enjoyed working in Buenos Aires. He returned off and on, in the following summers—of course, it was winter in the Argentine. He was always accompanied by artists who had worked with him in Italy, often with almost complete casts for operas he had done at home. That made things somewhat easier, since the leading ensemble did not have to be trained anew. But there was a different orchestra, and since it was not Toscanini's way to skimp in preparations, there were always enough rehearsals to keep him active.

There was a spirit of camaraderie in this company. Toscanini would occasionally join in the fun, and often he would look on with amusement. There were times, however, when sound musical procedures were disturbed, and then he was furious. There was the time in 1903 when Caruso and the young Giuseppe De Luca were singing together in an opera, and the tenor's voice broke just as he hit a high note. De Luca, rushing to the rescue, made his entrance sooner than required. The orchestra was thrown off, and Toscanini, never stopping in his beating of time, whipped it on until it caught up. After the act an irate Toscanini berated De Luca, who remembered in later years when he sang with Toscanini at La Scala and the Metropolitan that tenors must fend for themselves and that entrances must be made only when called for.

In one of those Buenos Aires seasons tragedy struck Toscanini and his wife. A third child, a boy, had been born to them, and they had named him Giorgio. One summer they took Giorgio with them to South America. The boy, then four, was stricken with diphtheria and died. Carla Toscanini was frantic. She wanted to leave her husband and rush home to Italy. When she got home, she could not bear to look at her other children. It took months for the shock to pass. And when their next and last child was born in 1907, the Toscaninis decided, with a touch of superstition, that they had done wrong to give the boy a name beginning with G. Their first two children had names beginning with W—a letter not used in the Italian alphabet—and everything had gone well. They looked around for another name starting with W and plucked Wanda out of the air. Now it would be safe to remember the departed little

97

brother, and Wanda received the middle name of Giorgina. Apparently the son, Walter, decided that it was a reliable tradition to follow, for when his only son was born he named him Walfredo. The daughters, in naming their children, ignored the W. Wally's daughter was named Emanuela, and Wanda's Sonia.

The first Buenos Aires season was satisfactory, and Toscanini returned to Italy in October full of vigor. In November he directed the world *première* of a new oratorio, *Mosé,* by Abbé Perosi, in the Church of Santa Maria della Pace in Milan, and then set to work on preparations for his fourth La Scala season. It began with Wagner again—*Die Walküre.* The contrary Milan audience did not take to it, though it had a stunning production. Thus at the very start of the new season Toscanini's growing irritation with elements of La Scala's public had something fresh to feed on.

There was an improvement with *Linda di Chamounix,* which introduced to La Scala Rosa Storchio, a beautiful and gifted young singer for whom Toscanini had a special regard. After *Hansel and Gretel,* in its first complete performance in Italy, there came a couple of memorials to Verdi—first a performance of his Requiem and then a restudied and refreshed production of *Il Trovatore.*

Toscanini had long thought of rehabilitating the operas of Verdi's middle period, works like *Il Trovatore, Rigoletto,* and *La Traviata,* that were the bread and butter of every provincial theater in Italy and, indeed, of the major opera houses of Italy and the rest of the world. He knew that an accretion of false traditions had encrusted these pieces. Routine performances in which singers took endless liberties had cheapened their value. They were loved but not understood.

What he did with *Il Trovatore* was the most eloquent tribute he could pay to Verdi's memory. He studied the opera anew. He insisted that it be played and sung just as Verdi had written it. New sets were designed that were in keeping with the grimness and passion of the story. The white plumes and the rattling sabers, which had become as much a part of *Il Trovatore* as horses, cowboys, and Indians are of an American Western film, were discarded. Everything was done to keep the mood of the opera tense, dark, and foreboding.

When word leaked out in the Galleria Vittorio Emmanuele, the gathering place of the musical world near the Scala, that Toscanini was uprooting *Il Trovatore,* there were the usual murmurs of opposition from people who liked to make up their minds before the event. The public arrived for the first performance, fearing the worst. But even the die-hards who whispered against Toscanini no matter what he did were forced to concede that *Il Trovatore* had been reborn. Time and time again the audience stopped the show with its demonstrations of enthusiasm. Toscanini had proved what he had believed all along and what he came to hold with undeviating conviction throughout his career—that the old operas, which have endured the batterings of generations of self-appointed improvers, have the greatest power if one goes back to first sources and does them truthfully.

The final operas of the season were Franchetti's *Germania,* in its world *première,* and Weber's *Euryanthe,* which had never been done in Italy.

With *Euryanthe* something occurred that was a presentiment of Toscanini's rupture with La Scala the following year. The Italians, like most of the rest of us, are superstitious folk, and in the ambient of the Milan theatrical world one of the gravest superstitions concerned a certain unprepossessing fellow believed to possess the evil eye. Opera folk avoided him as others might detour around the path of a black cat. Toscanini encountered the evil-eyed one on the day of the first performance of *Euryanthe.* His intelligence told him that the tales of the bad luck this character brought in his wake were purely coincidental, but there they were. He entered the pit glumly that night. He was in no mood to trifle with the goings-on of the noisy, demonstrative Milanese, and when they set up a furor in the middle of the performance for an encore and would not let the show go on, he threw down his baton and left the theater. He went home and sat there brooding that people were right—the evil-eyed one did bring bad luck.

Officials of La Scala rushed after him and pleaded with him to return, pointing out that the audience was waiting patiently for the performance to go on. Well, the fiasco had taken place; the evil-eyed one had done his work. Toscanini went back and finished the performance. The following year, as we shall see, there was no meeting with the evil-eyed one to precipitate events, and they happened all the same.

In the spring of 1902, Toscanini conducted four symphonic programs at La Scala, and for the first time he directed all of Beethoven's Ninth Symphony, giving it three performances. He began the winter season on December 22nd with Berlioz's *Damnation of Faust,* which had always been done as an oratorio in the past and which he insisted on putting on as a stage piece for the first time. This production remained high in his affections, and he still dreams of mounting a fresh revival. As he talks of the idea, he groans, "But where would I get the tenor?"

The tenor in 1902 was Giovanni Zenatello, who was to figure in the dramatic break on the final evening of the season. That came during a performance of Verdi's *Un Ballo in Maschera,* which had been revived during the season with the composer's *Luisa Miller.* Also in the repertory had been Antonio Smareglia's *Oceàna* in its world *première,* Franchetti's *Asrael,* Ponchielli's *I Lituani,* and a stage version of the third act of *Parsifal,* preceded by the Prelude, in its first Italian performance.

Toscanini's resentment at the continual clamor for encores had been rising over the years. He had had no use for them as far back as he could remember, and, despite his worship of the composer, he had condemned Verdi privately for not resisting encores at the *première* of *Falstaff*, when, he was wont to point out ruefully, three had been allowed. He had been heckled repeatedly about them at La Scala, and he had had about enough. His discontent probably had other reasons. He knew that certain elements in the company were rebellious against the severity of his discipline and the exigency of his demands. He knew that their friends were constantly creating disturbances aimed at him. In any case, he was in a fighting mood that final night of the season, and when the audience howled for an encore by Zenatello, he stood there immobile, waiting for the demonstration to blow over so that he could go on with the opera. But the tumult grew in volume; some in the audience were not howling merely for a repeat but were telling off Toscanini.

In a fury he swung around and flung his baton into the shouting mob. Then he turned and stomped out of the pit and out of the theater.

When he recalled this incident years later, his eyes flashed and his voice became sharp with anger, as though he were reliving the event.

When he walked into his home, he remembered, his wife looked up in surprise. "Is the opera over?" she asked.

"No!"

He sat down and refused to talk.

A lawyer from the Scala came hurrying into his home. At first he would not see the man. When he did, he would not listen to pleas that he return and finish the opera as he had the year before.

"You must conduct," the lawyer said.

"I turned on him," he recalled later, "and shouted, 'Conduct you!'"

The assistant conductor finished the performance, and Toscanini did not conduct opera at La Scala again until December, 1906.

The stories have it that he was so enraged that he packed

at once, took the first train out of Milan for Genoa, and boarded a ship the next day for South America, not to return to Italy for several years. The stories have been theatricalized. He was angry, all right, but his bags were packed and his train and boat passages arranged, for he had a contract to conduct in Buenos Aires that summer. He was merely leaving on schedule, if more dramatically than planned.

As for his aversion to encores, even this was not a consistent thing throughout his life. It is true that when he returned to La Scala several years later the programs always carried a note that encores were strictly forbidden, and the rule was adhered to. But there were times when it amused him to grant encores. There was the occasion some years later when an Italian composer came to him before the ninth and final performance of his opera to plead, in advance of the show, for an encore. Something told him, the composer said urgently, that there would be a demonstration. Something told Toscanini that the composer had arranged for the demonstration by hiring the services of a claque. The demonstration was punctual, just where the composer's "intuition" had told him it would come, and Toscanini, in an indulgent and pitying mood, granted the encore. After the performance the composer, with tears in his eyes, approached Toscanini backstage and said, "See how my public loves me." Toscanini ended the story with the comment, "Poor fellow."

In Buenos Aires, in 1903, Toscanini conducted a group of Italian operas as well as Wagner's *The Flying Dutchman* and *Die Meistersinger*. He returned to Italy in the fall, but instead of working he remained at home, keeping an eye on the operatic scene. He was eager to hear what was going on at La Scala, and his friends brought back reports of the new season under Cleofonte Campanini, his successor. If Toscanini was aware of Campanini's activity, the latter was even more conscious of Toscanini's existence. As Gatti-Casazza said, Campanini was no Toscanini, but he had experience and an instinct for the baton and the theater. He was haunted, as Gatti put it, by Banquo's ghost. Had Campanini but known, he would have been easier in his mind. For Toscanini was far from a threat to him. La Scala tried to get Toscanini to come back after a year's absence, but he refused because he felt that the theater should honor its three-year contract with Campanini.

The pressure, however, made Campanini nervous and irritable. Before he could complete his contract, he was the victim of a revolt in the Scala orchestra. The men felt that he was rehearsing an opera excessively and they refused to continue. Campanini stormed out and asked to be relieved of his job.

During Campanini's first season, Puccini's *Madame Butterfly* was on the agenda for its world *première*, and Toscanini watched developments with fascination. Puccini had brought the manuscript of his new score to Toscanini's house, but instead of playing through the whole thing, as he had done in the past, the composer played excerpts. Toscanini considered that a curious portent. He leafed through the score, absorbing its contents.

Madame Butterfly, in its first version, which was done at La Scala that season, was in two acts. The first act, Toscanini could see, was weak and long, and the second would take an hour and twenty minutes. "I thought at once," Toscanini recalled, "this length is impossible. For Wagner, yes. For Puccini, no."

Toscanini did not go to the *première*. He did not care to enter the theater, and what was more, he anticipated a fiasco. But he had an irresistible curiosity to know how it would come out. He commissioned a close friend who was planning to attend to come and tell him about it as soon as the performance was over. He sat up and waited for the report. The friend returned with the gory details. The first act was received coolly, but at least there was no outcry. In the middle of the second act the volatile Italian audience broke loose in an outburst of interruptions, catcalls, shouts of derision, and laughter. *Madame Butterfly* was a crushing failure. Toscanini listened to the recital and shook his head sadly. "The public is not wrong," he said. "The opera must be revised."

The next morning it was withdrawn and Puccini made revisions. In its new three-act form it was done in 1904 in Brescia under Campanini and in Buenos Aires under Toscanini, who was happy to find that it now was strong enough to make its way.

As the winter of withdrawal from activity wore on, Toscanini's hard feelings toward Italian audiences began to soften, and the urge to make music grew in him. When the Santa Cecilia Academy in Rome tempted him with an offer of symphonic concerts, he accepted. Then he went to Bologna's Teatro Communale for a couple of operas, *Die Meistersinger* and Meyerbeer's *Dinorah*. From May to August he was in Buenos Aires, and when he returned he did not take on any winter season. Again he sat in his home in Milan, read scores, received a few friends, and listened to news of La Scala.

In April, 1905, he went back to Turin for several concerts at the Teatro Vittorio Emmanuele with the Municipal Orchestra of the city. Turin was overjoyed to have him back. It greeted him wildly. But with the contrariness of Italian audiences, it gave him a terrible evening when he conducted a set of *Piedmontese Dances* by the Italian composer Sinigaglia. Apparently the folklike, popular treatment of the tunes did not sit well with the Turin listeners; as Piedmontese themselves they seemed to be offended by what the composer, a native of Turin, had done with the music. They set up a fearful racket that continued through the next piece and that subsided only when the police were called.

Toscanini, whatever he may have thought of the public, found the Turin orchestra responsive and agreeable to work with. Early in June he took it to Milan for a couple of concerts at La Scala. It would be hard to believe that he did not have something to do with arranging the visit, if only to propose it. One likes to imagine that it was, in part, his way of reminding the Milanese that he was still there; one also suspects that he was not above goading them with the capacities of a fine orchestra from another city. The Scala management, for its part, made its theater available, perhaps as a gesture of reconciliation. And Toscanini, in what may have been a response of cordiality, indulged the Milan audience by allowing an encore.

La Scala was ready to welcome Toscanini back, but Campanini was still there; he did not quit until after the season began. Toscanini conducted in Bologna in November and December, putting on *Madame Butterfly, Siegfried, Hansel and Gretel,* and still another new Italian opera, *Cassandra,* by Vittorio Gnecchi, a composer from Milan. For the winter season he turned up at his old stand, the Teatro Regio in Turin, conducting *Siegfried, Butterfly, The Damnation of Faust, Loreley,* and Giordano's *Siberia.* He followed this season with a series of concerts with Turin's Municipal Orchestra, and then took it on a tour of northern Italy, playing three times at the Teatro Lirico in Milan, and in Parma, Bologna, Venice, Trieste, Brescia, and Como.

In May he was in Buenos Aires again. When he returned late in August, he was invited to return to La Scala. This time he accepted. He recalled later that when he began preparations he found that all discipline had disappeared. Singers had resumed bad habits of making the music fit their own inclinations to show off. The orchestra played sloppily. At that time the musicians were busy organizing a union, and Toscanini, pausing in a rehearsal, wanted to know who was the president. The first trombone stood up.

"Are you writing your rules and bylaws?" Toscanini demanded.

"Yes, Maestro."

"I beg you, make this Article One: The orchestra must always play in tune."

"Yes, Maestro."

"Because you are scandalously out of tune today."

Toscanini was to find that the old contentions with sections of the audience prevailed anew. As he emerged to take his place in the pit on opening night for *Carmen*, there were shouts, possibly from the gang that had pursued him in years gone by. Several voices yelled, "Why don't you go back to South America?" Toscanini turned and shouted back, "Very soon, very soon."

The audience probably took umbrage at the printed notice that encores were forbidden. A Milan newspaper reported after the opening that "after greeting Maestro Toscanini with strong applause, the audience settled into the glacial severity of judges." As judges, though, they had to concede that they heard extraordinary productions that season of *Salome, La Gioconda, Tristan, Aïda, La Wally, Orfeo,* and Francesco Cilea's *Gloria* in its world *première*.

With *Salome* he achieved something rare even for him. He prepared the singers and the orchestra so painstakingly in their separate rehearsals and they responded so effectively to his instructions that when he brought all the elements together for their first joint rehearsal, he went through the entire opera without pause. Asked how it happened that he had not stopped, he said, "There were no errors." When Richard Strauss visited Milan to hear the production, Gatti-Casazza told him of Toscanini's feat, and the composer, who knew how difficult this score was, would not believe it.

This performance was the first in Italy for *Salome*, though only by a day. The Turin opera had it scheduled for performance on the very night of the Scala *première*, and it contrived to get Strauss to conduct. But Gatti-Casazza turned the Scala dress rehearsal into a full-fledged performance by inviting the subscribers and the critics to fill the house. Thanks to the speed with which Toscanini had put together the opera, it was possible to offer the finished product ahead of time.

The 1907-08 season broke new ground at La Scala. In addition to *Die Götterdämmerung, Tosca, Mefistofele, Paolo e Francesca* by Luigi Mancinelli, *La Forza del Destino,* and *Cristoforo Colombo,* the theater offered a pair of contemporary French operas. One was Gustave Charpentier's *Louise,* which had been done some years back in shabby fashion at Milan's Teatro Lirico, and the other was Debussy's *Pelléas et Mélisande,* which had not been done in Italy at all.

Louise, though it does not abound in the kind of tunes an opera by Rossini or Verdi would have, did not impose any insuperable obstacles. For the title role Gatti-Casazza had summoned Frances Alda, Australian soprano, young, red-haired, and attractive. She had spark, which was needful, and since she had made her own way, she understood Charpentier's heroine thoroughly. That she had a mind of her own she quickly proved to Toscanini. She had spent several months learning the role in Italian, and then she arrived in Milan and sang it for the conductor. He sat listening to her, his eyebrows knitted in a way peculiar to him when he is preoccupied, and did not interrupt once. When she finished, he said, "Tell me, dear, what language were you singing?"

The great majority of young singers would have collapsed at this sally, and Alda was appalled. But she had spirit, and she walked out. For three days she refused to come near the theater. Then Gatti persuaded her to relent, assuring her that Toscanini would work with her, syllable by syllable. And, as she freely admitted later, he restudied the role with her from beginning to end. She was willing to concede that, while his criticism was harsh, he knew what he was doing, for the tough Milan audiences would have been death on a young singer who could not handle their language intelligibly. Alda went on to admit that she, like innumerable other artists, could not sum up what she owed to Toscanini. In all the operas she sang under his direction at the Metropolitan, she said, he taught her everything.

Pelléas was a struggle, possibly the severest of Toscanini's years at La Scala. When he decided to chance it, he knew that it would create opposition, not only from the sources that had always attacked him but also from people of good will. For *Pelléas* was something different. Even today audiences accustomed to strange harmonies and stranger melodic lines do not take to *Pelléas* readily. One could imagine fearfully how the Italians of that period, raised in the tradition of round, fat tunes, would react.

Toscanini had encountered a score of *Pelléas* for the first time in Bologna some years before. He had just finished dressing for his evening performance of *Die Meistersinger* when he picked up the Debussy score. As he had leafed through it, he had been struck by its simplicity. As soon as he had finished conducting the Wagner opera, he had returned to his room and read through the entire score of *Pelléas*. He had been fascinated by its perfection. He had seen that it would be an elusive thing to mount and conduct properly, but he had decided that he must try it someday.

When the chance came, he was nervous. He conceded later that it was stupid to do the work in an Italian translation; the poetic text was all but untranslatable. When he revived the opera at La Scala in the twenties, he did not make the same mistake. He had it done in French and brought Fanny Eldy, a soprano from France, to sing Mélisande.

Toscanini slaved over the preparation of *Pelléas* in 1908. As Gatti-Casazza, who was there, testified later, he "transfused his entire being" to each of the singers. The dress rehearsal went well, but Toscanini kept on worrying. Debussy had promised to attend the *première* but could not make it, and the conductor was relieved. He was not sure how it would go, and he did not want the composer there if it turned out to be a failure.

Before the performance he told the entire company—orchestra and singers—that whatever happened, they must follow his beat. He had not underestimated the evening's ordeal. The audience was quiet during the opening scenes, probably out of puzzlement and hope that a tune it could hum would presently emerge. Soon it realized that the character of the music would not change radically. It began to murmur impatiently, then to shout its disapproval. In the scene of the subterranean vaults, where the basses in the orchestra groan ominously, the audience burst into an uproar. Toscanini recalled later that he had no idea how the orchestra played; he could not hear it for the bedlam at his back. Nevertheless, he kept on beating time, and the orchestra plugged away.

At one point Toscanini could make out what some of the loudest-voiced demonstrators were bellowing. "*Che bella musica!*" they were howling sarcastically. "What beautiful music!"

Still beating time firmly and vigorously, he turned and shouted a response: "*Si, si, per me, bella musica!*"

The din went on for many minutes. Gatti-Casazza recalled that "the public was positively indecent." Toscanini's determination to carry on hardened in the face of the opposition. Finally, even the noisiest in the audience paused to catch their breaths. They listened in spite of themselves. The scene between Golaud and little Yniold under Mélisande's window evoked a spontaneous ovation from the people who had come to give the new opera a fair hearing. After that the performance went on to triumph, and those who were set on creating a disturbance whether the opera was good or bad were forced to retire in silence.

At the end Toscanini, in a rare gesture, came out on the stage with the cast. He had worked like a dog for this moment of triumph, he recalled later, serving as coach, stage director, conductor, everything. But he did not come out to strut in the limelight and to lap up the applause. His purpose was to applaud the audience, and, as he did so, he called out admiringly, "*Molto intelligente, molto intelligente!*"

When Debussy was apprised of what had happened that night, he sent Toscanini a photograph of himself. On it he inscribed a passage from the scene between Golaud and Yniold and under the music he wrote, "This is where the tide turned."

In 1910, when he was in Paris, Toscanini went to the Opéra-Comique for a performance of *Pelléas*. It seemed to him appallingly bad. A few days later he visited Debussy and remarked that he was now sorry that the composer had not been in Milan for the Scala production.

"I was worried about our performance," he told Debussy, "and I see that I was wrong. If this is what Paris offers you, it is a pity you did not see what Milan could do."

Debussy began to make apologies for the Opéra-Comique.

"How does it happen," demanded Toscanini, "that there is so much noise here during the scene changes?"

"The Opéra-Comique has a small stage."

"We have a bigger stage at La Scala, and therefore it is harder to keep quiet. Backstage there was not a sound."

Toscanini did not tell Debussy that he had seen even to this detail. He had ordered the stage crew to do its work in stockinged feet.

It is entirely likely that a major source of the opposition to Toscanini in the 1907-08 season at the Scala was that word had leaked out that he and Gatti-Casazza might be leaving for New York. Certainly this news could not have endeared Toscanini to that section of the public already against him.

Apparently the news of his imminent departure set others against him, and before he left the theater, to be absent for many years, there was a parting dig. At the season's end he conducted two concerts and was scheduled to do a third. On this program he was ordered by the Scala officials to play two pieces by Gaetano Coronaro, a teacher of composition at the Milan Conservatory who had died the month before. Toscanini was not in the habit of taking orders. He declined to play the pieces, insisting that it was the conductor's, not the board's, prerogative to make programs. The concert was turned over to another conductor, and Toscanini brought suit. The court held against him on the grounds that the board had not renounced all control of the programs and that Coronaro's music was not such as would injure the reputation of a conductor.

Regardless of the court's decision, Toscanini felt that the board's action had been a gesture of revenge for his decision to leave. With this final indignity burning in him, he set his eyes toward New York.

12

At the Metropolitan

NEW YORK had beckoned to Toscanini in 1903. When Heinrich Conried began his five years of management of the Metropolitan Opera House at that time, he engaged Enrico Caruso and tried to hire the conductor with whom the tenor had made his debut at La Scala. In 1903 Toscanini had just broken with La Scala, and he was interested in the United States, but he did not get into serious negotiations, since he did not know enough about Conried and the Metropolitan.

Several years later Conried made fresh overtures to Toscanini. Probably the Italian singers in the company, led by Caruso and Scotti, had spoken highly of the little maestro with whom they had worked in Milan. When the offer came, Toscanini reflected and turned it down. He would not engage to work for a manager he did not know at first hand. He was not looking for just any job. True, the intrigues and opposition in Milan were irksome, but there his standards were accepted.

When it became clear that the Metropolitan wanted Gatti-Casazza, too, Toscanini became actively interested. He urged Gatti to negotiate seriously, and it was Toscanini's eagerness that made the difference in Gatti's decision to come to America. In the final stages of negotiations, when several problems arose, Toscanini brushed them aside. Otto H. Kahn, who was becoming and was to remain for a couple of decades the dominant figure on the Metropolitan Opera Board, had wired Gatti to inquire whether Toscanini would have any objection to serving on the same staff with Gustav Mahler, and Toscanini had replied that there could be no difficulty with an artist of Mahler's worth. Then Rawlins Cottenet, secretary of the Metropolitan Opera Board, arrived in Milan for conferences, and he informed Gatti and Toscanini that their three-year contracts would contain a clause permitting cancellation by either party at the end of each year. Again it was Toscanini who disposed of the problem. "Let's accept," he said. "We can feel absolutely sure of our ability. We won't be sent away after a year's trial."

Toscanini arrived in New York for the first time in the fall of 1908. There was curiosity about his career and personality, and his response then was exactly what it was to remain for the next forty-odd years. Newspapermen boarded the government cutter and went down the bay to interview the new maestro, but he would not talk. There were reporters at the pier, and they tried to get some information or comment out of him; he would not talk. A few journalists waited for him at the Ansonia Hotel, where he stayed in his first years in New York; he would not talk. From time to time they tackled him in the opera house but got nothing from him. In one newspaper of the period there is a long account of a reporter's encounter with Toscanini at the Metropolitan. Apparently the writer, who could speak Italian, cornered the maestro during a break in a rehearsal and, barring Toscanini's path, fired questions at him. To every one of his questions the reporter got the same answer, "*Non so* [I don't know]." Finally, the reporter let down his guard, and Toscanini slipped through the opening and fled backstage.

Toscanini was not unfriendly; he was merely uncommunicative when he was asked questions for publication. He recalled years later that when he was at the Metropolitan he got to know New York's music critics, met them upon occasion, and chatted freely with them. It was always understood, however, that the things he said were not to be printed as public declarations. One young newspaperman, encouraged by the maestro's agreeable manner toward him, got himself invited to the conductor's hotel. Perhaps he misunderstood, perhaps Toscanini misunderstood, but this young eager beaver thought he had a promise of a formal interview. When he arrived at the appointed hour, Toscanini appeared, and the young newspaperman asked his first question. Toscanini strode up and down the room, casting sad glances from under his knitted eyebrows at his visitor. The reporter tried another gambit. Toscanini brushed his mustache, and his eyes began to glower. The reporter made another attempt. Toscanini's pacing became more rapid and more intense. Suddenly he turned on his visitor and cried, "I don't know. Please go away." The unhappy young fellow went.

Toscanini had come to New York to conduct opera, and he was eager to get down to business. At his first rehearsal with the orchestra he chose to start with *Die Götterdämmerung*, which was to be his only Wagner work of the season. Gatti-Casazza, who knew the uses of psychology, insisted that he appear at the rehearsal without score. Early in the proceedings Toscanini stopped the cello section and said it had erred in playing an A-natural instead of a B-flat. The first cellist pointed to the A-natural in his part, insisting he had always played it that way. Toscanini sent for the full score, and it sustained him.

The men were impressed, and at the end of the rehearsal they gave him a spontaneous salute of applause and bravos. But don't get the idea that they labored together happily ever after. Some days later Toscanini tore into them savagely. His vocabulary of invective, particularly in Italian, can be sultry, and this time he flayed the orchestra. Quite a few of the men understood Italian, and they were offended. After the rehearsal a delegation went to see Gatti-Casazza to complain of the vile names Toscanini had called them. Gatti listened quietly, then shrugged his shoulders and observed, "You should hear what he calls me."

The men were not appeased. When Toscanini arrived at the Metropolitan for his next orchestra rehearsal, the players were not there. "I understood," he recalled later, "and I put on my coat and went home." As he sat brooding, there was a knock on the door. The solo flutist, an Italian, was waiting outside. He had come to Toscanini to explain the failure of the orchestra to appear. "Sorry," Toscanini said, "but that's the way I am. I was frank, and if they play miserably, I must tell them so." The flutist suggested that a milder way of speaking would be appreciated; if Toscanini would try, the men would be happy to return. Toscanini replied that he could guarantee nothing, but he made it clear that his comments, even if they reflected on a player's ancestry, were never meant to be personal.

The orchestra reassembled and Toscanini resumed rehearsals. He did not change his way or the tenor of his remarks. But the Metropolitan musicians finally realized, as have other players in other places and times, that Toscanini's swearing was not a personal attack but another aspect of his complete immersion in the task of bringing the music to life.

They found that he could hear the most incredible things. Once a fiddler in the second-violin section, either through forgetfulness or laziness, failed to remove his mute. Toscanini stopped the rehearsal and said, "I cannot see so far, but I hear a mute somewhere on one of the second violins."

Toscanini also tangled with the singers. Whether they were big names or unknowns, he was unrelenting in his demands on them. The first encounter, and perhaps the best known, was with a beloved prima donna, said to have been Geraldine Farrar. Whoever she was, she took liberties with rhythms and tempo, and Toscanini brought her up sharply. "Maestro," she told him loftily, "you must conduct as I sing, for I am a star."

Toscanini looked at her coldly and replied, "Signorina, the stars are in heaven. Here we are all artists, good or bad, and you are a bad artist."

He spared no one. Emma Eames later wrote that he was "amiable and charming" outside of the theater, but ceased to be these things once he took charge of a performance. In preparing a revival of Gluck's *Orfeo,* he hammered away at Louise Homer, the Orfeo, that she must not hold on to a climactic note in the aria *"Che farò senza Euridice."* Gluck's music did not require the note to be held, he told her, and he would not let the composer's intentions—or the dramatic requirements of the scene—be violated. At the performance the contralto, either forgetful or willful, clung to the note. Toscanini brought the orchestra crashing in with its final chord, and the singer was left holding on to her note, like a ship alone on a reef.

Caruso, who should have known his man better, tried to slip one by Toscanini one night. He landed on a high note with tremendous impact and, satisfied with the stunning effect it was making, held on to it as long as his breath lasted. Toscanini waited for the tenor to let go of the note, and when he did, he shouted at him across the pit, so that people in the audience could hear, "Have you finished, Caruso?"

In the rehearsals for *Otello,* Leo Slezak, in the title role, kept omitting certain measures, as though he had a mental block where they were involved. Toscanini kept reminding him of the measures, and on the evening of the performance went into Slezak's dressing room and carefully went over the passage, playing it on the piano for the tenor. Slezak promised that this time he would not forget. When he got to it, however, he skipped it once more. The fuming Toscanini yelled at him, *"Porco* Slezak! *Porco* Slezak!"

Another time a tenor in *Die Meistersinger* made a few blunders. At the end of the act, Toscanini came backstage. He banged his own head against the wall, moaning, "This tenor is a beast." The singer did the best he could the rest of the evening, singing with alertness, beauty of tone, and careful musicianship. Toscanini did not seem to soften. After the performance the tenor walked into the elevator of the Ansonia and ran into Toscanini, who saw him and pulled his hat over his eyes. The singer muttered a string of apologies and promised it would not happen again. Toscanini pushed up his hat, and his eyes were full of sorrow. Apparently he was relenting, but slowly. "My dear," he said compassionately, "you were terrible."

Toscanini made every phase of a performance his province—enunciation, acting, deployment of ensemble. Before the dress rehearsal of *Otello*, he told Alda, the Desdemona, how he expected her to play the fourth act. In her memoirs, *Men, Women, and Tenors*, she recalled the incident.

"*Senti*, Aldina," he told her, "you will kneel and sing the 'Ave Maria.' Then you will get up, without turning your face to the audience. There will not be one smile. Not one bow. There will be no encores. You will not lift your eyes. You will just get into bed like a good, pure virgin."

When he was preparing *Euryanthe*, he had a cast of German-trained singers. One of these was Margarete Ober, a contralto who had been born in Berlin and had sung throughout Germany in German. He stopped her at the first rehearsal and observed that her enunciation was poor. At this time he did not speak the language himself, but he could read and write it.

She was irritated. "You mean to say you do not like *my* German?"

"Yes," he said, "I do not like your German."

"It is my own tongue."

"Nevertheless," he said, "it is bad."

"I don't believe it," she cried.

"Well," he said patiently, "let us try. We shall see."

117

Before the rehearsal was over, she admitted that he had caused her to cease taking her German for granted and to improve her way of singing it.

If the singer's attitude was genuinely musical, Toscanini could be understanding and helpful in a time of emergency. One night Jacques Urlus, a tenor who was singing Tristan, found his throat tightening up in the middle of the first act, and thereafter he could scarcely sing. No substitute was available, and Toscanini carried on with the efficiency and thoughtfulness of a seasoned trouper. He helped Urlus at every opportunity. Where he sensed that Urlus might manage a passage he filed down the orchestral tone so that the tenor might be heard. Where the music was beyond Urlus's powers, he caused the orchestra to surge forth to cover the tenor's failings. He eliminated other passages entirely. He made it possible for Urlus to get through the show.

However, in the same season two leading singers found it inconvenient to be present for a rehearsal of *Tristan*, and Toscanini declared he would not do the work at all. The singers turned up eventually, but there was not enough time left to prepare the performance to Toscanini's satisfaction. It was not done at all. It was announced that Toscanini was "indisposed," and another Wagner work was hastily substituted under another conductor.

There were some singers who honored Toscanini for his insistence on musical rectitude and for his unsparing efforts to build fine performances. But make no mistake about it, there were others who resented him as long as they were in the same theater. There was a time early in Toscanini's stay at the Metropolitan when a group of principal singers signed a petition to the board demanding that Andreas Dippel, who was a co-manager of the company in Gatti's first two years, be retained. This was an open attack on Gatti, but the target was certainly Toscanini as much as, if not more than, Gatti.

Toscanini recalled years later that the atmosphere at the

118

Metropolitan was often full of tugging and dissension, with the Italian and German wings of the company ranged against each other in many of the internal differences. With Mahler, who conducted in Toscanini's first year, there was no conflict. Toscanini listened to him conduct *Tristan* and was surprised at how subdued it was. "There was no passion in it," he recalled, "but the poor man was tired and sick."

Nor did he care for Mahler's handling of Beethoven's Ninth, which he heard him do in New York. Again he was willing to make allowances for a man whose energy was ebbing perceptibly. But Toscanini would not forgive him for what he regarded as a tasteless and obvious tampering with the orchestration of Smetana's *The Bartered Bride*. He examined the score after Mahler had left the Metropolitan and in the place where Mahler had made the changes, Toscanini scrawled, "Shame on a man like Mahler!"

For Alfred Hertz, who conducted most of the German operas in Toscanini's years at the Metropolitan, the maestro had little short of pitying contempt.

"Poor Hertz," he once said in a reminiscent mood. "He had everything going triple forte nearly all the time. I remember one place in Wagner. The clarinet was blowing as if he were going to burst a blood vessel. His face was dark red. But he was not making a sound. Poor Hertz, he didn't know the man was acting."

Toscanini was no chauvinist when it came to heated exchanges with people in the company. He told off Italians as well as Germans and Americans and Frenchmen and individuals of any other nationality if they transgressed the just path of art. Giorgio Polacco, an Italian conductor, joined the staff of the Metropolitan while Toscanini was there. After a while, he became discontented. According to Toscanini, Polacco went about saying that he was getting few good operas to conduct because Toscanini was preventing it.

"It was not true," the maestro recalled later. "I told him so plainly, and I told him I wanted no more to do with him. After that he kept trying to telephone me to explain himself. After I left the Metropolitan, he would phone me in Milan when he was in Italy and I would not talk to him. One day, during the first war, Carla and I went to a hospital for wounded soldiers, and on the street we met Polacco. I wouldn't talk to him. Carla scolded me. 'You're impossible,' she said. So I told Polacco to come and call on us the next day at three. I meant to be polite. But when he came in, I got angry again, and I talked to him in the worst way. I told him everything. I was brutal."

As he recalled the harshness of his blunt talking, there was a faraway look in his eyes. "Later," he observed, "I was ashamed." Then his eyes blazed as he added, "But I told the truth."

The tensions and the disagreements at the Metropolitan were to accumulate over the seven seasons he was there until he could no longer endure them; but aside from scattered encounters, in which he fought to establish sound and artistic musical procedures, things started well. Toscanini conceded later that the Metropolitan in those years was blessed with important attributes; it had notable singers, a fine orchestra, and a fine chorus.

It posed difficulties new to him and Gatti. In Italy they had put on one opera at a time, letting it run continuously after its opening as long as the public wished to pay its way in. There had been occasions, as you will remember, when Toscanini had prepared two operas simultaneously, but that had been before the season began. At the Metropolitan the operas changed with every performance. An opera was rarely done more than six or seven times a season, and these performances might be spread over a period of several months. Fresh works had to be added to the repertory right through the season, which meant that singers, conductor, orchestra, and chorus had to fit in rehearsal time in addition to their regular performances. Conductors often competed with one another for rehearsal time.

These working conditions would be, as a matter of course, uncongenial to Toscanini, who had hitherto been the unquestioned master of his musical house wherever he had conducted. They were, in fact, to become intolerable to him before his stay at the Metropolitan ended.

At the start he was eager and determined to help build the Metropolitan into an opera house any musician could be proud of. And in his seven seasons there he achieved his purpose, certainly where his performances were concerned. Those who have watched the Metropolitan closely for decades agree that the house reached its artistic height in Toscanini's time. The nineties, when the Metropolitan had a gleaming roster of such artists as Lilli Lehmann, Nordica, Ternina, Sembrich, Calvé, Eames, Melba, the De Reszkes, Van Rooy, Plançon, Tamagno, Maurel, were denoted as the opera house's "golden age of song." But the singers were all-important then. From 1908 to 1915 the Metropolitan also had distinguished singers, as it has had them repeatedly since, and it had, in addition, Toscanini. And Toscanini made the period not merely a "golden age of song" but a golden age of opera. For under his direction, while there was ample opportunity for the singers to shine in all their splendor, the composer was sovereign. It was the total conception of the work that had to be served and projected. There was a saying that for a Toscanini performance even the side seats at the Metropolitan, from which one could see little or nothing of the stage, became highly desirable.

Toscanini made his debut at the Metropolitan on November 16, 1908, the opening night of the season. Save for the 1912 opening, when he was ill, he presided at all the first nights of his tenure. In 1908 the opera was *Aïda,* and the glittering cast was headed by Emmy Destinn, Louise Homer, Enrico Caruso,

Antonio Scotti, and Adamo Didur. There were new sets and costumes imported from La Scala, and the audience heard something fresh and vibrant in the way of an *Aïda* performance. Despite the prominence of the singers, Toscanini received the most attention. Henry E. Krehbiel called him "in the best sense, an artist, an interpreter, a recreator." There was only one dissenting voice, that of Reginald De Koven, who, writing in the *World,* averred that Toscanini did not understand *Aïda.*

On Thursday night of that first week Toscanini conducted *Madame Butterfly* with Caruso, Scotti, and Geraldine Farrar, whom he was to admire personally for a long time, as the Cio-Cio-San. He was struck by her poise and beauty, and despite the fact that he clashed with her in artistic matters, he admired her independence of character. Years later a friend warmly recalled Humperdinck's *Königskinder,* in which Farrar, wearing a long blond wig, made an appealing entrance. "Yes," Toscanini replied, "she was beautiful. Very beautiful."

On another occasion Toscanini recalled that some of the prima donnas had treated Frances Alda coolly when she arrived at the Metropolitan but that when she was married to the manager, Gatti-Casazza, in 1910, they became sweet and attentive. "Not Farrar," he said. "She didn't change a bit."

On Saturday afternoon of the first week of the 1908 season the scheduled opera was *Tosca,* with Eames, Caruso, and Scotti, and it had been rehearsed by Francesco Spetrino, who was to conduct. Spetrino fell ill shortly before the performance, and Toscanini, knowing that there was no time to get another opera ready, went to Gatti and volunteered to conduct *Tosca.* "But there is no time to rehearse," said Gatti, assuming that Toscanini would not undertake a performance which he had not had the chance to mold.

"Don't worry," Toscanini replied. "I'll do it without rehearsal."

He had time just for a hurried conference with the principal singers. Then he went out and conducted *Tosca*. What was more, he did *Tosca* as he felt it, not as Spetrino had rehearsed it. He changed tempos, made fresh nuances, kept the piece moving at a new pace. "The orchestra followed me perfectly," he recalled later. "That's how good it was." The leading singers and chorus did, too.

Other conductors have pinch-hit at short notice and have carried through performances of operas without rehearsal. But it is not likely that they dared to change the whole conception of the interpretation without prior preparation. Since Toscanini always had the reputation of holding out for the last split second of rehearsal time he required, his capacity to turn the trick of this *Tosca* is proof that he had the magnetism and courage to function in another manner, if the situation required it.

Toscanini next showed what he could do with a French opera, conducting a *Carmen* that had Maria Gay, Farrar, Caruso, and Jean Noté in the cast. Then he turned to *Die Götterdämmerung*, with a cast which had Olive Fremstad, Rita Fornia, Erik Schmedes, Allen Hinckley, Otto Goritz, and Adolf Mühlmann. While he did not present the music drama without cuts, he restored the Prologue and the Norn Scene, which had not been done since 1900. His Wagner in a theater which had had such eminent conductors of German opera as Anton Seidl, Felix Mottl, and Mahler made a profound impression. It was clear that here was a musician whose affinities far exceeded the limited and conventional repertories expected of an Italian conductor.

The rest of his repertory that season was hardly conventional, aside from *Cavalleria Rusticana*. He did *Le Villi*, Puccini's first opera (American *première*); *La Wally*, the best of his friend Catalani's operas (American *première*); and the most difficult and elusive of Verdi's works, *Falstaff*. In a special Good Friday performance he conducted Verdi's Requiem preceded by the Prologue to Boito's *Mefistofele*.

In his second Metropolitan season Toscanini's repertory expanded. To repetitions of *Aïda*, *Butterfly*, and *Falstaff*, he added *La Gioconda* (the opening-night opera with a brilliant cast of Destinn, Homer, Anna Meitschik, Caruso, Pasquale Amato, and Andrés de Segurola), *Otello, Tristan und Isolde, Orfeo, Germania* (in its American *première*), and *Die Meistersinger.*

There were memorable things in each of these productions. The Metropolitan had not seen *Otello* for some years, and it is to be doubted that it ever saw a more taut and dramatic version. The *Tristan*—and Toscanini had three different Isoldes in the one season, Johanna Gadski, Fremstad, and Nordica—was filled with passion and sustained song. The *Orfeo,* which had always been a vehicle for a prima donna, became an integrated and touching human drama, with lovely, young Alma Gluck as Euridice to complement the stateliness of Louise Homer's Orfeo. *Die Meistersinger,* it was agreed, was radiant with youth and wisdom.

At the end of the season the Metropolitan Opera made its first and last trip abroad. Thanks to the support of Otto H. Kahn, a season was arranged in Paris, and at the Théâtre du Châtelet seventeen performances were presented. The operas were *Aïda, Pagliacci, Cavalleria Rusticana, Otello, Falstaff,* and *Manon Lescaut.* The singers were the famous names of the Metropolitan plus Lucrezia Bori, who made her debut with the company in Paris in *Manon Lescaut.* Toscanini, of course, conducted.

He was keen to show Europe what this American opera company could do and even passed up an engagement in Buenos Aires at a higher fee to make the trip to Paris. But before he got the first opera, *Aïda,* ready, he had occasion to wish he had gone to Buenos Aires instead.

The Metropolitan had taken along, besides its leading singers and conductor, its chorus, ballet, sets and costumes. The one thing it recruited in Paris for these performances in May and June was the orchestra. The players were drawn in large measure from the orchestra of the Concerts Lamoureux with a few from the orchestra of the Concerts Colonne. Toscanini found them a careless, undisciplined lot. They did not play the Italian or German operas well at all, he thought, and he hoped, as he said later, that there was something to be said for them in French opera.

The first rehearsal was something he did not forget. He had expected to do all of *Aïda*, but got through the first act only. Alda recalls that at one point he became enraged and took his watch out of his pocket and flung it over the heads of some of the players against a wall. It was one of those old-fashioned, sturdy timepieces; the works inside were undoubtedly knocked askew but the case was not shattered. Alda picked up the watch and handed it to Toscanini, who slipped it into his pocket without stopping his instructions to the orchestra and without glancing at the watch to see what had happened to it. A little later the orchestra ignored instructions and again he pulled out the watch and dashed it against the wall. Again Alda picked it up and handed it to him, and again he took it and replaced it in his pocket, as though this were the most natural routine in the world.

The watch-throwing, the tongue-lashings, and the constant pressure woke up the French musicians, who had not known such discipline or such demands for concentration in a long, long time. Toscanini got additional rehearsals, and there were further explosions.

After he had finished berating the men savagely one day, a player spoke up. "We played this music for Nikisch, and he thought it was all right."

That was like prodding Toscanini with a load of burrs. "This is not Nikisch," he shouted. "This is Toscanini! Not Nikisch but Toscanini!"

Then he told them he didn't care whom they had played with or what traditions they thought they knew. The performance would follow his ideas. He walked off the stage and threatened to quit. The Frenchmen, who had heard a little something through the international grapevine of the musical world about Toscanini's severity, murmured that this Italian was worse than a mad dog.

Evidently they got something out of those rehearsals and performances. In the middle of a rehearsal before the concluding performance of the Paris season, they invited Toscanini to join them in the foyer of the Châtelet. There he found long tables covered with white cloths, heaped with food and wine. They drank champagne together. The men toasted "*le cher maître.*" In bidding him their own farewell, they even went so far as to wish he would be back soon.

The Paris season was, of course, a glittering social and artistic event. But here, too, Toscanini found that the kind of opposition he had known at La Scala awaited him. As he came out for the second act of the opening-night *Aïda* and gave the starting beat, he was greeted by an outburst of stamping, shouting, whistling, and catcalling. It was aimed not only at him but at the management. It was obviously a prepared thing. No one knew for sure how or why it was precipitated. Gatti's theory was that several artists not re-engaged for the ensuing season at the Metropolitan had engineered it. Other observers thought that French artists who had not been invited to sing with the Metropolitan were responsible. Still others assumed that friends of the orchestra Toscanini had bedeviled were repaying him in kind. To Toscanini it must have seemed like home. He kept on conducting, and finally the noisemakers let up.

By the beginning of 1910-11 season it was clear that Toscanini had become, beyond question, the dominant musical personality at the Metropolitan. Mahler had conducted only one opera the season before, and now he was gone. Toscanini did not receive the official title of artistic director, and he did not care. Titles had never worried him. Artistic policy had, and at last he seemed to have a controlling voice in the Metropolitan's artistic destinies. The achievements of the theater in the next few seasons reached their highest peak. Friction and backbiting subsided for a time.

Just glance at the operas Toscanini himself conducted in 1910-11 and bear in mind that each was repeated a number of times: Gluck's *Armide* (in its first performance at the Metropolitan), *Aïda, Madame Butterfly, La Bohème, La Gioconda,* Puccini's *The Girl of the Golden West* (in its world *première*), *Orfeo, Tristan und Isolde, Die Meistersinger, Germania, Tosca, Otello,* and Paul Dukas's *Ariane et Barbe-Bleue* (in its American *première*). Even at La Scala he had not shouldered so heavy a load. He carried it willingly and delightedly. In one week he conducted *The Girl of the Golden West, Tristan, Orfeo,* and *Otello* while preparing *Ariane.* Here were variety, novelty, and authentic greatness—in sum, a tremendous challenge for a musician who liked nothing better than solving demanding artistic problems.

Puccini, with whom Toscanini had consulted in Italy in the final stages of writing his latest opera, came to America for the *première* and rejoiced at the production. He said, perhaps more optimistically than the quality of the opera itself warranted, "I have no doubt now of its success," but it could not be denied that he was not overshooting the mark when he called the performance perfect.

In the season of 1911-12, Toscanini was still satisfied with the way things were going at the Metropolitan. In December, 1911, he signed a new three-year contract, and his work for the season was, as usual, formidable. His repertory consisted of *Aïda, The Girl of the Golden West, Tristan, Madame Butterfly, La Gioconda, La Tosca, Armide, Orfeo,* Ermanno Wolf-Ferrari's *Le Donne Curiose* (American *première*), *Ariane et Barbe-Bleue, Otello, Die Meistersinger,* and *Manon.*

Massenet's *Manon* was done in a cleaned-up version that Toscanini prepared anew from the ground up. With Farrar,

Caruso, and Léon Rothier in the cast, it struck listeners as something more than a neatly made French opera with some pretty tunes. It had fire and dramatic impact, thanks to Toscanini. And Caruso, who had not been outstanding in French opera, handled his role with an expertness that was attributed in part—and rightly—to Toscanini's guidance.

Wolf-Ferrari was in New York for his opera and said, "I have never realized what was in my opera until I heard it today for the first time in Italian, and under the direction of Signor Toscanini."

Two seasons later another Italian composer was to win a greater success with a new opera in New York than he had in Italy. He was Italo Montemezzi, and his opera was *L'Amore dei Tre Re*. In Italy, in fact, *L'Amore dei Tre Re* had been a failure. When a musician asked a representative of the opera's publisher how it could possibly have failed in Italy, the latter nodded in Toscanini's direction and replied, "They never heard it in Italy."

After the long and exhausting season of 1911-12 Toscanini did not take a rest. He headed for Buenos Aires, where his schedule was even heavier than it had been at the Metropolitan. He conducted a total of twenty-two different operas. As if this were not sufficient, he paused in the course of a brief holiday in Milan in November to conduct two programs of music by Beethoven and Wagner for the new audiences of the Teatro del Popolo. Nor was this the first time he conducted in Italy after his departure from La Scala. In 1909, after his first Metropolitan season, he had agreed to lead an orchestra of teachers and students of the Milan Conservatory in the first of a series of popular concerts.

And while he remained inflexible in his resolution not to conduct opera in the regular Italian opera houses, he was to make an exception in 1913 for Busseto, the town near which Verdi was born and in which he grew up. Here, in a tiny theater seating little more than five hundred, he was to help observe the hundredth anniversary of the composer's birth with loving performances of *Falstaff* and *La Traviata*.

His return to the Metropolitan for the 1912-13 season was delayed until December. Once he resumed work, he did a heavy share. In addition to nine of the operas that had been on his schedule in preceding seasons he conducted Donizetti's *Don Pasquale* and Mussorgsky's *Boris Godunov* in its American *première*.

The production of *Boris Godunov* was one of the great ornaments of Toscanini's career at the Metropolitan, and it remained one of the finest productions mounted in the twenty-seven years of Gatti-Casazza's stay as general manager. That it was done at all was attributable to Toscanini's insistence. He and Gatti had seen the brilliant production in Paris in which Chaliapin had made such a stirring impression on him, and he argued for its production. Chaliapin, who had had a bad time of it at the Metropolitan during the season before the arrival of Toscanini and Gatti-Casazza, could not be tempted back to New York at that time, and Gatti could not see how *Boris* could be done without him. Toscanini thought that Adamo Didur could be turned into a fine Boris, and his idea prevailed. Gatti purchased the sets and costumes that had been prepared for the Paris production and that were lying in a warehouse unused, and Toscanini went to work.

He began rehearsing the singers and the chorus in January. Rehearsals went on through February and into March, with the orchestra being brought in. At the *première* on March 19th, the Metropolitan had a production which had cost Toscanini as much sweat as any opera he had ever prepared. But it was worth the trouble. What emerged was a performance that drew attention to the originality and magnificence of the score, not to any single element on the stage or in the pit.

In his final two seasons at the Metropolitan, Toscanini continued his arduous labors. In 1913-14, besides nine operas of previous seasons, he added *Un Ballo in Maschera*, in a grand revival in honor of the Verdi centenary; *L'Amore dei Tre Re;* and Wolf-Ferrari's *L'Amore Medico* (American *première*). In 1914-15 he did fourteen operas; new to his repertory at the Metropolitan were *Euryanthe,* Giordano's *Madame Sans-Gêne* (world *première*), Mascagni's *Iris,* and *Il Trovatore.* For this last opera he turned the very trick he had managed at La Scala. He stripped away the dross that had gathered around it and restored its native feeling and vitality. And as at Milan, there were dissenters. In New York they reminded him that there was a difference between operatic and symphonic conducting, as though to censure him for bringing out the unity and tautness of the opera as one might handle a symphony by Beethoven.

Probably this was also a dig at his temerity in undertaking to conduct a symphonic concert, which is precisely what he had done on April 13, 1913. On this occasion he had made his American debut in this role. He had conducted the Metropolitan Opera orchestra in Beethoven's Ninth, with the opera chorus and with four singers of the company—Frieda Hempel, Louise Homer, Karl Jörn, and Putnam Griswold—as the soloists. The program, which had been repeated five nights later, had begun with Wagner's *Faust* Overture and Strauss's "Till Eulenspiegel."

In his final Metropolitan seasons Toscanini was beginning to feel intolerable resentment, though his toil was undiminished. In an eleven-day period in December, 1914, he conducted five operas in six performances—all, of course, without score. Later on he did *Tristan* on one night and *Tosca* the next. All this time he was preparing his novelties and revivals. And not content to handle his assignments for the current season, he was forehanded enough to begin preparing some sections of the company for a revival of Borodin's *Prince Igor* for the following season. He was not there to conduct it.

All through his last season there were rumors that he would

not return after the spring of 1915. He had made clear to Gatti and members of the company that various things had annoyed him. There was the matter of repertory. While he had the ultimate say as to what he would do, he had strong convictions as to what the Metropolitan's scope should be. At one time he had suggested a production of *Louise,* and Gatti had vetoed it on the ground that Oscar Hammerstein's Manhattan Opera House, which had been the Metropolitan's stiff competitor during Gatti's first two seasons in New York, had mounted the opera with Mary Garden and that New Yorkers might compare any new production unfavorably with the old one. Toscanini replied that this need not be so. But Gatti won his point.

Some time later while Toscanini was spending part of the summer in Milan, he received a wire from Gatti, who was in Paris. Gatti had just seen a new opera, *Julien,* by Charpentier, and he said that it was a beautiful work. He urged Toscanini to conduct it in New York the following season. He promised an outstanding cast with Farrar, Caruso, and Scotti and the best artists in the secondary roles.

"I knew about this *Julien,*" Toscanini recalled later. "I had the score and I had studied it. I would not conduct it. It turned out to be a fiasco."

Then there was the question of *Cyrano,* an American opera with music by Walter Damrosch and book by William J. Henderson. It had its *première* in February, 1913. There is a story that Toscanini created a scandal while the piece was in rehearsal. The tale has it that he walked into the auditorium one day, listened, and then shouted that it was a shame to do such an opera. Many years later I asked the maestro whether any such incident had occurred. He denied it. His part in the *Cyrano* business had been simpler, he said. His opinion, however, had been just as drastic.

One day he was present when Damrosch went through the score at the piano for a group from the Metropolitan. It can be imagined that Toscanini showed his distaste for the piece, if not through sheer impoliteness, through silence and dark looks.

When Damrosch completed the playing of his opera, Otto Kahn turned genially to Toscanini and said, "Would you like to conduct it?"

"Thank you, no," said Toscanini. He insisted later that his excuse was thoroughly polite. "I don't understand English," he told them.

Some time later he went to dinner at Reginald de Koven's house and sat through a piano reading of that composer's new opera, *The Canterbury Pilgrims*, which the Metropolitan was to do after his departure. Alda, who was present, recalled that all through the audition Toscanini sat with his eyes down and his face as foreboding as a thundercloud, and after it was finished said not a word.

Differences over repertory were only part of Toscanini's dissatisfaction. Some of the things that happened when the Metropolitan toured—it visited a number of cities outside New York each season—were another source of irritation. After the event he could probably forgive as an unforeseeable accident that the sets for an opera in Philadelphia arrived late and the curtain went up almost an hour beyond the scheduled time. Probably he could forgive, but that evening he conducted everything at break-neck speed without looking up at the stage. The orchestra and the poor singers were like breathless pointers chasing after a wild animal.

He could not forgive so readily the affair of the stage trumpeters in *Aïda*. The company was in Chicago for several performances and the day before *Aïda* was to be done, he discovered that the trumpeters, who appear in the triumphal scene, had not made the trip. He wanted to know why and was told that competent substitutes could be found in Chicago inasmuch as that city's opera company regularly did

Aïda. Icily he retorted that he had rehearsed the men in New York and that he would not conduct if they were not on hand. A wire was rushed to New York, the trumpeters were mustered and piled onto a train, and they reached Chicago just in time for the performance.

Incidents like these could be forgotten, if not forgiven. What irked him most was the concern with keeping the Metropolitan Opera's finances in the black. After 1910, when Hammerstein's competing venture was bought out by the Metropolitan, the theater began to operate at a profit, and there was a determination to keep it so. Toscanini was indifferent as to whether the budget was balanced or not. He did not mind if this happy result were accomplished without harming artistic standards. But he would not endure skimping on rehearsals, on salaries for good singers, choristers, and orchestra players, on expenditures for sets and costumes. He held out for every moment of rehearsal he needed, and he got what he wanted. But he could see that other conductors had to make do with what they were offered. He was in recurrent contention with singers who did not care to submit themselves unstintingly to his discipline. He was, in short, getting fed up.

In discussions for the season of 1915-16 it became clear to Toscanini that, because of the war in Europe, the directors of the Metropolitan wished to cut down costs. Toscanini urged Gatti to quit with him, arguing that the Metropolitan would come to book if together they held firm. Gatti could not see it this way. Many years later Toscanini said bitterly, "Gatti was Kahn's man."

In the middle of that final season Toscanini had probably made up his mind to leave, and apparently the Metropolitan sought to dissuade him by tempting him with a plan for a tour with the opera orchestra and a quartet of soloists—Hempel, Sophie Braslau, Giovanni Martinelli, and Amato.

This plan must have appealed to him and undoubtedly gave him pause. But there were new irritations and he turned all offers down.

However, through April he took pride in his work at the Metropolitan. One night, when *Carmen* was scheduled, a group of singers and the conductor, Tullio Serafin, from La Scala, who were in New York en route to Havana, were in the house. Toscanini heard of their presence and told his colleagues to do their best because he wanted to show the delegation from La Scala what the Metropolitan could do. But things went awry. Amato was ill and another baritone was an awkward Escamillo. Farrar was not in good voice. The orchestra made several blunders, and the stage band entered ahead of cue. Toscanini was in a frenzy of anger.

He conducted one more performance that season, and then it was announced that he was "indisposed," though he was seen in public at the very time another conductor was directing his operas. He even canceled a symphony concert scheduled for that month.

It is also probably true that he was suffering under the strain of a personal emotional crisis at this time, and this has been mentioned as the fundamental reason for his departure from the Metropolitan. It may have played its part, but I believe that the overriding reason was discontent with artistic policy.

When he left the Metropolitan that spring, it was for good. During the summer, when he was in Italy, he was asked by Metropolitan Opera officials to change his mind. He was offered the title of artistic director, which meant full control of artistic decisions, but he was through.

His parting with Gatti could not have been cordial, and eventually there grew the tale that there had been an abrupt and scathing break. Much was made in 1932 of the fact that there had been a reconciliation between the two men after they had not met or spoken to each other for seventeen years.

The facts do not sustain this tale entirely. In the winter of 1920-21, when Toscanini led an orchestra of Italian players in an American tour, he was greeted at the pier upon his arrival by Gatti and Alda. He was at the Metropolitan on Christmas Eve of 1920 when Caruso, singing in *La Juive,* appeared in what turned out to be his last performance. Toscanini went backstage to visit Gatti, and they talked concernedly about Caruso's health.

There is no doubt, however, that Toscanini's opinion of Gatti remained low after the periods of conflict at the Metropolitan. He recalled a dispute with Gatti—this one took place long after they had parted company—about the merits of a conductor then at the Metropolitan. Gatti had conceded that the conductor in question was no more than a *routinier* but had added that the public came to hear the singers, not to look at the conductor's back. Toscanini had snorted wrathfully: "That's why your performances are spineless."

In 1939 Gatti was ill, and his wife, the former ballerina Rosina Galli, begged Toscanini to come and visit his old collaborator. After refusing, the maestro gave in. When he arrived, the two embraced, and they were left alone—apparently warm and cordial to each other. Presently they could be heard in a near-by room. Their voices were rising; they were in the midst of a knockdown argument.

Toscanini always held it against Gatti that he had taken as one of his first principles the remark of Verdi: "Always remember that the box office must be filled, not empty. If the theater is not filled, the opera is a failure." I once heard Toscanini cry out indignantly at Verdi for having uttered such monstrous words. To him the test of an opera house was the quality of its performances, not the size of its audiences. To those who might have to meet the bills, the problem might look different. But for Toscanini there could be no compromise, and he would not have been what he was if it had been otherwise.

For the Metropolitan in the decades after his departure he professed to have little regard. When Edward Johnson was general manager, he tried to get the maestro to return for a special production of *Falstaff*, but the answer was no. He spoke on occasion with distaste of much of the Metropolitan audience, reviling the stupid, social elements which, he contended, had no interest in music. That had not changed, he said, over the years.

He had had several tussles with the audience in his days at the Metropolitan. During his first performances of *Tristan* he had the doors barred for the playing of the Prelude, and latecomers were forced to wait in the corridor. During a performance of *Euryanthe*, he stopped in the middle of an orchestral interlude because he was bothered by the whispering behind him, and he held up the show until the audience became silent. There had been times when, in a rage at the noise of shuffling down the aisles and of murmurs of whisperers, he would cease to conduct with his usual concentration, and with a grim look in his eyes would race through a performance as though it were a contagious infection to be rid of speedily.

And yet he had given the Metropolitan seven long seasons, and whether he really despised the theater or not, it remained in his blood stream. He kept informed of what was going on in the place. I remember one night recently when we were chatting of other things far away. He stopped suddenly and, leaning forward confidentially, said, "What about the Metropolitan? What about this new director, Bing?"

13

War Years

ONCE he had broken with the Metropolitan, Toscanini could not wait to get back to Italy. His son Walter, now seventeen, was enlisting in the Italian Army, and he wanted to see him before he went off to service. New York reminded him of countless irritations, and he wanted to get as far away as he could from the scene of his troubles. He had booked passage on a large luxury liner, but decided to leave some days earlier and set out on an older and slower vessel. The ship he had planned to travel on was the *Lusitania*, on her last, fatal voyage.

The war had come very close to him, and it was to remain uppermost in his mind and emotions as long as it lasted. It had already disrupted one plan. He had arranged to conduct in Russia for the first time in the fall of 1914 before returning to the Metropolitan, but the outbreak of fighting had wiped out that commitment, and he never did get to conduct in that country.

In 1915 he did not grieve over a lost engagement. He followed the news of the fighting with avid interest. Like his compatriots he suffered when his country's arms met defeat. Possibly he suffered more deeply, and in his moments of black despair he would not talk, eat, or sleep. There were times when he barricaded himself in his room and kept himself incommunicado even to his family.

When the news was good, he rejoiced. He cheerfully offered his services for charitable and patriotic performances, and when he got his chance he headed for the fighting front to lead a military band.

All the conducting he did between 1915 and 1920, however, added up to very little for a man who in years gone by had carried killing schedules at La Scala, the Metropolitan, the Colón in Buenos Aires. Save for a few special benefit performances of opera, he did not conduct in the theater during this period.

His failure to conduct opera was not for want of invitations. He had returned from New York with an inflexible resolution: he would never again conduct opera in the conventionally organized theater. He had given almost thirty years of his life to opera houses governed either by impresarios or by rich men, and he had had enough of both. Art could not flourish in such opera houses. There might be promises of earth and heaven, and for a time the promises would be kept. Then there would be the inevitable trimming and compromising. He would no longer be a party to any of it.

One can imagine that this decision, while it gave him grim satisfaction, must have been hard to hold fast to. While he had often known intolerable anguish when performances had not gone as he wished, he must have endured almost as much pain not to be conducting. The theater was a snare and a curse, but to be without a theater was a punishment, too. During the war years he had occasional outlets for his energy and his need to make music; afterward, for a time, they were scarce, indeed.

He accepted no money for appearing at benefits, and for a long time there were no paid engagements. His family lived on savings, and when they ran out the house he had purchased on the Via Durini in Milan was sold; he was to repurchase it some years later when he began to earn money once more. With finances running low, his wife urged him to accept some of the offers he was receiving. He would not be budged. He got out his cello, which he had not used for years, and began to practice. He would work hard and get his fingers back in shape; he would rather be a cellist earning a modest living than an illustrious maestro beating his brains out against the thick walls of stupidity and ignorance of the average opera house.

The strain of inactivity lay most heavily on him in 1919. Opera houses were resuming their seasons in many parts of Italy. Major theaters were functioning in other European countries, in the United States, and in South America. Managers and audiences had not forgotten Toscanini and they knew that he had no engagements. But he clung determinedly to his resolution; all feelers and offers were rejected out of hand.

It was not quite so bad from 1915 through 1918. In July, 1915, he undertook the organization and direction of a concert for the benefit of the Red Cross. He trained an ensemble of almost three thousand, including hundreds of instrumentalists and thousands of choristers, and in the open-air arena of Milan before an audience of forty thousand he conducted a popular program ending with the national anthems of the Allies. At one point he turned his back on the massed orchestra and chorus and led the fervid Italian audience in thunderous singing of the "Garibaldi" and "Mameli" hymns. It was growing dark, and many in the crowd rolled up newspapers and put matches to them, waving them like torches to the swing of the patriotic tunes.

In the fall of that year he conducted opera at the Teatro dal Verme in Milan in a series of benefit performances. There were forty-odd performances, and the repertory was *Pagliacci, The Secret of Suzanne, Tosca, Un Ballo in Maschera, Falstaff*, and *Madame Sans-Gêne*. Caruso, back in Italy during the Metropolitan's off-season, sang in *Pagliacci*. The net receipts were three hundred and sixty thousand lire for the season.

In 1916 Toscanini conducted benefit concerts in Rome and Milan, and each time he ran into trouble because he persisted in conducting music by Haydn, Mozart, Beethoven, and Wagner. During the First World War, you will remember, the hatred of Germany and Austria in the Allied countries extended even to music by German and Austrian composers long dead. At the Metropolitan Opera, Wagner was interdicted. In Italy they banished even the composers of earlier generations. Toscanini considered this attitude silly and stupid. "How can they call Mozart German," he demanded, "when his best operas are written to Italian texts?" How could they be against Beethoven and Wagner when their music spoke for all men?

At a concert opening the Augusteo season his program was largely Italian music by Corelli, Martucci, and Tommasini, but he included two Wagner excerpts—"Waldweben" from *Siegfried* and the "Funeral Music" from *Die Götterdämmerung*. Count de San Martino, president of the Augusteo orchestra, advised him to omit the Wagner music, but he refused. There were murmurs of anger during the "Waldweben," and during the "Funeral Music" there was a demonstration of antagonism that must have reminded him of the old days at the Scala. Someone yelled bitterly, "That's for the dead of Padua." The reference was to a recent bombing of the north Italian city by Austrian planes. From other parts of the house there came indignant shouting and cries for the national anthems.

Toscanini tried again in Rome with a program that contained the Beethoven Ninth. Edward Johnson, who was then at the outset of his career as a tenor, working in Italy under the name of Edoardo di Giovanni, was one of the soloists. He recalled later that the maestro prepared for this performance with an intensity that must have been deepened by his consciousness of the tragedies of war. At the first rehearsal for piano the contralto, who had never sung with him and was understandably nervous, made a poor entrance. Toscanini called, *"Da capo,"* and they started afresh. Another bad entrance, and another fresh start. At the third try the girl opened her mouth but no sound came forth; then she began to weep. Toscanini sat there glowering, and Johnson and the other two singers braced themselves for fireworks. They did not come. When the contralto stopped crying and dried her eyes, Toscanini ran his fingers over the piano and said, *"Da capo,"* and then as though speaking to himself, he added, "And they say that I am impatient."

At the performance he geared himself for opposition. As he remembered the incident later, there were two men who set themselves up as defenders of the faith against German music. They kept shouting until they were joined by others in the audience. Luigi Mancinelli, who was down in front in the audience, counseled him to play the "Royal March" when the racket was at its height. He followed this advice, and then resumed the performance. The two obstreperous fellows kept yelling throughout.

Toscanini was so incensed that he did not conduct in Rome again until 1920. And in Milan, where the opposition to his playing German music was led by a newspaper, he went personally to see the editor, a Socialist journalist of promise named Benito Mussolini. Toscanini remonstrated with Mussolini about his benighted views, and Mussolini defended them. Toscanini ended by delivering a tirade and walking out.

This was the first meeting between these two. They were to clash violently later, but during the war years and the period shortly thereafter the journalist's bold, liberal views and his seemingly ardent devotion to the welfare of Italy appealed to Toscanini.

There is no need to gloss over the truth. There is no man who has not made some miscalculation or misjudgment at some time in his life, and Toscanini later conceded without hesitation that he erred in his early estimate of Mussolini. He was beguiled by the journalist's professions of love for Italy. After the war he thought there was some hope for the chaotic, stricken land in Mussolini's program, and he gave it his support. It is true that Toscanini ran for deputy on Mussolini's ticket in the general elections of 1919, and they were both defeated. But for Toscanini his candidacy was not motivated by a desire for public office; it was a moral stand against the disintegration and turmoil that consumed Italy.

It is also true that Toscanini still felt some hope for Mussolini as a man who might deliver Italy from its difficulties when the latter took over the government in 1922. But disillusionment was not long in coming. Toscanini soon began to distrust Benito Mussolini, become Il Duce, and his distrust turned to unappeasable hatred when Mussolini started suppressing civil liberties and setting up a monolithic one-party state.

To grasp fully how ardently Toscanini gave himself to the cause of his country, one may look back at his behavior in 1917. He could not bear to be sitting in comfort in Milan while the battle raged to the northeast. He contrived to get himself appointed to lead a military band. There are photographs of him in this role, showing the slight figure in a uniform with puttees around the legs and the dark mustache and heavy eyebrows bristling under an overseas cap.

He led band concerts on an open-air stage set up among green meadows encircled by rocky hills not far from an encampment. He played marches, waltzes, patriotic pieces, gay and exalting things, and it made him feel that he was part of the war effort.

During the battle of Monte Santo, when the Italian forces went over to the offensive, Toscanini and his band were on hand. An account in the New York *Times* of September 3, 1917, told this story:

In the midst of the fighting and at a time when the Austrian barrage fire was at its height, Signor Toscanini led his band to one of the advanced positions where, sheltered only by a huge rock, he conducted a concert which did not stop until word had been brought to him that the Italian soldiers had stormed and taken the trenches of the Austrians to the music of his band.

He was decorated with a silver medal by the Italian Government for bravery under fire.

This was not the first time he had been exposed to fire. Some time earlier he had visited his son at the Isonzo front. Walter was then a captain of artillery, and he took his father for a stroll along a road that had recently been the scene of fighting. At one point they reached a big puddle that filled the road, and they separated to walk on opposite sides in the fields. At that moment a shell zipped by, following a path directly over the puddle.

"Father has always been lucky," Walter said later. "If it had not been for that puddle, both of us would have been hit."

In the winter of 1917-18, Toscanini conducted a series of twelve concerts at the Milan Conservatory for the benefit of indigent artists, realizing one hundred thousand lire. At these concerts he included Beethoven's Ninth. No matter how strongly he felt as a patriot, he still refused to submit to the practice of eliminating German music from his programs.

At the war's end in 1918, La Scala, which had been closed since 1917, was reopened briefly for a victory season, and he prepared and conducted Boito's *Mefistofele*.

During rehearsals for a performance of Beethoven's Ninth in Turin, Toscanini gave vent to one of his outbursts of rage and injured a violinist in the eye as a result of a swing of his baton. The musician brought suit against the maestro for assault. The judges listened to the evidence and handed down their decision. It is amusing at this distance to read the following excerpt from a report in the New York *Times* of December 31, 1919:

Toscanini usually insists on the rigorous exclusion of all but performers on such occasions [rehearsals], but had made an exception in favor of Professor Pastor, a psychologist of renown, who was engaged in preparing a scientific study of *Enthusiasm*. This courtesy was well rewarded, for the Professor, in the role of principal witness for the defense, delivered a philosophical plea for the irresponsibility of genius which won a verdict of acquittal.

He stated that what really happened was that Toscanini struck out mightily but involuntarily with his baton, causing the violinist's bow to snap and rebound into his eye. Pastor went on to say that he had made a special pathological study of Toscanini and had found that on great occasions this prince of conductors becomes so possessed by sublime frenzy that his normal personality forsakes him. He becomes transfigured by genius, beside, or rather outside of, himself, so that the inhibitory nerves are completely paralyzed. In a paroxysm of inspiration he falls a tragic prey to the tyranny of art, and the faculty of distinguishing good from evil is subordinated to the extreme ebbs and flows of sensibility. Stupendous words and vivacious deeds break forth with volcanic force.

So impossible is anything like a quiet return to normal equilibrium that throughout the night after a performance he continues in a state of pitiful, nervous exaltation. He cannot sleep, his teeth chatter incessantly, his muscles and arms and legs become painfully rigid, and his whole organism vibrates like the subsoil after a terrific earthquake.

The judges decided that a superman cannot be dealt with after the manner of ordinary mortals and that it would be a flagrant injustice to penalize a musical genius like Toscanini with even so much as the infliction of a fine.

Eloquent Professor Pastor! Toscanini must have squirmed uncomfortably when he heard the defense his lawyers had cooked up. He was certainly remorseful about the bodily harm done the violinist, for he privately gave the man a sum of money to see him through his medical expenses. The guff about being a genius must have fretted him fearfully. He had hated the term when applied to him as a boy in the Conservatory; he despises it now. One day he showed a friend a copy of the score of Verdi's *Falstaff*, indicating where slight changes had been made by the composer to transform an ordinary passage into a moment of genius.

"That is genius," he declared. "I am no genius. I have created nothing. I play the music of other men. I am just a musician."

Perhaps the judges of Turin were not taken in by Professor Pastor's erudite appeal. It may be that with the straight-faced, even-handed way of justice they were letting Toscanini off not because he was a genius but because they thought him an extraordinarily good musician.

14

Back to La Scala

W𝚒𝚃𝙷 the end of 1919, Toscanini had had enough of retirement. The urge to work with living musical forces was too compelling to resist any longer. Probably he did not admit openly, while he studied his scores or worked at the piano or cello, that he missed the excitement of watching his own conception of a symphony or an opera take shape under his hands. But when an offer came from the Augusteo orchestra in Rome, he accepted, even though he had not forgotten the nasty demonstrations of 1916.

In January of 1920 he conducted a series of five concerts in Rome and returned in May for another group of programs. In Padua he did a series at an agricultural exposition. In the meantime, ideas important to him were beginning to take shape in Milan.

La Scala was closed, and many Milanese felt that it was a disgrace that the opera house, long the most honored in Italy, was not restored to activity. They bethought themselves of the conductor living in their midst, and tentative approaches were made to entice him back into the theater. Toscanini was forthright. If the plan was to reopen La Scala on the old terms, with an impresario or a good-hearted Maecenas like Duke Guido Visconti di Modrone or his son, Duke Oberto, who had carried on from his father's death in 1901 until 1917, the answer was irrevocably no. If some way could be found to finance the theater so that it would not be dependent on the whims of any individual or group of individuals and if the theater could then be run on strictly artistic principles, he might be interested. He wanted to be assured that this time there would be no nonsense. The best interests of the music and the drama must prevail over all other considerations.

The people behind the movement to restore La Scala bestirred themselves to devise a setup that would satisfy Toscanini, and the fact that they had the possibility of getting Toscanini's services made their task manageable. With Toscanini in the center of the picture, they found that all the forces in the community were eager to co-operate.

The scheme finally fixed upon was to organize an autonomous corporation, which would be in complete charge of La Scala's affairs. To this Ente Autonomo della Scala the city of Milan turned over its rights of ownership in the theater. The box holders went along with the municipality in ceding their proprietary claims. Millions of lire were contributed by private citizens for the renovation of La Scala, and these people neither asked nor were offered any privileges in return, not even the privilege of having a controlling voice as to how the money would be spent. Finally, the city authorities passed an ordinance placing a small tax on all places of amusement —cinemas, theaters, sports arenas—with the proceeds to be used in the operation of La Scala.

Toscanini was consulted every step of the way, and he found the plan good. He was named chief adviser of the Ente Autonomo, and he began slowly to put an organization together. He met with the architects who drew up plans for the modernization of the house. He conferred with the expert called in to see to it that the theater's fine acoustics were not disturbed. He began to think about repertory. Since the death of Arrigo Boito in 1918, Toscanini had had a firm conviction that his unfinished opera, *Nerone*, must be completed and mounted, and he had taken it upon himself to carry out this memorial to his departed friend. Yes, *Nerone* would come as soon as possible. But before the specific operas, there must be a solid basic musical organization—a good orchestra, a good chorus, a good ballet.

A good orchestra, equal in all its elements and truly responsive in all situations, cannot be built overnight, and Toscanini sought for the means to assemble and develop an ensemble at his own pace, not in the rush and tension of the few weeks that precede the opening of an opera season. The work on the reconstruction of La Scala would take months; the house could not be ready for opera until late in 1921. Here it was the middle of 1920, with a year and a half in which to get something done. Why not organize the orchestra at once and take it on a tour? In the course of a long stretch of playing together it could be welded into something fine.

No sooner had Toscanini indicated that he would like to organize an Italian orchestra and tour with it than there were offers from the United States from people willing to arrange sponsorship. London also heard about the plan and beckoned. Italian patrons said that they would be willing to support visits to the cities of the peninsula. The tour in Italy and the United States was arranged, and Toscanini began to organize the orchestra.

From all over Italy the most renowned instrumentalists came to Milan to audition for Toscanini. Selections were made exclusively on merit, not on reputation; it did not matter to Toscanini that one man had held a solo post while another had sat far back in a section. He insisted on a second-violin section that was equal in quality to the first. He took pains to balance each group within the woodwind and brass sections so that it made a harmonious unit. This is a subtle but important consideration; if you have a third horn player whose tone is stronger than that of the others in the section he may throw all the horns out of proportion, and you may have to let him go even though he happens to be a capable musician.

Having assembled the orchestra, Toscanini spent a month

rehearsing it. In October he let the Italian public hear what had been wrought. There were five concerts in Milan and appearances in nineteen other northern Italian cities. One of these took place in Fiume, which the poet Gabriele D'Annunzio and his legionnaires had taken over in the name of Italy. Always the ardent patriot, Toscanini was proud to give this salute to the men who had restored Fiume under the Italian flag. When he stepped out on the stage, someone led a cheer "for the man of the battle of Monte Santo." Before the concert he had been the guest of honor at a military review and had been presented with a gold medal. D'Annunzio had delivered a flowery oration, extolling the magic Toscanini could unleash with his baton and hailing him as a leader of the people.

The orchestra sailed for the United States on November 30th from Trieste on the *President Wilson* and arrived in New York on December 13th. The first engagement was not a concert but a trip to Camden, New Jersey, where Toscanini made his first recordings. These sessions were a trial and exasperation to him. He had always been his own master before the orchestra; now he had to take guidance from engineers. It was the days as acoustic recordings, and the results he got were scarcely commensurate with the effort he put into the work. Recording was to remain a painful experience to him through the years, but he learned to accept it with a martyrized air. Those early disks, released by the Victor Company in its Red Seal series, were either single- or double-faced. They contained short pieces, and they may be found in shops that trade in second-hand records. Their reproduction of the sound of the orchestra was hopelessly inadequate, and their value today is chiefly as curiosities or collectors' items.

The American tour began at the Metropolitan Opera House on December 25th, and for Toscanini at least it was a triumphal progress. Some New York critics thought that the orchestra was not up to the standards of the best American ensembles. On Toscanini there was no dissent; he was cheered and praised to the skies. The leading musicians of the country came to the concerts. The newspapers ran laudatory reviews. In Boston it was suggested that Toscanini ought to be imprisoned to make sure that he would remain to conduct the city's orchestra. The Boston Symphony had, in fact, made him a formal offer to become its conductor several years before, but he had declined because he had not wished to leave Italy while the fighting was still going on.

It was an arduous tour with an incredibly exacting schedule. There were fifty-nine concerts in all, and once the entourage left the East, Toscanini and his men were on trains night after night. The maestro had done a bit of traveling with the Metropolitan, but even he had not realized the size of the country and the distances of the jumps. As for the men in the orchestra, they were overwhelmed. They were also annoyed from time to time by their accommodations, and they brought their complaints to Toscanini.

When Toscanini was touring America with the N.B.C. Symphony Orchestra in the spring of 1950, he was asked when he got to this town or that whether he had been there with the Italian orchestra. Some cities he was certain he had visited; others he could not remember. A friend teased him one day by asking how it was that Toscanini, with his vaunted memory, could not remember where he had played thirty years before.

"At a certain point in that tour," he replied mildly, "I was so furious at the managers and some of the orchestra that I didn't know where I was or what I was doing."

It must have required extraordinary self-restraint for Toscanini to stay with the orchestra and complete the schedule. All kinds of irritations confronted him. In one town he was so besieged by well-wishers after the concert that he could not get away to catch his train, and it left for the next stop carrying the orchestra without him. He had to wait hours for the next train and arrived just in time to rush into his dress clothes for the start of the concert. Everywhere else he had taken the trouble to rehearse the orchestra and to test the acoustics of the hall. Having to forgo this preparation here, he was nervous and irritable. In another city the mayor offered to walk out on the stage with him to introduce him to the public. Toscanini assured him that he need not discommode himself, that he was quite used to walking out on his own. But the mayor would have none of it; he was determined to make a speech of introduction.

Through January, February, and more than half of March, 1921, Toscanini and his orchestra trouped through America, traveling as far south as Richmond and as far west as Des Moines, Kansas City, Topeka, Omaha, and Tulsa, in addition to stops in several Canadian cities. In the towns that had large Italian colonies there were special celebrations. Everywhere there were honors not only for Toscanini and the players but for the country of their origin. The homage paid Italy touched Toscanini and made him feel proud of the venture.

The programs contained standard pieces by Beethoven, Brahms, Schumann, Debussy, Wagner, Rossini, and Strauss, and among the contemporary composers represented were Respighi, Lualdi, Sinigaglia, Malipiero, Tommasini, Bloch, and Roussel. The performances, of course, were not standard or conventional. There was some critical comment that they were not traditional, to which one musician replied, "Thank heavens!"

On April 3, 1921, the orchestra and its leader embarked on the *Argentina* for the trip back to Italy. Several thousand persons gathered at the New York dock to wave bon voyage to the departing visitors. Moved by this tribute, Toscanini sent the men for their instruments and struck up "The Star-Spangled Banner."

Back in Italy, the orchestra started the second half of its

home tour with a concert in Naples and then visited another twenty cities in that part of the peninsula which had not heard the ensemble before the trip to America.

The orchestra Toscanini brought back to Milan with him was a seasoned, sensitive musical instrument. He had nothing to fear about its share in the revival of La Scala, which was soon to unfold. He spent the summer lining up his repertory, engaging singers and choristers and all the other staff members, including an administrative crew. The up-to-date backstage equipment required a new approach to sets, and he plunged boldly into the problems of design.

In those days—and in the years to follow at La Scala—he was almost literally a dynamo. Though he did not prepare every opera and conduct every performance—he engaged a group of promising young maestros to help him carry this burden—he kept a close watch on his colleagues. He was concerned with everything that happened in the theater. When he was not rehearsing or conducting, he was likely to turn up to watch other rehearsals and performances. The company never knew whether he was in the audience or backstage; it was seldom in doubt that his eyes and ears were on them.

He was annoyed one day by the colorless way in which one of the staff co-*répétiteurs* was pounding the piano for a singers' rehearsal. He rushed over to him and slapped his wrists sharply, crying, "Where is your blood?"

Another time, when the ballet corps was doing a dance during a rehearsal, he slammed down his baton, ran up a set of stairs he had had installed for ready access from pit to stage, and went chasing ballerinas, shouting and swinging at them and scattering them like frightened sheep. Among the girls who felt his wrath that day was Cia Fornaroli, who became his daughter-in-law.

On a later occasion, when *Nerone* was in the final stages of preparation, he became annoyed with the way in which one of the backdrops showing St. Peter's in Rome had been painted. The *première* was several nights off, but he did not wish to leave the repainting of this drop to chance. After he finished the rehearsal that night, he sent for the scene painters and forced them to sit up all night to repaint the drop. He remained at his place on the podium all night, too, watching every move they made, guiding and commanding, just as though he were conducting a performance.

The revivified Teatro alla Scala opened on December 26, 1921. All the planned remodeling backstage had not been completed, and in later years Toscanini blamed himself, for the unfinished work did not get done at all. Another six months were required to complete the job. In the meantime, a sum of two million lire had accumulated from the tax imposed for La Scala's benefit, and under the terms of the law the money would be forfeit if there were not a 1921-22 season. He could not bear to see so much money turned aside from opera, and he did not wish critics of the tax to have fuel for propagandizing against it. He would rather have waited, but it was safer to go ahead while the money was available and there was good will on all sides.

The first opera was *Falstaff* with Mariano Stabile, a young baritone, who was to sing later with Toscanini at Salzburg in the piece, in the title role. It was a *tour de force* of ensemble performance. In the past *Falstaff* had had the respect of the Italian public but not its affection. The tightness of its structure and the subtlety of its details had perhaps impressed the knowing, but the average operagoer felt that the absence of grand arias in the style of the earlier Verdi was a failing and he did not bother to go to the theater when it played. This time it caught on. It was staged with loving attention to detail; it was sung and played with a humanity that reached out to nearly all. It revealed that Toscanini's conception of the piece had deepened.

The Ente Autonomo was off to a brilliant start, and *Falstaff* was a triumph for Toscanini, the conductor; Toscanini, the stage director; Toscanini, the administrator.

There were twelve operas that season, and Toscanini assumed personal direction of five. Besides *Falstaff* he did *Boris Godunov, Mefistofele, Rigoletto,* and *Die Meistersinger.* He lavished endless attention on the Mussorgsky opera, and though it was hailed on all sides, he spent the next few years polishing and improving it each time it returned to the repertory. At one point, when he had to leave for several months to conduct the New York Philharmonic, he turned over his cherished production of *Boris Godunov* to another conductor on the staff, begging him to take care with it. The conductor replied that after Toscanini had set it so firmly on its path, it would be easy for him to follow.

"The stupidity of some conductors," Toscanini shouted years later as he recalled the affair. "He thought he was doing exactly what I had done, and in one rehearsal, one rehearsal, I tell you, he succeeded in destroying this *Boris.*"

He attacked *Rigoletto* as he had approached *Il Trovatore* years before, and as he was to work with *La Traviata, Lucia di Lammermoor,* and *Il Trovatore* again in the seasons to come. He studied it as though he had never seen it before. He forced the company to treat the old warhorse in the same way. He gave it a production that had freshness and dramatic impact, and he caused audiences to appreciate it anew.

Speaking of the effect made on audiences by the old operas done without any of the worn-out customs, he observed years later, "Work, work, work. That's what does it. I have worked all my life, and the hardest struggles were with the operas everyone took for granted."

In the season of 1922-23 he took on more than his fair share of work. Out of seventeen operas, he conducted twelve, among them *Manon Lescaut, Lucia, Luisa Miller,* and *Lo-*

hengrin in revivals, and a new Italian opera—Pizzetti's *Debora e Jaele*. He labored hard to give *Lucia* a vivid, freshened production, but he reserved perhaps his most arduous work for Mozart's *The Magic Flute*. Here was another opera that had never gone well in Italy, and he was determined to make it go. He did all that he could in the way of performance, and one cannot doubt that it was a striking production. The public, however, remained aloof. Many stayed away, and those who came were cool. It was suggested to Toscanini that it might be the better part of discretion to withdraw it, and he replied, "We will repeat it until the public comes."

In addition to the operas, he found time to prepare a performance of Verdi's Requiem just as he had found occasion at the end of the previous season to do Beethoven's Ninth Symphony in the course of a symphonic series.

During the 1923-24 season he conducted fourteen operas in eighty-one performances. He revived Gluck's *Orfeo* and *Tristan und Isolde*. For the Wagner work he brought in Adolphe Appia to do the *mise-en-scène*. This was a further example of his audacity. For Appia's ideas were original; they were opposed to the old literal and naturalistic way of setting Wagner; they were not in keeping with the Bayreuth "tradition." In Germany the epoch following the First World War had begun—to last briefly until Hitler imposed his vapid taste—in which new operas and new ideas in staging and scene designing were welcomed, but in Italy there was no comparable flowering of energy, save for the bold, old fellow of almost sixty at La Scala.

Toscanini's major novelty that season was Boito's *Nerone*. At the turn of the century Boito had promised Gatti and Toscanini that he would finish it at once for La Scala, but he could not get it done. It remained for Toscanini to put on the finishing touches, to pull it together, and to fill out the orchestration where it had been left incomplete. The *première* was an event of national importance. Bologna had pleaded for it, and had asked Toscanini to name his own price. He had replied politely that Bologna's stage was too small. Bologna enlarged its stage. But Toscanini had never planned to do it first in any theater other than La Scala. This was the house Boito had loved and for which he had designed *Nerone*. After the Scala *première,* Toscanini took the production to Bologna.

For three years Toscanini had worked with consuming intensity. His son Walter recalled years later returning home one night and finding his father asleep at his desk with a score in one hand and a photograph of a stage set in the other. He had received offers at tremendous fees from other theaters, and although he had had no signed contract with the Ente Autonomo, he had steadfastly replied that he had a moral obligation to La Scala. But it was more than a moral obligation that held him. He was enamored of his work. For the first time in his life he had complete control of every aspect of a theater, and he had it running to suit his ideals. There can be no doubt that this is why he always treasured the memory of those years.

But it was his fate not to be allowed to concentrate on his work undisturbed. By the spring of 1924 a new, troubling force intruded itself on his work and peace of mind. It was Mussolini and his Fascist party.

Shortly after Mussolini captured the government, he sent word through his party functionaries that every opera house and theater in Italy must make prominent display of photographs of himself and the King. The other theaters fell into line, but La Scala did not seem to hear. Representations were made to the influential gentlemen on the board of the Ente Autonomo, and they mentioned the matter to Toscanini. He refused to have the photographs put up. No one dared to make an issue of it with him, though there was constant pressure on the people connected with La Scala.

Years later Toscanini declared proudly, "As long as I was

156

at La Scala, until 1929, we had no pictures of Mussolini and the King in our lobby."

The Fascists did not suffer his resistance cheerfully, but they hesitated to insist on the photographs. On April 21, 1924, which, as the birthday of Rome, was designated as a national holiday, he was requested to preface the evening's performance with "Giovinezza," the Fascist hymn. He refused.

"I shall not allow my orchestra to play 'Giovinezza,'" he said. "The Scala is not a beer garden or Fascist propaganda territory. If you want to play it you can play it to your heart's content in the square outside the opera house or in the Galleria near by. But not here!"

Toscanini knew thereafter that he was being watched. He was not alarmed for his personal safety, but the Fascists were an intrusion that rubbed some of the sheen off his work at La Scala.

There was no further difficulty that season. Still a bear for work, he took the Scala orchestra for a tour of a number of Swiss cities in June. Another post-season orchestral tour to Switzerland the next year was cut short because of the dishonesty of an impresario, and Toscanini made up the loss to the orchestra by giving two special concerts in Milan. In the 1924-25 season he conducted fourteen operas, including Giordano's *La Cena delle Beffe* and Zandonai's *I Cavalieri di Ekebu* in their world *premières*, *Pelléas et Mélisande* in the original French in a production which he remembered with pride twenty-five years later, and *Il Trovatore* in a production that was even more modern and fresher than the one he had done at the Scala decades before.

On April 21st the question of playing "Giovinezza" in honor of Rome's birthday, which Mussolini was now turning also into Labor Day, Colonial Day, and Empire Day rolled into one and which he wanted observed with ceremony throughout the land, arose once more. This time Toscanini had no need to make speeches about the availability of the piazzas and the Galleria. It just happened that an important rehearsal was scheduled for the evening of April 21st, not a public performance.

The next year, 1926, the holiday of April 21st was to be solemnized with greater grandiosity. The Fascists remembered that the theater had been closed to the public the year before and they began their pressure ahead of time to be sure that they were not confronted with such a situation again. They raised hob with the dukes, counts, industrialists, and merchants who had given their names to the board of the Ente Autonomo della Scala: this year they must have "Giovinezza" played. A deputation of these fearful gentlemen went to Toscanini to ask him to relent. He would not budge. Once again the theater was closed, this time for the rehearsal of Puccini's posthumous opera, *Turandot*.

However, the matter was not dropped so readily. Toscanini had been in New York for his debut with the New York Philharmonic in January and part of February. Possibly there was additional hostility against him for going off to America, even if this meant an opportunity to earn sizable sums, which he needed to augment the modest fees he had set for himself at La Scala. Possibly there were some who had realized that this very act of going to New York was a sign that Toscanini would not trifle with unreasonable demands at La Scala.

A day or two after the celebration of Empire Day in 1926, Mussolini arrived in Milan. Members of the directorate of the Ente Autonomo—not Toscanini—visited him and begged him to honor the theater with his presence on the evening when *Turandot* would have its *première*.

Writing in the New York *World* some weeks later, John Lucas described this interview:

Mussolini, who had been amiable to them up to that moment, put on his tyrant's mask—chin out, brows knit in a Napoleonic frown, hands crossed Napoleonically—and strode up and down the room roaring like a bull:

"How dare you even ask me to La Scala while you keep that rebel Toscanini there? How dare you allow him to remain when he has defied my orders? Yes! MY orders, to play 'Giovinezza' on Empire Day!"

The visitors stood silent—Mussolini rarely asks his callers to take a seat. He went on:

"Either that man goes or I never cross the threshold of your place again! Take that as final! I always mean what I say!"

The Scala directors shuffled out of the august presence and turned toward the theater. As they walked they decided they must speak to Toscanini. He would not leave rehearsals to meet them. Later that day they met with him, giving him a gentle version of their meeting with Mussolini.

"If you want 'Giovinezza' played," he told them, "get some-body else to conduct *Turandot*."

He walked out on them.

Confronted with Toscanini's decision, the governing board of the Ente Autonomo conferred late into the night. It dared not do *Turandot* with another conductor and it dared not set *Turandot* aside. Worldwide interest had been drummed up in this *première*, and the loss of prestige would be grave. Furthermore, there was business at the box office to consider. In Toscanini's absence in America, attendance had been poor; with his return it surged up. What would the Milan public think? Finally, what would Mussolini think?

The board took a chance and let Toscanini conduct. There was no "Giovinezza" to preface the *première* of Puccini's last opera. Toscanini dramatized the occasion more forcefully. Puccini had not quite finished the opera, and the final scene had been written by Franco Alfano. At the *première*, when Toscanini reached the point at which Puccini wrote his last music, he laid down his baton, turned to the audience, and said that here death had stopped Puccini's hand. He left the pit; the performance was over.

Shortly after this performance it was announced that Toscanini was ill. He went off to the Italian Riviera, leaving the rest of the season to other conductors. While he was gone, Milan seethed with rumors. The news was cabled to the world that Toscanini was breaking with La Scala because of a rift with the Fascists.

Some weeks later he was back in Milan, obviously in the best of health, seeing friends, studying new scores, going about his affairs without any appearance of fear or worry. In the showdown between art and Fascist demands, he knew, the Scala had chosen art—at least for the time being. Toscanini had got away with his defiance of the dictator.

15

Dual Role

FROM 1926 through half of 1929, Toscanini took on a dual role during the height of the music season. While he retained full control of the policies and management of La Scala and continued to conduct a large share of its operas, he found time for trips to America to conduct the New York Philharmonic each season.

Clarence H. Mackay, president of the Philharmonic Society, who had heard Toscanini during his stay at the Metropolitan as well as during his tour with the Italian orchestra, had listened to him abroad and had decided to try to bring him to New York. But Toscanini felt that his first allegiance belonged to La Scala. Max Smith, who as a music critic for the New York *Press* and New York *American* had become friendly with Toscanini, was commissioned by Mackay to go to Italy and to conduct negotiations. Toscanini gave the New York offer much thought. The question he kept asking himself was, "How can I leave the Scala even for a short time without neglecting my duty to it?"

He asked no questions about the fee he would be paid until he had studied the Scala situation thoroughly and had worked out a plan that would enable him to be gone for about six weeks without any break in that institution's schedule. Of course, it was a handsome fee. But it was not money that brought him to America. Much as he loved opera and La Scala, he had wanted also to do symphonic music. In Italy he could find time only for an occasional series. In New York it would be the orchestra only, and the Philharmonic, he assumed, would be an ensemble of high quality. He had always liked to travel and undertake new ventures, and the call to New York had a strong appeal for him. Later on his detractors in Italy suggested that his New York engagement was a premeditated preparation for his eventual departure from La Scala. Certainly La Scala grew less attractive as the Fascists exerted their pressure, but late in 1925 he was still coping with them on his own terms.

Toscanini conducted his first concert with the Philharmonic on January 14, 1926. His program consisted of Haydn's Symphony No. 101, in D; Respighi's *Pines of Rome*, in its first New York performance; Sibelius's *Swan of Tuonela*; Wagner's "Siegfried's Death" and "Funeral Music"; and Weber's Overture to *Euryanthe*. This was a fair sample of what his programs were to be in succeeding seasons.

It is odd that the "Funeral Music" from *Die Götterdämmerung* happened to be on the first program. On another occasion some years later it was to cause him untold anguish, and he was to forswear playing it again with the Philharmonic. On that occasion—a wintry evening—the trombones broke badly at the crucial point. Otherwise, the orchestra had played splendidly, but Toscanini finished the performance beating time mechanically, a black expression on his face. When the audience burst into thunderous applause, he blew up. To think that those people would approve of such a performance! He did not go out on the stage for bows, but dashed out of the rear exit of Carnegie Hall on Fifty-sixth Street. Still wet with perspiration and still wearing his dress suit, he scurried down Broadway. He had not bothered to take a hat or coat, and friends chased after him as he went hedge-hopping through the crowds and the traffic of midtown Manhattan at theater-closing time. He arrived safely at the Hotel Astor, where he stayed during his years with the Philharmonic, and was in an ugly, uncommunicative mood for hours. His friends and family regarded it as a miracle that he was not injured in the traffic and did not come down with a bad cold.

He conducted the Philharmonic only for a few weeks in that first season, and by the middle of February was back at La Scala. By March 4th he was able to conduct the Italian *première* of Debussy's *Le Martyre de Saint Sébastien,* so rapidly and intensively did he prepare this novelty. By the end of the 1925-26 season in Milan it was discovered that his work at home had not diminished measurably despite his absence in New York. He had been responsible for fifty-two performances, and besides the Debussy work and *Turandot,* he had revived *Un Ballo in Maschera, L'Amore dei Tre Re,* and *Faust,* revealing in the case of the Gounod opera, a staple of staples in all opera houses, new insight and fresh vitality.

He had also been in a new law suit. This time a violinist in the Milan orchestra brought him into court on the charge that Toscanini had injured his feelings, health, and reputation by criticizing him savagely in front of the other musicians. According to the press reports of the time, Toscanini allegedly said, "Weaklings are not wanted here. You're awfully feeble." You can bet that Toscanini's language was stronger. In the end, the violinist withdrew his suit. Perhaps someone told him how the court in Turin had ruled in 1919.

In the summer of 1926, Toscanini repaired to Busseto for a repetition of the labor of love of 1913. In observance of the twenty-fifth anniversary of Verdi's death, he did *Falstaff* again with Stabile in the title role. He was moved once more by the compassionate humanity and wisdom of the opera, and in the little theater of Busseto his conception was projected on a scale where every subtlety of inflection and detail—in the singing and playing and in the staging—could not be missed. He led the company in pilgrimage to Le Roncole, the village where Verdi was born, and to Sant' Agata, the large farm on which Verdi had lived in his last years.

His love for this opera had never wavered from his first acquaintance with it more than thirty years ago. With each new revival—at the Metropolitan, at La Scala, at Busseto— he had probed for new things in it. Even though he had put it on in a memorable performance at La Scala upon his return in 1921, he had continued to study the score each year when the time came to remount it. And in 1923 he had made a discovery that had deepened the emotions *Falstaff* awoke in him. He had been troubled about a certain point in the score and had asked the house of Ricordi, Verdi's publisher, to let him look at the original manuscript.

He was alone with the manuscript that day, and having checked the musical point that had interested him, he turned the pages, looked at the music, and admired the meticulous hand in which Verdi had written. The very writing—controlled, precise, and yet with an unmistakable touch of poetry —moved him and evoked the image of the old composer at his desk at the age of eighty. And as he leafed through the pages, he found near the end of the score a farewell letter in Verdi's hand. He picked it up with excitement, and as he read, he wept. Verdi had written: "All is finished! Go, go, old John. . . . Find your way, as far as you can. . . . Diverting type of rascal; eternally true, under different masks in every time, in every place!! Go. . . . Go. . . . Walk, walk. . . . Farewell."

Somehow it was not merely an apostrophe to *Falstaff* but Verdi's farewell as a composer of operas. The humility and pathos of it tore Toscanini to bits, and at Busseto the remembrance of that letter pervaded every thought and feeling as he prepared and conducted *Falstaff*.

Toscanini kept that Verdi letter by his side in the years that followed. When he had returned the manuscript score to Ricordi in 1923, he had told them that in view of his work at Busseto in 1913, his friendship with Verdi, and his discovery of the letter, they ought to present it to him. They were glad to. Later on he had copies made and framed and presented them as gifts to special friends.

"But just think of it," he said recently in recalling the finding of the letter. "I had looked through that manuscript score several times before and hadn't seen it."

In September and October he conducted a series of concerts in Milan and Turin on the eve of the centenary of Beethoven's death. He knew that he would be occupied with other things on the actual date—Beethoven had died on March 26, 1827—and he was eager to make his devotions. In both Italian cities he did all nine symphonies. The Turin management, grateful for the extraordinary success of the concerts, sent Toscanini an extra check in addition to the set fee. He returned it; he thought he had been paid enough.

For the Scala season of 1926-27, his Beethoven observance took the form of a production of *Fidelio*. As at Salzburg later, he introduced the "Leonore" Overture No. 3 before the final scene of the opera. He gave the work a luminous performance, and those who heard it were particularly moved by the chorus of captives with their yearning for liberty. Toscanini was not unaware that the theme of this opera had a moral for his own country.

He did not fear the anger of the Fascists. Nor was he downcast by the failure of the public to throng the theater. As with *The Magic Flute*, he felt that it was his obligation to repeat *Fidelio* until the public came.

Despite the fact that he suffered from a nervous ailment that winter, he conducted eleven other operas at La Scala, including an impressive revival of Verdi's *Don Carlos*. In February, 1927, he was in New York, but because of his illness he conducted only several of the fifteen concerts he had promised to do. In two of them he directed Beethoven's Ninth with Elisabeth Rethberg, Louise Homer, Richard Crooks, and Fraser Gange as soloists. Miss Homer, his Orfeo of years ago, was brought in at short notice. The girl who had been engaged

riginally had been unsure of words and music at the first re-
h arsal, and Toscanini had been summary with her. In her
presence and in the presence of the other singers, he had said
to an official of the orchestra, "This lady will not do. Get me,
at once, another contralto."

Upon his departure, snide rumors were circulated about
him. One had it that he did not like America, which was untrue, and the other had it that he had received and accepted
payment for the full fifteen concerts of his contract when he
had conducted only three in New York and one in Philadelphia, which was equally untrue.

Far from disliking America and the Philharmonic, he had
agreed to become co-conductor of the orchestra for the 1927-
28 season, sharing these duties with Willem Mengelberg. The
guests were to be Sir Thomas Beecham and Bernardino Moli-
nari. Furthermore, he had promised to be responsible for all
the concerts from January 26, 1928, until the end of the season on April 1st.

And he carried out his agreement to the letter. After a rest
in the summer of 1927, he returned to his task at the Scala full
of vigor. He put on *Otello* with new sets, and after he returned
from America he conducted the world *première* of Pizzetti's
Fra Gherardo. All told, he conducted eleven operas in forty-
three performances that season. In addition, he concerned
himself with all that happened in the theater in a season when
new operas by Pedrollo and Wolf-Ferrari and important revivals such as *The Marriage of Figaro* were prepared and put
on by his associates.

He returned to New York with fire in his eye. He had heard
that the previous season Mengelberg had talked patronizingly
of him as "the Italian conductor." In fact, the Philharmonic
in more than eighty years of existence had not had an Italian
conductor before, but Toscanini did not regard it as a national
honor that he was the first. When it came to music, he did not
think in terms of his nationality, and he resented the way

Mengelberg had talked. He had heard, too, that in the previous season Mengelberg had made remarks about his indisposition and failure to do all his concerts. What irritated Toscanini most was that Mengelberg hung around New York after he had completed his share of the season, trying to absorb the limelight and, what was worse, giving him advice on how to conduct.

Mengelberg had the reputation of delivering endless discourses during rehearsals. It got so that a deputation of players went to the manager to complain about the long, boring lectures. Apparently, he gave Toscanini the benefit of his knowledge, too. As the maestro said years later, "Talk, talk, talk. That was Mengelberg. Once he came to me and told me at great length what was the proper, German way to conduct Beethoven's 'Coriolanus.' He had got it, he said quite seriously, from a conductor who supposedly had got it straight from Beethoven. Bah! I told him, 'I get it straight from Beethoven, from the score.' "

Before the season was over, it was clear that Toscanini had become the dominant figure in New York's orchestral world. It was decided to merge the New York Philharmonic and the New York Symphony, which Walter Damrosch had conducted and Harry Harkness Flagler had supported for many years. Toscanini was named the principal conductor of the merged ensemble for the next season and received authority to choose the new orchestra from the players in the older two. Mengelberg remained an associate conductor for a while but soon quit New York for good, complaining that Toscanini had intrigued against him.

While it was true that Toscanini did not like Mengelberg as a man and did not admire him as a musician, he did not and would not have plotted against him. No matter what the Mengelberg adherents might say, it was the quality of performances that made the difference. Toscanini's concerts were received joyfully by public and press, both in New York and on a tour in which Toscanini led the Philharmonic in Philadelphia, Washington, Baltimore, Buffalo, and Pittsburgh.

Toscanini's programs in 1928 leaned heavily on the standard repertory, but they contained contemporary pieces by Sinigaglia, Honegger, Respighi, Pizzetti, and Victor de Sabata. In the course of ten weeks he managed to conduct, in New York and on tour, a total of forty-two concerts. It is interesting to observe, in studying the details of his programs, which were reasonably characteristic of his work throughout his tenure with the New York orchestra, that he seasoned his fare of the staples of the classic repertory with the music of other men who were, properly speaking, contemporaries—*his* contemporaries. While he did not turn, then or later, to many of the composers who were young and belonged to the *avant-garde* of 1928, he did conduct representative pieces of men like Elgar, Ravel, de Falla, Busoni, and Martucci. The appearance of Martucci's Second Symphony on his programs was perhaps the first indication New York had of how he felt about this late nineteenth-century Italian composer, whose music was to play a central role in one of the most turbulent incidents of Toscanini's life three years later.

Toscanini ended his New York season in 1928 with another performance of Beethoven's Ninth, with Nina Morgana, Sophie Braslau, Richard Crooks, and Ezio Pinza as his soloists this time. Then he hastened home to resume his duties at La Scala.

In the fall he conducted three concerts in Milan, and then began to work on what turned out to be his final season at La Scala. New York wanted more of his time, and the situation in Italy was becoming oppressive. The Fascists had not let up in their pressure on La Scala, and while Toscanini remained outwardly impervious, it was a constant irritation to him.

Apparently Il Duce had attempted to take a hand directly and had summoned Toscanini into his presence on one occasion. The maestro had gone unwillingly, but had decided he must go through with the meeting. Fearing that if he spoke his mind to Mussolini there would be a crackdown on La Scala, which might even lead to the closing of the theater and the loss of jobs for hundreds in the company, he made up his mind to listen silently. Mussolini kept Toscanini standing and de- livered a furious diatribe. The conductor stood there, watch- ing a point on the wall above Il Duce's shaven head. He would not answer Mussolini; neither would he agree to any of Mus- solini's demands. The harangue lasted about an hour, and then Toscanini was dismissed. Mussolini had got a lot of angry words off his chest, but he had not won a single con- cession from the little maestro.

The bulk of the Milan public was not disturbed by the un- concealed enmity of the local Fascists. It turned out jubilantly to pay homage to Toscanini on the evening of December 26, 1928, when the thirtieth anniversary of his debut at La Scala was celebrated with a performance of *Die Meistersinger*, the very opera he had conducted in his 1898 debut. Toscanini conducted, and everyone at La Scala as well as the people of Milan and of all Italy joined in doing him honor. Even the Government paid its respects officially; whatever its leaders thought privately of the conductor, they found it wise to go along with the sentiments of the people on this occasion.

There was talk of raising a large fund to present to Tosca- nini, but when he got wind of it, he served notice that he would have none of it. He did not object, however, when money was collected and set aside in a foundation bearing his name, to be used for the care of children of the Scala com- pany, particularly the children of the members of the or- chestra.

One of the first operas to be done in the new season was *Fra Gherardo*. Toscanini had ended the 1927-28 season with the piece, and he did not look forward to resuming rehearsals with it in the fall. He did not like the opera particularly, and he could not bring himself to wrestle with it anew. He called together the company and said, "We did it last night really, and we don't need rehearsals. Let's go." It was a difficult work, but it went satisfactorily without rehearsals.

Speaking of rehearsals years later, he exploded the theory that he needed more than any conductor in the business. Of course, he insisted on rehearsing a piece until it met his requirements, but once it was set, he did not keep fussing with it. He recalled that when he had done *Die Meistersinger* with La Scala in the twenties, he had had a number of rehearsals with piano and six with orchestra for the first season. In succeeding seasons, one rehearsal session—and, he pointed out, it would take two sessions to go through the whole opera—would suffice. The same procedure was employed with *Falstaff* and many other works, some of extreme complexity.

"There is no need to rehearse," he said, "when the company knows the opera."

Even though he had a heavy commitment in New York, Toscanini conducted thirteen operas in his final season at the Scala. They were *Die Meistersinger*, *Fra Gherardo*, *Otello*, *Lucia*, *Parsifal*, *Pelléas*, *Aïda*, *Rigoletto*, *Germania*, *Falstaff*, *Manon Lescaut*, *La Forza del Destino* (in another of his rehabilitations of a Verdi work), and Giordano's *Il Re* (world *première*). The first performance of *Il Re* took place on January 12th, and then he headed for New York.

He conducted the Philharmonic-Symphony from February 21st to April 1st, taking it on a week's tour again as far west as Pittsburgh and introducing new works by Respighi, Pizzetti, and Tommasini. His work with the orchestra, in rehearsal and performance, was intensive as usual, but it seemed to be simple compared with the demands made on him in the opera house.

He was now sixty-two. He told himself, in moments of self-analysis, that he was growing old and that he must drop some of his burdens. It is amusing to observe that when he reached seventy he felt that the end of his career was in sight, and at eighty he spoke humbly of being too old to keep working. He did not stop at those later stages, and certainly in his early sixties he had the physical vitality and the compelling urge to keep working in music.

The truth, more probably, was that he had spent eight exhausting and exciting seasons at La Scala. He had proved to his own satisfaction and to the Italian public that an opera house could be run on a sounder basis than any attempted before. He had now an irresistible urge to turn to other forms of musical expression, and he wished to devote himself to the orchestra. The pinpricks of the Fascists had their effect, too. The board of the New York Philharmonic-Symphony wanted him to give much more time to the orchestra. The dual responsibility of the New York orchestra and the Milan opera house was heavy. The time had come to choose, and he chose the orchestra.

But he had a final fling with the Scala company. It had always been one of his greatest pleasures to take a musical group he had trained to his taste on a tour of other cities and countries, to show, as it were, what could be accomplished where it came from. In May, Toscanini set off with the Scala forces for performances in Vienna and Berlin. He took along not only the leading singers, orchestra, chorus, ballet, costumes, and sets but the Scala stagehands, and he was accompanied by a sizable delegation of Milanese laymen, traveling with the representatives of national achievement much as passionate baseball fans might follow their team on the road.

At the Vienna Staatsoper, the company performed *Falstaff* and *Lucia*. Public and press were enchanted. The demonstrations in the theater were almost frenzied; the notices in the newspapers were ecstatic. There were receptions and banquets for the troupe as Vienna turned itself inside out to welcome Toscanini. It may be imagined how he glowed at the thought that this was the city of Mozart, Beethoven, and Brahms and that it was now acknowledging the power, passion, and humanity of Verdi and Donizetti.

The special train moved on to Berlin. At the Staatsoper and the Städtische Opera of Charlottenburg, Toscanini conducted *Falstaff, Lucia, Rigoletto, Il Trovatore, Manon Lescaut*, and *Aïda*. The German theaters, encouraged by the Weimar Republic, were then at the height of their adventurous postwar careers, and it is likely that the German audiences looked forward to the Scala performances with a certain amount of show-me reserve. Toscanini showed them. He had carefully chosen his repertory, you will notice, from the Italian school, and he led performances the like of which the Berliners had never known. Verdi had been rediscovered in Germany in a great wave of revivals in those years, and Toscanini gave the Germans four Verdi operas. The audiences were filled with visitors from all over the country. They were wild with enthusiasm, and the critics companioned their mood and reaction. The vogue for Verdi received new impetus.

The company returned home like conquering heroes. Even Mussolini, who had an enormous appetite for conquering heroes that was not to receive too much gratification, must have been pleased by this artistic conquest. It may even be that he and his Fascists had a moment of regret when they realized that Toscanini was now finished with La Scala. It may be—but it is much more likely that they were delighted to be rid of a difficult, recalcitrant musician. For the public of Milan, however, it was a time for sorrow.

Toscanini, too, undoubtedly knew more than a twinge of regret. These had been years of enormous accomplishment at La Scala. He was leaving much of himself in the old house, and he was carrying away more than a thin slice of it.

16

Virtuoso of Virtuosos

ON OCTOBER 3, 1929, Toscanini was in New York to conduct the opening of the Philharmonic season for the first time, and he directed all the concerts until November 24th. While guest conductors took over, he sailed for a brief visit at home in Italy where, you may be sure, he kept close watch on how La Scala was faring. He returned to New York in February, and from the 27th through April 20th he conducted the Philharmonic-Symphony again. All told, he was in charge of sixty-one concerts, averaging three or four a week.

His repertory was now reasonably predictable. Some pieces new to the orchestra as well as some new to New York and America were introduced. They were by Paer, Tommasini, Busch, Wetzler, Pizzetti, Ravel ("Bolero"), Goossens, Kodály ("Summer Evening"), Castelnuovo-Tedesco, and Respighi (the transcription of Bach's Passacaglia and Fugue in C minor). The music of Stravinsky, Respighi, Roger-Ducasse, Sibelius, and Honegger was also represented. There was little here to make the *avant-garde* among laymen and musicians happy, and the American contingent of composers began to carp at Toscanini's failure to recognize its existence.

The public at large did not complain. It found the Toscanini concerts enormously exhilarating. For a showpiece like the "Bolero" it reacted wildly, and it rejoiced at the precision and splendor attained by the orchestra. It felt that New York at last had a conductor and an orchestra that the city's size and pre-eminence deserved. For some years the Boston Symphony under Serge Koussevitzky and the Philadelphia Orchestra under Leopold Stokowski, in their periodic seasonal visits, had been commended as superior ensembles. The New York orchestra could now stand comparison with any group in the country and the world.

As for Toscanini, he was now accepted as having achieved a niche all his own. He was treated not as just a conductor but as the reigning star of the musical firmament. The man who had fought against stars in the opera house all his life was acclaimed as the brightest light of them all. Many in his audiences were not just listeners but worshipers. It was held a high privilege to watch him and to hear him in whatever music he chose to conduct. The name of Toscanini assumed a new magic at the box office and in the hall. It was as though people came for him alone, and even the orchestra took on secondary importance in their eyes.

It was a remarkable ascendancy, and it fitted in well with the phenomenon of the era—the predominance of the virtuoso conductor. In the nineteenth century the singer and then the virtuoso violinist and pianist had been all-prevailing. Into the twentieth century these performers held their sway, and even in our day they have their legions of devoted admirers. But the virtuoso conductor moved up to equality and, in America, where orchestras are more widespread than opera houses, assumed dominance. In this climate Toscanini naturally came to be regarded as the virtuoso of virtuosos. To some extent it had been true even when he was at the Metropolitan; now that he was with the Philharmonic it was true beyond question. It was true, for that matter, all through Europe, where he loomed as the conducting star of the first magnitude.

It must be remembered that at this time Toscanini's name and work became known to millions where thousands had been able to hear him before. The Sunday afternoon broadcasts of the Philharmonic had begun and were carried throughout the United States. He now also made recordings which, thanks to the recently developed system of electrical reproduction, enabled him to transmit much more of what he could do onto the black disks.

Had you asked him what he thought of the new public fascination with his life, his person, and his career, he would probably have given a short, nasty answer. The very phrase "virtuoso conductor" would have irked him. He continued to consider himself a musician, with the orchestra as his indispensable instrument. He knew when he and the orchestra had made music satisfactorily; and while he could not but be pleased by the audience's wild admiration, he did not need it for corroboration. And when he knew that the music was below par, he would revile the audience for its undiscriminating applause. He could be drastic with it when he felt that it was not properly respectful to the music. One evening at Carnegie Hall he paused in the middle of a piece to glare at a group of latecomers who were hurrying down the aisles and shouted at them, "You are late!"

Another time, he was presented with a huge floral wreath after a performance, and the sight of it caused him to run off the stage in a fury.

"They are for prima donnas and corpses," he said. "I am neither."

During the second half of that 1929-30 season with the Philharmonic he seems to have been in an unusually docile and obliging mood. Rehearsals no doubt had their moments of stress, with scores flung to the ground and trampled and with batons snapped in two while the orchestra's librarian went charging off to get a new supply, shouting, "Lumber, lumber!" But Toscanini, it may be guessed, was happy. Plans had been completed for his European tour with the New York Philharmonic in the spring, and for the first time he was to conduct at Bayreuth in the summer. The prospect of these adventures, both close to his heart, made him agreeable to proposals that

175

he would have rejected out of hand in other circumstances.

Thus we find him on March 5th at Georgetown University in Washington, D. C., receiving an honorary degree and saying a few, brief words of graceful acknowledgment. On March 22nd we find him on the stage at Carnegie Hall at the final concert in the children's series conducted by Ernest Schelling. Not only did he hand out the medals and ribbons won by the youngsters but he made a little speech. Yes, Toscanini, making a public speech! It contained only a few sentences, but the very idea of his saying them before an audience moved the *Times* to report them in full.

"It is dear to me," he said, "that my friend, Maestro Ernest Schelling, has wished me to convey the annual prizes to the children. I love and always have loved children. To give them joy is just like giving air and light to flowers. Flowers and children are pretty things, and we are all fond of them. In the heart of children there is always some music to be called out by a touch of sympathy and love. Therefore, I have accepted today this very sweet task."

He was a "prize winner" himself that morning. Mr. Schelling pinned on his lapel a red ribbon like those presented to the youngsters, and Toscanini wore it in public for days, which was more than he did with the many decorations that he had received in the past. And at the end of that morning's concert he conducted the Prelude to *Die Meistersinger*.

Three days after the season's end on April 20th, Toscanini and the orchestra embarked for the tour through Europe. It was a tour that cost the supporters of the orchestra more than two hundred thousand dollars in additional deficit, but they made the contribution as a gesture of good will to Europe and, one may guess, to Toscanini. They knew that he wanted this tour very badly and they were willing to go to great lengths to keep him happy.

For Toscanini this was more than just a tour. He was proud of this orchestra, and he wished to show it off in Europe. He wanted to reveal to the connoisseurs in cities with ancient musical cultures how America organized and sustained an orchestra. It is reasonable to assume that with this orchestra he wanted to make music in cities that had long beckoned him to come as a guest. It must be remembered that although he was now sixty-three and had accumulated a fabulous world-wide fame he had rarely conducted symphonic music in Europe outside of Italy, save for brief visits to Switzerland.

The tour opened at the Paris Opéra on Saturday evening, May 3rd. It began, aptly enough, with Beethoven's "Eroica," and the program continued with Brahms' "Variations on a Theme of Haydn," the Nocturne and Scherzo from Mendelssohn's *Midsummer Night's Dream* Music, and the Prelude and "Liebestod" from *Tristan.*

In the course of the ten-day ocean voyage there had not been much opportunity to practice, and some of the players were not in top form. The lips of the brass players were soft from inactivity, and the first horn player, an accomplished musician, reached the final, sustained note of his solo in the Mendelssohn Nocturne in a winded, red-faced condition. Toscanini saw that the man was heading for trouble, possibly a bad, cracking sound as his stamina gave out, and he signaled that the note be cut short long before it was due to end. This was a breach of musical rectitude. Normally it would have infuriated Toscanini, and on this occasion, when he was so eager to have Paris hear music made in perfect taste, it must have been a wrench for him to condone such procedure. But in the heat of his performance his mind remained intensely alert and could adapt itself, in instantaneous decisions, to the necessities of the situation.

The following evening there was another concert at the Opéra. This time, in addition to music by Haydn, Pizzetti, and Wagner, Toscanini conducted two French pieces—Debussy's "La Mer" and Ravel's "Bolero." Years later he recalled that after hearing this performance of "La Mer," the French always asked for it from him. Ravel was in the audience to hear his piece, and he complained of the rapid tempo Toscanini took for the piece. The maestro later got hold of a recording Ravel himself had made and proved that the composer's pace was like his own.

The audiences and the critics of Paris, in their excitement and panegyrics, set a tone that was to be standard throughout Europe. To take one sample, Emile Vuillermoz, writing in *Excelsior*, said, "Toscanini has crossed Paris like a meteor, like a scintillating star. Here, in all truth, is a Master, not only a conductor but the master of all conductors." What held true in America applied in Europe. Conductor of conductors, virtuoso of virtuosos, Toscanini was regnant everywhere.

Zurich was the next stop, and then came two concerts in Milan at La Scala. Back in the old theater to which he had given so many years, he must have had a moment of regret and then a strong sense of gratification that he could bring so fine an orchestra to show to his old friends and enemies. And they, listening to Rossini, Schumann, Pizzetti, Mendelssohn, Bach-Respighi, Wagner, Mussorgsky, Tommasini, Franck, and Ravel, lamented their loss and shouted their bravos, like all Europe.

On to Turin, where the Princess of Piedmont was to be in the audience. Here there was a dilemma. It was traditional that the "Royal March" must be played at the outset of a concert if a member of the ruling family was in the audience, but Mussolini had made it a fixed rule that the "Royal March" must always be followed immediately by the Fascist hymn. Toscanini acceded to the "Royal March," but he would not, under any circumstances, lead the Fascist hymn. There were many conferences and much scurrying about until a solution satisfactory to everyone was hit upon. With the orchestra in its place on the stage and with Toscanini standing, arms folded, on the podium, a ragged-looking, oompahing brass band filed out sadly and hesitantly in front of the footlights and played the "Royal March" and "Giovinezza" in embarrassed and slovenly fashion. Then the concert went on.

Two concerts followed at the Augusteo in Rome, one in Florence, one in Munich, two at the Staatsoper in Vienna, one in Budapest, one in Lucerne, one at the Gewandhaus in Leipzig, where Mendelssohn and Nikisch among many others had shed luster on the city's symphonic seasons; one in Dresden, two in Berlin, one in Brussels, and four in London—two in the Albert Hall and two in Queen's Hall. The final concert took place on June 4th. In one month and two days Toscanini and the orchestra had played twenty-three concerts in sixteen cities of nine countries.

The much abused phrase "triumphal tour" would have to be shined up in all its pristine significance to describe the sensations created by this trip. Old Julius Klengel, cellist, who had played in the Gewandhaus orchestra for years, came backstage in Leipzig to tell Toscanini that he had cried when he had heard the "Eroica" played as he had always known it should be played. In London, Toscanini received a letter from eighty-year-old Sir George Henschel—the man who had been the Boston Symphony's first conductor and who had later written a book of his reminiscences of his friend Brahms—praising the performance of the Brahms Second Symphony. Henschel said that he had heard all the conductors in his life and for him Toscanini was the best. A former London music critic named Bernard Shaw was there at the first London concert, wearing a raincoat and beaming under his dancing eyebrows. "It was a good concert," he said. King George and Queen Mary were there. Toscanini waited for them to take their seats in the royal box and then cheerfully led the orchestra in "God Save the King."

All through this tour Toscanini was in the rarest of good humor. On the ship crossing the Atlantic and on train trips, he went among the men, making sure that they were comfortable and pausing to have a glass of wine with them. While many of them were musicians who had been born and trained in Europe, he treated them as if he were their host on a journey through new lands.

The one thing he would not do, well disposed though he might feel toward the whole world, was grant interviews to the newspapermen throughout Europe who pleaded for personal meetings. Dorle Jarmel, in charge of publicity for the Philharmonic-Symphony, accepted this attitude; she had had enough experience to know that he could not be changed. She did not try to expose him to European reporters, but she felt that the investment made by the supporters of the orchestra for this trip abroad justified an effort to have more than routine reports sent back home. For the rail trip from Rome to Florence she invited an Associated Press man to come along. Carefully she concealed the fact that he was a reporter. When Toscanini came through the train, she introduced the man as a friend to whom she was giving a lift to Florence. She hoped that the maestro would sit down and chat, as he had done earlier on the trip. But Toscanini's eyes gleamed. Talk? Not at all. He was too delicate for intrusion on such an occasion. He winked at Dorle and went on. He had made up his mind that this was a tender reunion. Being a man of sentiment, he would not, no matter what Dorle would say, stop to chat and waste the time of his friend and her visitor.

17

Bayreuth and Bologna

WITH the tour over, Toscanini rested for a few weeks in Italy and then moved on to Bayreuth. At long last the invitation had come from Siegfried Wagner, the composer's son, to conduct in the theater that Richard Wagner had founded and that Toscanini looked upon as a shrine. For him this was not just another engagement. In fact, when he was offered payment for his services, he returned the check indignantly, saying that it would be like taking money from Wagner. It was a rare privilege to conduct at Bayreuth, and he went to it as on a holy pilgrimage.

From his student days, when he had discovered Wagner's music, Toscanini had studied and admired it. He had conducted it with pride and devotion in the opera houses of Italy and South and North America. He had read every word Wagner had written and nearly everything written about Wagner. He loved Wagner not only for his creations but for the intelligence and clarity of his mind, especially where it dwelt on musical matters. While he had not been able to condone Wagner's preoccupation in his last years with meretricious doctrines of race, he had had nothing but admiration for the precision with which Wagner had evaluated the musical scene. Of Wagner's essay on conducting, Toscanini had always had the highest opinion, and only recently he called it the most perceptive, if not the only worth-while, analysis of the subject.

Thirty years earlier Toscanini had visited Bayreuth, and thereafter he had followed with absorption what happened there. If he had hoped for an invitation from Cosima, Wagner's widow, who ran the place, he had not said so. He had known that the Germans were bears for traditions and that at Bayreuth they would not dream of bringing in an Italian conductor to conduct festival performances. Singers from other countries had been invited from time to time, but an Italian to conduct? What would the German public say? What would the *Kapellmeisters* think? How could an Italian understand Wagner? Had not the Italians always held out Verdi as their champion?

Had Siegfried consulted with his mother when he made the precedent-breaking decision to invite Toscanini? Perhaps, although the crusty, strong-willed woman was in her ninety-third year when she died on April 1, 1930. Toscanini held no resentment against her. On the day of her funeral in Bayreuth he ended his program with the Philharmonic-Symphony in New York with the "Funeral Music" from *Siegfried* as a tribute to her memory.

Toscanini came to Bayreuth with a heart filled with devotion for the man who had made it possible. But he was still Toscanini. Having agreed to conduct *Tannhäuser* and *Tristan*, he did not intend to accept productions just as they had always been. Traditions at Bayreuth might be sacred, but he would not be bullied into doing just what had been done in preceding seasons merely because it was regarded as traditional. He went for his source of information and tradition to the scores of Wagner. Where there was doubt in his mind, he repaired to the original manuscripts in the Villa Wahnfried and studied them.

At one point in *Siegfried*, conducted by another man, Toscanini insisted that the staging was wrong. He felt that the evidence of the music was clear indication that the brightest lights were required. He was assured by the upholders of tradition, the people who had been watching Bayreuth festivals for years, that this had never been the case. He went to Wagner's manuscript, and there in the composer's handwriting, over this scene, was the instruction, "Full light."

Since he did not have the final say at Bayreuth, he took such musical forces as had been assembled for the festival that year and went to work with them. Sets, costumes, and staging were fixed, and while he did not agree with all the equipment and ideas, he did what he could with them. He struggled to improve the action, but most of all he waged relentless battle to have Wagner's works sung and played not like venerated museum pieces but like fresh and vivid masterpieces.

For weeks he worked with the leading singers and chorus. At a first rehearsal with one singer, Toscanini merely remarked, "Beautiful voice." At the next he tore into imperfections of phrasing and style. At the third the singer had corrected the mistakes of the previous day, and Toscanini paid him the high compliment of saying that he had paid attention to instructions. Other singers did not respond so quickly and so intelligently. And the orchestra was dismaying in its lack of quality.

Bayreuth had no permanent instrumental ensemble. Players from all over Germany were recruited for the performance at the Festspielhaus. They made a variable and indifferent band. Some were first-rate musicians; others were *routiniers.* In sum, they were a far cry from the New York Philharmonic-Symphony, which he had conducted only a few weeks before. There was no equality in this Bayreuth orchestra, no subtlety of response, no possibility for perfect balance and integration.

Rehearsals drove him to despair. Was it for this that he had come to Bayreuth? He had planned to serve Wagner to the limit of his capacities, but how could he get things done his way with this crowd? In black moods, he would dart out of the rehearsals, leaving the orchestra to sit there, startled out of its stolidity. He would return and blow up again. He would shout abuse, and curse in German, Italian, and English. Things would go well for a while, and then there would be another explosion. This time, he yelled, he was leaving for good, never to return to this miserable, unhappy theater. But he would cool off and come back. Probably, if this had not been the holy of holies to him, he would have walked out before the festival started.

Toscanini's performances of *Tannhäuser* and *Tristan* were hailed as new things for Bayreuth. He brought to both an ardor and an intensity that had not been heard for years. *Tannhäuser* had youth and freshness. The "Venusberg" scene seethed with sensuousness, and elsewhere there was a wonderful spaciousness. As for *Tristan,* it was radiant and passionate and heartbreakingly tragic.

Toscanini at Bayreuth was news to operagoers. They came from all over Europe, America, and the other continents to hear what he had done. The German musicians were no less eager to make acquaintance with his conception of Wagner. Years later Toscanini chuckled over his memory of those performances. Leading conductors of Germany would file into the pit behind the musicians—furtively, they thought—and watch and listen from this vantage point throughout the performance. Toscanini later called the roll of the famous names hidden in the pit, observing, without false modesty, that he hoped that they had learned something.

For himself, despite the heartaches of the preparations and the occasional falls from grace of the orchestra during performance, Bayreuth was the ideal place to conduct. The pit in the Festspielhaus is down lower than in any other theater and the conductor is invisible to the audience. This, to Toscanini, was a heavenly arrangement. He did not bother to wear full dress, and he did not trouble himself with applause and curtain calls. He was scarcely conscious of the audience and could concentrate with undeflected attention on the task in hand—the unfolding of Wagner's works.

"For two years," he said recently, "I took no bows. Imagine, not a single bow."

As his second season at Bayreuth was coming to a close in the summer of 1931, Frau Winifred Wagner, widow of Siegfried—Wagner's son died at Villa Wahnfried on August 4, 1930, while the festival was in progress—and now presiding authority of all that went on at the Bayreuth observance, came to Toscanini and said, "For two years scarcely anyone in town has seen your face."

After much persuasion he let her take his arm and march him through the cafés and through the restaurant of the Festspielhaus, where the throngs looked up from their beers and *Schinkenbrot* to stare at the little maestro on display. Having played his part in this ostentatious comedy once, he had had enough, but Frau Wagner, wishing to show off her lion again, tried to lead him on similar tours. He resisted, but his annoyance with her, initiated by other things, grew.

When he had finished with his part in the 1930 Bayreuth festival, Frau Winifred invited him to return in 1931. Naturally, he was eager to continue at Bayreuth, but this time he set conditions. The most important was that the orchestra must be improved. With Wilhelm Furtwängler, artistic director, and Heinz Tietjen, the intendant, or general administrator, she joined in promising that this would be done. It was agreed that he would repeat *Tannhäuser* and take over *Parsifal.*

After a rest in Italy he returned to the United States and the New York Philharmonic-Symphony season, conducting sixty-two of the season's concerts. New to the orchestra's programs were some further Bach transcriptions by Respighi, pieces by Pizzetti and Kodály, Shostakovich's First Symphony, and Verdi's Requiem and Te Deum, with Elisabeth

Rethberg, Matzenauer, Mario Chamlee, and Ezio Pinza as the soloists in the former. There was a smattering of Italian composers such as Martucci, Sammartini, and Tommasini, and, as additions to the maestro's own repertory, Bruckner's Seventh and Sibelius's Fourth Symphonies. He managed also to find short American pieces to conduct—Abram Chasins' "Flirtations in a Chinese Garden" and "Parade."

In the fortnight between November 24th and December 7th, Toscanini traded orchestras with Stokowski. His concerts in Philadelphia went well, and the orchestra, though it got more than a touch of severity, responded cheerfully to his wishes. But the relations between the New York orchestra and Stokowski were another story. There were rows between the conductor and some of the men; several were banished from performances for the two weeks, and the atmosphere was tense all the time.

Stokowski's troubles with the Philharmonic are more relevant to the story of Toscanini than they would seem at first blush. It was not the first or last time that a conductor who followed Toscanini found himself bedeviled. Part of the explanation, one would guess, was that Toscanini had been so insistent on unlimited output of energy and concentration from the men that they were weary and tended to let up when another man took the podium. The men might also feel that the new conductor did not have Toscanini's knowledge and imagination or his capacity to convey what he wanted, and they might turn unco-operative and insubordinate. In this case, Stokowski left little doubt that he knew just what he wanted in the way of sound and pacing and shading. The chances are that since he was a man of temperament himself and since this was his first appearance at the head of the New York orchestra, he would brook no obstacles. The fact remains that his difficulties must be considered, in part, a legacy of Toscanini's way with an orchestra.

During a midseason pause of some four or five weeks early

in 1931, Toscanini took a holiday at his Milan home, where Winifred Wagner visited him. She brought him the reassuring news that the Bayreuth orchestra would be strengthened by the engagement of some of the best players from the Berlin Staatsoper.

Back in New York, he resumed his concerts with the Philharmonic on February 26th and conducted steadily until the end of the season on April 19th. Since his next commitment was not until summer at Bayreuth, he had agreed some time before to take part in two performances at Bologna in memory of Giuseppe Martucci, a musician whom he had admired and who had been his friend. Toscanini had directed his music many years before and had received the composer's acknowledgment that he was a coming man among conductors. Toscanini liked Martucci's music and respected all that he had done to spread the practice of symphonic music in Italy. Some years earlier Toscanini had come to Naples, Martucci's native city, to conduct a commemorative concert after the composer's death in 1909 and had told some of the musicians, "I owe to Martucci my understanding of the greatness of Beethoven."

On that occasion Toscanini had conducted Martucci's First Symphony, a large and intricate work, which was rarely played and which he had never directed. The Naples musicians were astonished when, on reaching the podium, he closed the score and said, "Let's begin." He worked with that orchestra for a solid eight hours. One of the musicians said later, "It was as if the vanished musician were sealed up in him."

Honoring Martucci was an act of devotion for Toscanini. He told the Bologna people who were arranging the concert that he would take no payment. He spent arduous hours rehearsing at the Teatro Communale in Bologna, and then the public performances never took place.

These concerts which never took place created a furor that

was followed throughout the world. The first was scheduled for May 14, 1931, and for weeks thereafter the press was full of reports of what had happened. Taking advantage of the maestro's veneration of Martucci, the Fascists had set a trap for him. An exhaustive account in the New York *Times* of June 15th, sent from Lugano, Switzerland, told the background of the Fascists' machinations as follows:

To the Fascisti, as one of their organs candidly put it recently, "Toscanini, by refusing to play the Fascist hymn, succeeded in making a name for himself in politics."

It seemed that Fascist animosity had died down last year when Signor Toscanini made his triumphal tour of Europe, including Italy, with the New York Philharmonic-Symphony Orchestra. Premier Mussolini then sent him a telegram expressing Italy's gratitude at the honor he had brought her. Signor Toscanini replied politely, but perhaps he nettled Premier Mussolini then by failing to make any reference either to the Duce or to his regime.

Perhaps, as reported, too, whisperers told the Premier that Signor Toscanini, when among his friends, left no doubt that he was against Fascism. At any rate, we are informed that Premier Mussolini made a remark to the effect that Toscanini had gone too far and was taking advantage of his good nature.

His remark was interpreted by the fervent Guido Arpinati, Undersecretary of the Interior, as an order to make Signor Toscanini pay public homage to Fascism by playing its song or be punished.

Signor Arpinati is boss at Bologna—he headed Fascismo there before he became its Governor. Into his bailiwick he sought to bring the illustrious offender to bear in such a way as to make it hard for him to refuse to play "Giovinezza."

The first plan was to invite Signor Toscanini to open the season at the municipal theater, which had just been restored, the idea being that once Signor Toscanini arrived it would be impressed on him that since the theater had been restored under Fascism it would be necessary to open it with "Giovinezza."

Signor Liparini, who is *Podesta* (Mayor) at Bologna, went to Salsomaggiore, where Signor Toscanini was taking the cure, to invite him as "the greatest orchestra conductor" to give the special solemnity which Bologna desired for this ceremony. Signor Toscanini declined, excusing himself as being ill.

Then it was decided to organize at Bologna two big concerts in memory of Signor Toscanini's friend, the late composer Giuseppe Martucci, whose music alone should be played in them. Seeing no possibility of politics in this invitation, Signor Toscanini was delighted at the honor to Signor Martucci and agreed to conduct both concerts free.

Without saying anything to him, his hosts arranged to hold at Bologna, on the same days as the concerts, a Fascist festival, to be attended officially by the father-in-law of the Duce's daughter, Count Costanzo Ciano, who was Postmaster General, and by Arpinati. These dignitaries planned to be at the concerts and it was expected that their presence would oblige Toscanini to play the official anthems.

Toscanini was forced by personal reasons to postpone the first concerts to May 14th, and the Bologna Fascists postponed their ceremonies to the same day. Some hours before the May 14th concert, a delegation from the Mayor waited upon Toscanini to inform him that the high officials would be at a banquet until 9:30 P.M., and to request him to delay the concert's start. He made no issue over this, agreeing to hold up the concert provided the public received advance notice. The delegation had something else on its mind: The maestro, it suggested respectfully but firmly, must play the royal hymn and the Fascist anthem in honor of the official guests. Toscanini flatly refused. They knew his principles, he said; politics had no place in a concert commemorating a musician. They pleaded with him, they demanded action, but he was adamant.

Fascist hoodlums under a certain Regazzi, notorious in Bologna for violence, were posted outside the theater. Inside, several were stationed in the conductor's box to keep Toscanini out. Into this ugly situation the maestro, accompanied by his wife and daughter Wally, rode up in his car. They got out at the door of the theater. Squads of Fascisti surged threateningly around. Young bucks armed with heavy canes roughly ordered the playing of "Giovinezza." Toscanini refused, and they fell upon him.

Recently Toscanini remarked, "Carla took the hardest blow, while I got hit on the back of the neck and on the shoulder." Twenty years later he made light of the physical injuries he had suffered, but indignation still raged in him.

There was a handful of police around the theater that night, but they did nothing to intervene. The maestro had to defend himself and, with the help of his chauffeur, he got his wife and daughter into the car, and they all drove back to the Hotel Brun, while the mob hooted at them. The Fascists, led by Mario Ghinelli, secretary of Bologna Fascismo, paraded to the hotel. They stood under the maestro's window and shouted insults. There were even cries of "*A morte* Toscanini!"

During the night, after the mob had dispersed, Toscanini and his party slipped out of the hotel and drove to his house on the Via Durini in Milan. The first thing the maestro did was to send the following wire, couched in formal, honorific language:

To His Excellency, Benito Mussolini:
Last night, when I came with my family to the Teatro Communale in Bologna to perform a delicate act of love and friendship to the memory of Giuseppe Martucci—invited by the Mayor of the said city not for a gala evening but for an artistic commemoration—I was assaulted and struck repeatedly on the face by an unspeakable gang, even though the Undersecretary of the Interior was present in Bologna. Not satisfied with this, the gang, swollen into a mob, gathered under my window at the Hotel Brun —where I was staying—shouting all sorts of insults and threats at me. Not only this, but one of the leaders sent Maestro Respighi to warn me to leave before 6 A.M., otherwise my safety would not be guaranteed.

This message goes to Your Excellency because of the silence of the press and because Your Excellency might get inexact information and because the facts remain in the memory. Greetings, Arturo Toscanini.

Mussolini never deigned to reply.

Until he was granted permission to leave Italy on June 10th, Toscanini and his family were kept under rigorous police surveillance. Uniformed men and detectives were stationed around his house, and carabinieri patrolled the streets near by. Letters addressed to the maestro and his family were opened by the censors, and Italians who had the temerity to write had their homes entered and searched by way of Fascist reprisal. Toscanini's passport was taken from him, and threats were made that his property would be seized.

Word of the outrage, which was not reported in the press, got out and aroused indignation in Milan. There were demonstrations for Toscanini and against Fascism. On Sunday evening, May 17th, students gathered in a square and began to shout, "*Evviva* Toscanini!" and "*Abbasso il Fascismo!*" They were joined by passers-by, and police were called to break up this gathering. Two students were thrown into jail. The next night, during a symphony concert at La Scala, another demonstration broke out, and the police had to be summoned to quiet it. Again there were arrests.

In time the Fascist press got around to making oblique mention of the affair. Its purpose was to praise the ruffians and abuse the victim. *Libri e Moschetti*, organ of Fascist students, called Toscanini a "monster, not a genius," and regretted that his assailants "did not spit in his face." The Fascist press did not print Serge Koussevitzky's letter to La Scala refusing to fill a promised date in Italy until amends had been made to Toscanini. Word of the Boston conductor's action reached Toscanini as did reports of the demonstrations of the Milanese. These things greatly moved him.

The day before Toscanini was allowed by the Fascists to

leave Italy, Ossip Gabrilowitsch, pianist and conductor of the Detroit Symphony, came down from Switzerland to see how he was. Toscanini was fighting mad. He still spoke his mind freely about the Fascists.

"We must have truth and freedom of speech at any price, even if that price be death," he told Gabrilowitsch. "I have said to our Fascisti time and again, 'You can kill me if you wish, but as long as I am living I shall say what I think.'"

Reports had it that Mussolini had taken personal charge of the case. If he planned to keep the maestro in "protective custody" for a long time, he was obliged to change his mind. Indignant comment outside Italy had its effect on the Fascists, and after three weeks of being held a virtual prisoner, Toscanini was allowed to leave Italy. With his family he went to St. Moritz. The days in the quiet and beauty of Switzerland were a healing interlude. Toscanini needed time to soothe his nerves and to turn his thoughts to the work that lay ahead. The duty and privilege of conducting *Parsifal* at Bayreuth bulked large to him. He had a special regard for this last work of Wagner's. In some ways it seemed to him Wagner's most moving and most memorable score. It was his dearest wish to do justice by it.

Toscanini opened the Bayreuth festival with *Tannhäuser* and then put on a *Parsifal* that had an unforgettable amalgam of solemnity and color. There were not many persons around who could remember *Parsifal* as Hermann Levi, to whom Wagner entrusted its *première* at Bayreuth in 1882, had done it, but it was agreed that for purity and spaciousness there had not been such a performance in years. Recently I asked him how this *Parsifal* had gone, and he replied, simply, "Was good."

The orchestra was improved this year, but Toscanini had to struggle to get what he wished. His labors were complicated by pain in his right shoulder and arm. He was suffering from bursitis, an occupational hazard for conductors. Considering that Toscanini had not spared himself in more than four decades of conducting, it was astonishing that bursitis had not caught up with him earlier. In 1931 the ailment had been aggravated no doubt by the blows struck by the Fascist hoodlums in Bologna.

Friends who visited the maestro's dressing room during the long intermissions at Bayreuth found him reclining on his left side. Occasionally he would clutch at his right arm as twinges of pain shot through it. But he asked for no relief at Bayreuth; carrying out his promised engagements. There were times when he stood on the podium with his right arm hanging limply at his side, relying entirely on his left to beat time, give the cues, and shape the nuances of the performance.

The personal joy he derived from doing *Parsifal* at Bayreuth was marred by other irritations. Winifred Wagner, as the new chatelaine of Villa Wahnfried and the Festspielhaus, was obviously throwing her weight around. She was dabbling in politics, both national and musical. Toscanini thought her activities were subject to expedience and commercialism.

It seemed to be his fate. Whenever he found a theater or a musical organization in which he thought he could at last make music on the highest artistic plane, disturbing elements began to creep in. Bayreuth, it appeared, suffered from the ailment; it was not, wholly and undeviatingly, a place consecrated to art.

At the end of the season, Winifred Wagner sent Toscanini a gift of an original letter written by Richard Wagner. By now he was furious with her. He returned the offering, telling her frankly just what he thought of her artistic and personal leadership of Bayreuth. Clearly, if things went on as they had in the summer of 1931, he would not conduct again at Bayreuth.

He did not return to Bayreuth, but there were even more

compelling reasons when he made his final decision. It was the custom of the Bayreuth festival to run for two successive summers and to remain closed each third year. Thus, 1932 was a year of inactivity. In 1933, Adolf Hitler had come to power.

18

New York Philharmonic

TOSCANINI returned to New York in the fall of 1931 prepared to fulfill his commitment to conduct two eight-week periods of concerts even though his right shoulder and arm were still ailing. He should not have conducted at all. Whenever he moved his arm darts of pain raced through him. Determined to live up to his contract, he began his season on November 26th.

His first appearance evoked a demonstration more cordial than usual. The American audience was paying its tribute to the courageous little man who had stood up to the Fascisti. This attitude was made even more explicit when a shower of pastel-hued paper slips, carrying the words "Liberty is essential to Art—*Evviva* Arturo Toscanini!," was thrown from the balcony of Carnegie Hall and drifted into the laps of the audience below. Several nights before, Dino Grandi, Mussolini's Foreign Minister, had attended a performance at the Metropolitan Opera House, and similar paper slips had been tossed from the gallery; their message had been "Down with Fascism" and "Long live Toscanini."

Toscanini conducted fourteen concerts in four weeks, and then he had to bow to the pain that was racking him. He begged to be excused, and guest conductors were found to replace him. Returning to Italy, he set out to find a cure. He took a long rest, and he went to various doctors. Months of inactivity helped more than the doctors. It was not until more than ten years later that Dr. Irvin Stein in Philadelphia, to whom Toscanini had been sent by Eugene Ormandy, helped clear up the trouble.

Early in 1932, Toscanini tried all kinds of physicians. Some months ago he was recalling his experiences with the medical men, laughing at his encounter with one fellow in Milan who was regarded an expert on arthritic ailments. This man had a tiny office and an immense reputation. Toscanini said that on busy days some of his patients had to wait in the street, so crowded was the office, and they stood outdoors patiently even in the rain. The doctor would line up three or four sufferers, mostly old women, and inject some mysterious substance into them. He worked so hard, the maestro chuckled, that he once fell asleep with his head pillowed against the broad back of a patient and his hand still clutching the hypodermic.

"He was crazy," Toscanini said. "He had a strange ending—he was assassinated. I don't think," he added, "that he helped me."

Due back at the end of February, Toscanini notified the Philharmonic management that he was still unable to conduct. Sir Thomas Beecham, Ottorino Respighi, and Hans Lange took his place. But by March he was feeling somewhat better, and he agreed to make a special trip to the United States to conduct one concert for the benefit of unemployed musicians. The Philharmonic was happy about this gesture, since it would offer proof to subscribers that the maestro had recovered his health and would be on hand the following season.

On April 28th at Carnegie Hall he conducted a program that contained excerpts from *Parsifal* and Beethoven's Ninth, with Rethberg, Matzenauer, Martinelli, and Pinza as soloists. He arrived in New York a couple of days before the concert; this was another occasion when he showed he could manage a memorable performance with little rehearsal time. The concert realized twenty-six thousand dollars. That, and the fact that his arm bore up well in action, made him feel that the trip had been eminently worth while.

He sailed back for Italy to continue the treatment of his arm and to rest until the fall. He interrupted this regimen in June with a trip to Paris to take part in a program commemorating Debussy. On June 17th a Debussy monument by Jan and Joel Martel was dedicated on the Boulevard Lannes near the Bois de Boulogne, and in the evening at the Théâtre des Champs-Élysées Toscanini conducted "La Mer" and Mary Garden took part in a performance of the fourth act of *Pelléas et Mélisande*.

Apparently time moved slowly during the inactive months. There had been no opposition to his return to Italy, but he had made up his mind that he would not conduct there again so long as Mussolini and the Fascists remained in power. He held his peace and was unmolested. He spent a good deal of time in Milan and on the Isolino di San Giovanni, the tiny island on Lago Maggiore opposite the town of Pallanza, where he was surrounded by his family and a few friends and by his books and scores.

When the *Börsen Zeitung*, a Berlin newspaper, sent him a questionnaire about his musical preferences, he actually answered it. He must have been indeed eager for some sort of activity. His remarks are worth reprinting, not only for the light they threw on his point of view then but because they revealed what was to remain his fixed position.

"I love everything I conduct in concert and in the theater," he wrote, "because I conduct only what I love. In the symphonic domain, my preference is for the greatest—Haydn, Mozart, Beethoven. In the last years I have studied deeply the monumental symphonies of Bruckner. I leave to other conductors the production of modern works. Among the operas I esteem above all others those of Wagner and Verdi. It is difficult for me to give a preference among Wagner's works. I have noticed that when I conduct or play a Wagner opera at the piano it is always that one which possesses my heart. And then, every time I glance at a score of *Parsifal*, I say to myself: This one, it is the most sublime. Of Verdi's operas I appreciate not only their melodic richness but the force and sure power of their musical drama. When I conduct *Falstaff* at Busseto, I dream of creating a Verdian Bayreuth on the model of the Wagnerian Festspielhaus. These two masters are truly the representatives of national German and Italian music."

This was an honest statement of faith, and yet if Toscanini had been taxed with whether the first sentence was utterly accurate, he might have had to admit that even he made occasional concessions to the needs of the moment. For in the Philharmonic season of 1932-33 he conducted a number of compositions that he could scarcely have loved. *Noblesse oblige*, yes; enduring affection, no. A conductor who undertakes to lead sixty-five concerts in a single season has no alternative.

The fact that Toscanini was able to handle so many concerts was proof of his amazing recuperative powers. He opened the Philharmonic-Symphony season on October 6th and remained in charge until November 27th. Then he took over again on March 1st and conducted until the season's end on April 23rd.

He had indeed studied Bruckner, and he offered his Fourth Symphony. Among the contemporaries on his programs were Schönberg, although only in a Bach transcription; Tansman, de Sabata, Respighi, Castelnuovo-Tedesco; two Russians, Veprik and Mossolov; and two Americans, Bernard Wagenaar and Howard Hanson. The latter's Second Symphony had its first New York performance and the former's Second its *première*.

The Wagenaar symphony was filled with advanced harmonies and with dissonances that bothered Toscanini because they seemed to him often to have no purpose. In a moment of exasperation he wrote a concluding C major chord on the last page of the score, circled it in red ink, and scribbled under it, "My chord, Arturo Toscanini."

Tchaikovsky was returning to his repertory. The "Manfred" Symphony was on the programs. There was also a Beethoven cycle for Sunday afternoons, and it was welcomed by the management not only as an artistic enterprise but as a shot in the arm to the box office at a time when the depression was at its deepest.

At the final concert of the season, which happened also to conclude the Beethoven cycle, the soloist was Vladimir Horowitz. This was the first time that Toscanini and Horowitz had played together. Toscanini had heard of the young pianist, of course, but he did not know that his daughter Wanda had been to hear him play in Italy two years before and that she had formed the opinion that he was the finest pianist around. Horowitz later teased his wife about this remarkable restraint. "They are funny people, the Toscaninis," he said smilingly. "They never talk to each other."

Toscanini certainly did not realize at this time that his daughter was attracted to Horowitz in ways other than musical. Wanda and the pianist became friends during the preparations for the performance of the "Emperor" Concerto. Undoubtedly she helped to ease the tensions of the nervous young man as he steeled himself for the worst. The rehearsals turned out to be painless; there were no outbursts and no scenes.

That summer Horowitz visited the Toscaninis at the Isolino, and eventually, in old-world style, he asked the father formally for his daughter's hand. The marriage took place before the year was out.

Momentous events were taking place in 1933, and Toscanini was not indifferent to them. On January 30th, Hitler moved into power, and shortly thereafter the persecution of thousands for political and religious reasons began. Toscanini was outraged. When he was asked in April to join with a group of famous musicians in signing a cablegram directly to Hitler asking that the persecutions be stopped, he wrote, "Not only can you use my name but, if there is no objection and if it is possible, I would like to have my name at the head of the signers of this message."

There was a sound reason for his wishing to lead the signers. Winifred Wagner, whose friendship with Hitler had provoked Toscanini to wrath in 1931, had sought all through 1932 to convince Toscanini that things would be different if he would return. Because conducting at Bayreuth meant so much to him, he had allowed himself to be persuaded that the atmosphere of the festival would be restored to the artistic plane on which it belonged. With the accession of Hitler, the chatelaine of Bayreuth undoubtedly began to worry whether her conducting lion would be on hand in 1933, after all. Possibly she transmitted her fears to Hitler; in any event, Toscanini received a personal letter from Der Führer early in 1933. Now that Germany and Italy were following the same course, Hitler wrote, it would be an affirmative act for Toscanini to conduct at Bayreuth.

Having his signature lead all the others was by way of an answer to Hitler's appeal. Toscanini waited to see whether there would be any change in Nazi behavior, and then he wrote to Hitler personally, telling him what he thought of him, his party, and all their works.

Hitler, not Toscanini, was at Bayreuth that summer. But there were people connected with the Wagner shrine who grieved. Young Friedelind Wagner, daughter of Winifred and Siegfried, was one of those who saw what was happening to Bayreuth and to Germany, and some years later when she escaped to Switzerland, it was Toscanini who befriended her and then helped her to get to the United States.

Hans Paul Freiherr von Wolzogen, who had been closely associated with Richard Wagner during the last years of his life, had seen all the Bayreuth festivals and had been editor for fifty years of *Bayreuther Blätter,* sent Toscanini a touching, personal letter in the summer of 1933. With the maestro's permission it was offered for publication to the German press, but it was not printed.

"We now have the decision," Wolzogen wrote, "which neither at present nor in the future can separate us. The decision was recognized by both of us as a necessity, which must be considered tragical. It is a tragedy to which everybody great is subject. There are two who must suffer profoundly from this tragedy—not only Bayreuth but you yourself, Bayreuth's master and friend. You must realize that I, as a citizen of Bayreuth, understand your sorrow and sympathize deeply with you. But we, the faithful ones of the Festival Hill, know also that inwardly you belong always to Bayreuth, to this artistic ideal which owes to you in such great measure its realization. May the peoples of the world go their predestined ways through history. But before and above them remains for all time the idea and the work of Bayreuth, and—as a part thereof—the indestructible memory of your participation. And to this memory I wish to give expression in these lines."

With the decision to avoid Germany, Toscanini listened more readily to offers from Austria. Where he had hesitated before when Austria had sent invitations, now he accepted. It was his way of reminding the Germans that he was still active and that he was willing to appear in free lands. In November he conducted the Vienna Philharmonic in two programs. Earlier that year he had also appeared in Paris, conducting the Concerts Straram, and in Denmark and Sweden, his first visits to those countries.

The concerts with the Vienna Philharmonic were, he admitted recently, in the nature of a trial run. The Salzburg festival, eager to profit from Bayreuth's loss, had made overtures to him, but he had decided privately that he did not wish to go through the miseries of slaving with a poor orchestra, as he had at Bayreuth. The concerts with the Vienna Philharmonic, which played at Salzburg, would give him a chance to test its capacities.

The agreement with the Vienna Philharmonic gave him the right to as many rehearsals as he wished. Four sufficed for the two programs. The musicians expected fireworks and found that, while they were worked intensively, everything was reasonable. They were staggered when, in rehearsing Beethoven's Seventh, he accused them of playing a wrong note and it turned out that their edition of the score had errors that no previous conductor had caught.

Playing music dear and familiar to Vienna, such as the Beethoven symphony and works by Mozart and Brahms, Toscanini once again followed an old habit of conducting in a new city the very pieces that had become part of the community's tradition and that had had the benefit of attention by the most eminent conductors. Call it a gesture of pride; call it also a determination to be measured by the most exacting local standards.

The Vienna orchestra pleased Toscanini. Perhaps it did not have the brilliance and crispness of the American symphonies, but it had warmth and mellowness, and the men were intelligent and responsive. The concerts created a stir, and the question of Salzburg was posed anew. Toscanini agreed to come, not yet for opera but for concerts.

He returned to the New York Philharmonic-Symphony on January 11, 1934, and remained, with breaks of a week here and there, until the end of the season. He conducted forty-four concerts in all, but to make up for the reduction in total concerts he undertook a large number of big works for soloists and chorus, which required much more of his time for preparation. There was another Beethoven cycle with the Ninth Symphony and the *Missa Solemnis*. There was a special Bach program, and a series of three grand Wagner concerts.

These programs were designed by Toscanini, with the encouragement of the management, to stimulate the box office at a time when people were thinking twice about spending their money for music. During the depression years Toscanini was left in no doubt that budgets for musical organizations were difficult to balance. First the Metropolitan Opera then the Philharmonic had gone to the public appealing for contributions. Toscanini made no secret to his friends that he thought the begging appeals on the radio were undignified. He felt that it was disgraceful for a rich country like America to fail to support its leading musical institutions.

Years later he recalled that he had had a discussion with Fiorello H. La Guardia, New York City's Mayor, on the subject.

"Why don't you place a tax on radios and turn the money over for music?" he had asked.

"Can't!" the explosive little mayor had shouted. "Freedom of the air."

"Shame on New York," Toscanini had replied. "Look at Milan, a small city in comparison. Milan supports La Scala and has a much longer season than New York."

Remembering the conversation, Toscanini went on, "I still think New York doesn't support its music in the best way."

Toscanini had been induced to come to the Philharmonic by the stand of men like Clarence H. Mackay that they did not care what the cost might be, they meant to have the best conductor in the world for their orchestra. Well, the cost had been high and the ladies and gentlemen who sat on the boards of the Philharmonic-Symphony Society and its auxiliary, while they enjoyed the *réclame* Toscanini and the orchestra received, probably wondered how they would be able to keep on meeting the inevitable deficit. Toscanini could not but be conscious of their anxieties.

At any event, the seeds of discontent had been planted in him by the undignified pleading for public contributions. They were to sprout under the impetus of a plan brought to him by Bruno Zirato, then assistant manager of the orchestra.

In a trip to Italy in December, 1934, Zirato, serving as an emissary, placed before Toscanini a proposal to merge the orchestra with the Metropolitan Opera. The basic purpose of the scheme, of course, was to save money for both organizations by using one orchestra and one theater.

The idea was placed gently before Toscanini. It was just an idea, and his expert judgment was wanted. He gave his opinion, violently no doubt. A merger, he said, would not help either organization artistically. In brief, he was ag'in it. Zirato's message to Arthur Judson, manager of the Philharmonic-Symphony, put it tactfully: "The maestro, however, wishes you to tell the members of the board that this honest opinion should not carry any weight in their minds or arrest any negotiations if they still consider the merger advantageous to the Philharmonic."

Toscanini's "no" laid the kiss of death on the merger plan. The people at the Philharmonic understood the carefully worded message. They had every reason to believe that if they went through with the merger, they would find themselves without Toscanini.

They were dead right. The very idea of their entertaining such a plan irritated Toscanini. To him it was a breach of artistic faith, and even abandonment of the scheme did not mitigate the crime.

In the 1934-35 season he conducted only thirty concerts, which included a couple of novelties by Castelnuovo-Tedesco and Giulio Cesare Sonzogno, a Brahms cycle topped by the *German Requiem,* and a repetition of Beethoven's *Missa Solemnis.* In the 1935-36 season he conducted only thirty-nine concerts; highlights were a special Debussy program and Beethoven's Ninth.

The reduction in the number of his concerts was his own idea, since he wished to lighten his burden. But little things were happening to make him dissatisfied in New York. Perhaps he magnified them; there is no doubt that he can be unreasonable when he is angry.

There had been the problem one season of an extra rehearsal with the Schola Cantorum, a New York chorus which was to join him in a performance of Beethoven's Ninth. The maestro had declared on a Monday that he must have another session with the chorus the next day. It had been impossible to find time on Tuesday for a rehearsal. In the daytime the members of the chorus, who were amateur singers, were busy at their jobs, and in the evening Carnegie Hall was to be used for a concert of the Philadelphia Orchestra. To Toscanini, in an impatient mood, these had seemed poor excuses and he had fumed, and finally the management of the orchestra had arranged a Wednesday morning rehearsal by agreeing to pay the choristers for the time lost from their jobs.

There had been a slight difference one year over the maestro's total fee. It had been one of the seasons when he was to conduct a great many concerts. In the letter from the board stating the terms of his engagement—each year such a letter constituted the only written agreement between the orchestra society and the conductor—it had been set down that the maestro's net fee would be $100,000, with taxes to be paid by the society. The exact sum should have been about $102,000, but Clarence H. Mackay, chairman of the board, had recommended offhandedly to make it a round number. On receipt of the letter Toscanini had immediately pointed out that $100,000 was less than he was entitled to, and when he had been told that it was a round figure, he had protested. "Why didn't you make it $110,000!" he had wanted to know. "That is also a round number." And the final figure had become $110,000.

In the late summer of 1935, when Toscanini had found that he would have to miss several weeks of his Philharmonic engagement early in the coming season, the board had engaged

Sir Thomas Beecham as guest conductor. This step had been taken without consulting the maestro, and in September he had sent a cablegram to the management, saying, "Please inform the board of directors not to count on me for the season after next."

Bruno Zirato, who, because he had known Toscanini since his days at the Metropolitan, had been engaged by Mr. Mackay personally to serve as an aide to the maestro in his early years with the orchestra and who was by this time on the managerial staff of the society, did not open discussions for the 1936-37 season until February of 1936. Toscanini had arrived in January, and since he had made no mention again of his threat to leave the orchestra, Zirato thought he had forgotten the cable of the previous September. But Toscanini had not forgotten, and in February he told Zirato that he was tired and would like to be free of long contracts. Arthur Judson, manager of the orchestra, lunched with the maestro at the Hotel Astor, and he failed to budge him in his determination to leave. Zirato tried another tack on Toscanini: Why not pass up the 1936-37 season and return the following year for a special Toscanini festival of any music of his choice? Toscanini was not interested. The Philharmonic, he was told, would like to celebrate his fifty years as a conductor by arranging to have him do a special opera or series of operas by Verdi or Wagner at the Metropolitan some time in 1936. Toscanini was still not interested.

Possibly the maestro had private moments of regret. After all, the Philharmonic was his orchestra. They had worked, traveled, and done fine things together. He would miss it. The truth is he never lost interest in it. When John Barbirolli was engaged for a three-year term the following year, Toscanini was offended that no one had seen fit to notify him of the decision, even though he was no longer with the orchestra. In hurt tones he complained that the society had never offered him a three-year contract, and he was not mollified by the reply that he could have had a contract for life if he had asked for it. And when, some years later, there was a bitter rupture between the society and its conductor, Artur Rodzinski, the maestro wanted to be kept abreast of every development.

In February, 1936, Mackay went down to the Astor for a conference with the maestro. Toscanini would not change his mind. As he was leaving, Mackay said, "Maestro, you always had a friend in Clarence Mackay. If at any time you feel like coming back to us, please remember a little bell that answers to my name. Just press that button and I will answer with the same great enthusiasm that I always have." Marshall Field, president of the society, wrote a letter in longhand to Toscanini expressing the society's sorrow at his decision. Both Mackay and Field had given Toscanini repeated evidence of their personal regard. The former had provided the maestro with a car and had stocked his wine cellar. Field had sent gifts of rare game from his farm in the South. Other members of the board had made all sorts of gifts to the maestro.

Toscanini was through, although some people connected with the Philharmonic hoped to bring him back sooner or later. An era of Philharmonic glory was over. In eleven seasons Toscanini had conducted four hundred and fifty concerts, and had helped to bring the orchestra to the pinnacle of world fame. No one else had given such consistently enkindling performances. Toscanini made his farewell appearance on April 29, 1936, in a Beethoven-Wagner program with Jascha Heifetz as soloist. At his request some of the proceeds were turned over to members of the orchestra, the personnel of Carnegie Hall, and the society's office staff, and the rest went to the Musicians' Emergency Fund and the orchestra's maintenance fund.

The farewell concert drew a big crowd at high prices—hundreds were turned away—and it ended in unexpected ex-

citement. As the concert closed with a hair-raising performance of "The Ride of the Valkyries," a storm of applause and
shouting broke out. Toscanini came out for a bow, and a
photographer who had slipped down the center aisle shot off
a flash bulb. The maestro stumbled off the stage, and though
the audience stood and shouted for further curtain calls he
did not return.

I remember the evening well. I hurried back to the office of
the New York *Times* to write a report of the event and was
getting ready to go home shortly after midnight. Telephones
began to ring throughout the office. Was it true, the question
was asked repeatedly, that Toscanini had gone blind? News
reports on the radio had said so, and the town was filled with
wild rumors. The night managing editor got hold of me and
said, "I want you to go and check personally, and you're not
to go home until you've seen Toscanini for yourself."

Toscanini, I knew, was giving a farewell party for the men
of the orchestra at the Hotel Astor. I went over reluctantly,
knowing that these affairs were private and thinking that I
would not be welcome. I rode up to the Astor roof and managed to get in. The party was gay, indeed. The maestro had
provided food and drink, and the orchestra players thronged
the room.

This did not look like a wake for a man stricken with blind-
ness. At the end of the room I saw Toscanini. He was seated
on a sofa flanked by a couple of attractive girls who worked in
the offices of the Philharmonic-Symphony, and was chatting
with animation. He was not blind. His eyes, weak and myopic,
had been blinded by the flash, but it had been momentary. He
could have returned for further bows after a few minutes, but
he had been so angry that he had refused.

Now he was cheerful and friendly. He did not wish to talk
about the photographer, and he did not care to say much
about the years he had spent with the Philharmonic. He had

agreed some weeks before to go to Palestine in the fall to help launch a new orchestra made up in large part of refugees from Nazi Germany, and this project was uppermost in his mind. He had no desire to grow sentimental about the past; he was thinking of the future. Over and over he said, "*Andiamo in Palestina.*"

In succeeding seasons of the Philharmonic, when performances were below the standards Toscanini had set, it was said that Toscanini, with his drive and flaming intensity, had used up the orchestra. Poor concerts, the charge went, were an inevitable Toscanini aftermath; the same thing had happened elsewhere. It cannot be denied that Toscanini's successors, wherever they had to follow him, were unable to match the fire and purity of his performances, and it is probably true that orchestra players and singers relaxed after he was gone. Could that really be held as a reflection on him?

A week after his farewell, on the eve of his departure for Europe, Toscanini was moved to make an exception to his long rule against public statements. A letter from President Franklin D. Roosevelt, expressing regret that Toscanini was leaving and adding "my word of appreciation for all that you have done for music during your stay among us," was made public, as well as the maestro's reply:

"I am deeply touched to receive your letter. It will remain among the most precious of the souvenirs which I shall take from your country, where I have spent so many happy years. I shall never forget with what kindness and true understanding I have been received by the American people. I leave with sadness in my heart but with memories to enrich the years to come."

The statement expressed his "personal good-by" to "the thousands who have come to my concerts, to the men of my orchestra who have worked so faithfully and magnificently with me these many seasons, to the innumerable unknown friends who have sent me messages and letters, and to the board of directors and the management of the Philharmonic-Symphony Society."

The emotion of parting encompassed all. The maestro had tidied up all his human relations. And it was seemly that he should. After all, he had no intention of returning to America.

19

Salzburg

TOSCANINI's first contribution to the Salzburg festival was modest. In August, 1934, he conducted several orchestral concerts and had Lotte Lehmann as his soloist. She had made her first appearance with him in New York, in February of that year, as a soloist in a program of a special radio series. She had long been drawn to him as an artist, but the stories of his exigence had frightened her off when she had been invited in the early twenties to sing Eva in *Die Meistersinger* at La Scala. When she had finally come to work with him, in fear and trembling, she had found that, while he had been exacting, he had been movingly and profoundly intelligent, sensitive, and inspiring. He had found her equally attractive as an artist and a woman and had even gone to hear her in recital; and though she had always felt secure in the *Lieder* she adored, her voice and breath had failed her momentarily when she had caught sight of him in the audience.

Before going to Salzburg that summer, Toscanini had conducted six concerts at the Champs-Élysées in Paris. The concerts at Salzburg with Lehmann were high points of the festival, and he realized that his taking part in a summer season so close to the German border could not be concealed from the German people, even though Goebbels distorted and suppressed the news. The Vienna Philharmonic was at hand, musical standards were high, and if his adherence to this festival instead of Bayreuth were interpreted rightly by Germans as a slap at the Nazis, so much the better.

He found himself in sympathy with the Austrians, and in the fall he was back in Vienna for several concerts. When Chancellor Engelbert Dollfuss was assassinated, Toscanini considered it a grave privilege to be invited to conduct the Verdi Requiem in his memory. Again he chose, in his music, to make clear beyond any shadow of doubt exactly where he stood with respect to the Nazis. As a mark of gratitude, Chancellor Kurt von Schuschnigg, in behalf of his country, presented Toscanini with a first-edition score for voice and piano of *Fidelio* with corrections scrawled in Beethoven's bold hand.

The question came up: Would he conduct opera at Salzburg the following year? He had resolved that he would not conduct opera again save under special conditions. Salzburg was special, he was reminded, like Bayreuth. After all, Salzburg was Mozart's city, just as Bayreuth was Wagner's. Perhaps it was not quite the same thing, but it was undeniable that Salzburg in these days had a special significance. Well, he might consider it. How about *Fidelio*? Yes, he would like to do *Fidelio* with Lehmann. That was quickly settled. What about a second opera? Discussing the matter with Bruno Walter, artistic director at Salzburg, Toscanini proposed doing an Italian opera. He recalled years later that Walter seemed taken aback. Would not Italian opera be out of place at this festival?

"No," Toscanini replied. "I have in mind an Italian opera that can stand beside Mozart and Wagner for a festival of this kind. I would like to do *Falstaff*."

That, too, was gladly accepted. He proceeded to fill his fall, winter, and spring engagements but found time to consult about casts, sets, and staging for Salzburg.

He arrived in Salzburg in the summer of 1935 and plunged into his work. He had been promised as many rehearsals as he needed, and he took them. He was, as usual, relentless in attention to detail. He spent endless hours with the singers, chorus, and orchestra. He took pains with the staging, rushing up to show the singers how they must stand and move. Some of the singers who worked with him at Salzburg observed that he pounded at them with such tenacity that by performance time they were tense. This meant, they said, that the first performance of a work was not necessarily the best, but once the piece was set, the repetitions became experiences that none of the artists would have cared to miss.

Toscanini prepared *Fidelio* and *Falstaff* simultaneously, working with an expenditure of energy and time that would have been strenuous for a conductor half his age. The cast of *Fidelio* was so unnerved by the constant pressure that it assembled one day to discuss ways of seeking relief. The singers agreed that Lehmann, who knew Toscanini best, must go and beg him to let up a little or they would all fall apart. With halting step, she went to his dressing room and managed to get out a few words telling him what the cast thought. Toscanini stared at her more in sorrow than anger. "I thought," he said, "you were all as interested in the opera as I am."

He would shout and threaten and then behave with baffling temperance. Lehmann made a terrible blunder in a performance of *Fidelio* and expected the worst, but he acted as if nothing had happened. He could overlook an error on occasion, if everything else went well.

He was pleased with the results that season. He knew that his conception of *Fidelio* was different from that of the German conductors, and it pleased him when Arnold Rosé, the venerable and accomplished concertmaster of the Vienna Philharmonic, told him that it was the first time he had heard the opera taken in the right tempos.

In addition to the operas, he conducted a number of orchestral concerts at Salzburg, and in the next two festivals he added to his duties. In 1936 he did a third opera, *Die Meistersinger*, and in 1937 a fourth, *The Magic Flute*.

He remembered years later that he required so many rehearsals to prepare *Die Meistersinger* that another conductor demanded more rehearsal time for his operas the following year. If Salzburg had thought that things could be rough with the way Toscanini waded into *Fidelio* and *Falstaff*, it found out that they could get even stormier with *Die Meistersinger*.

There was, to begin with, the affair of the Hans Sachs. Toscanini had consented to the engagement of a baritone who had had a great career in Europe and America. The singer had turned down other offers, had rented a house for the season, and had brought his car to Salzburg. After three weeks of rehearsals with piano, Toscanini blew up.

"I can't stand that man," he said. "I won't do *Meistersinger* with him."

"But why?" a close friend, who had sat through many of the rehearsals, asked. "You agreed to him yourself."

"He's not Hans Sachs," Toscanini cried. "Wotan, with a patch over his eye, yes. Sachs, no."

"But the poor man has gone to an awful lot of trouble and expense to be here," the friend protested.

Toscanini stared at his friend icily. "Whom do you care for," he demanded, "this man or Wagner?"

The friend insisted that the thing would have to be managed considerately, if that were now possible. Toscanini was prodded into writing a letter to the baritone, suggesting that he was unwell and needed a rest. The baritone, a good sport as well as an intelligent man, replied that this was true and that he was withdrawing. A new baritone was flown in from Munich.

Toscanini worked on that *Meistersinger* as though it were a new opera. With Erich Leinsdorf at the piano, he labored with the singers for three weeks, clapping his hands to beat time. The singers were all veterans; they had all sung Wagner in leading theaters of the world. That made no difference to him. For days he kept them going through the score, insisting only that the proper rhythms and tempos be maintained. "No expression," he would warn them. Once he was satisfied that

214

the pacing was right, he began to fill in the details, seeking for flexibility of phrasing and nuance of tone.

When he discovered that some of the leading artists were not in the habit of taking part in the singing of the grand fugue that closes the second act, he almost turned purple. "With me," he shouted, "you sing the fugue!" He had raised the roof with a tenor long ago at La Scala when the latter had said proudly that the fugue was for the chorus only. He forced the Salzburg singers to go to work with Leinsdorf and to learn their share of the scene.

There was a row over the deployment of the chorus in one scene. The choral group, which was from the Vienna Staatsoper, insisted it had always done the scene this way, and after all the Vienna Staatsoper had some notion about Wagner tradition. Toscanini got out the score and showed them that their "tradition" was not sanctioned by Wagner, whereas he was following the composer's instructions.

He stopped a rehearsal and shouted from the pit to Charles Kullman, who was singing Walther and who was standing a far piece from him, "Stand up straight. You're playing a nobleman." Kullman squared his shoulders and drew himself up, murmuring, "I thought he was nearsighted."

Every production at Salzburg went through this ordeal of Toscanini's fire. When he undertook to do *The Magic Flute*, he knew that it would be a battle to get it done his way. In the end, he got what he wanted.

"*The Magic Flute*," he said reflectively, years later. "I had always slept through it. That's what I told Bruno Walter when he suggested I do it at Salzburg. I changed the tempi at Salzburg. It had life. After the performance, Bruno Walter congratulated me and I said to him, 'You cannot like it; you were trained on the slower German tempi.' "

Toscanini's presence at Salzburg made the festival the foremost in the world. The little city on the banks of the Salzach, with its narrow streets in the old part of town, its cafés, and its surrounding hills with the castles perched on them, became a gathering place for people from all over the world. Americans, Britons, Frenchmen, citizens of the free world filled the city's hotels and pensions. Some came because it was the thing to do, and if Toscanini knew about this manifestation of snobbism, there was nothing he could do about it, save to leave Salzburg altogether. And if he did, what then? Wherever he went now, the same crowd would be attracted. One day a maharajah walked into a Toscanini orchestral concert after it had started, and the maestro stopped the music and turned a withering look on him.

To the objective visitor, there was something sad about the crowds of local people assembled along the paths leading to the theater to watch the arrival of the grand cars of the wealthy foreigners decked out in their finery. The visitors meant good business for the town and for Austria. Nevertheless, one had a disturbed feeling that these remarkable performances ought not to be for the few and the prosperous. There was no answer to this dilemma then; television today might serve to spread wide such performances, but alas, it is too late to recapture the magic of Toscanini's contributions there.

Before the beginning of the 1937 Salzburg season, Toscanini discovered that Wilhelm Furtwängler had been engaged to conduct Beethoven's Ninth. His attitude toward the tall German conductor had changed since 1936, when he had recommended him to the Philharmonic as his successor. The Philharmonic had engaged Furtwängler and then had been forced by public protests to call it off. Toscanini had learned in the interval that Furtwängler had continued to lend his name and prestige to Hitler.

When he heard about Furtwängler's engagement, Toscanini was furious. He sent a letter to Bruno Walter that he would not return to Salzburg. Why had no one consulted him, Toscanini demanded. Walter admitted that this had been an error. The Austrian Minister of Fine Arts hurried down to see Toscanini, pleading with him that, since he had agreed to do four operas and since it was too late to make changes, his failure to take part would mean a disaster.

Toscanini saw Walter and said, "You or Knappertsbusch or I could have done Beethoven's Ninth."

Walter agreed, but said sorrowfully the commitment had been made.

Toscanini remarked later that he understood what was up. Salzburg wanted to engage several singers from Germany. The officials calculated that the Nazi powers, fretting over the fuss made about Salzburg throughout the world, would not be co-operative, and the engagement of Furtwängler, the maestro thought, was a sop to them.

After listening to much pleading, Toscanini agreed to return to Salzburg on two conditions—that he would not have to see or have anything to do with Furtwängler and that Furtwängler would never again be asked back.

One day Furtwängler walked into Toscanini's dressing room. As the maestro recalled the meeting years later, he smiled at the way the German, though he towered over him, seemed to be afraid of him.

Toscanini glared at Furtwängler and said, "I don't want to see you."

"Why?"

"Because you're a Nazi."

"It is not true," Furtwängler protested.

"Yes, you are," Toscanini insisted, "whether you have a party card or not. In London you lunch with Jews to make a good case for yourself so that you won't lose your position in the West. In Germany, you work for Hitler."

Toscanini turned his back on the tall man, who slowly walked away.

The stand against Furtwängler was not the first Toscanini had taken against dealing with Nazism at Salzburg. In 1936 the Austrian Government, which was still trying to live with the Nazi Government in Germany, had cooked up a plan for an exchange of broadcasts. The Salzburg operas were to be sent to Germany by air, and the Bayreuth operas were to be broadcast to Austria. The performances led by Bruno Walter were not to be airwaved from Salzburg, since the Nazis did not wish to have music conducted by a man of Jewish antecedents. When Toscanini heard of this plan he sat on it hard. Broadcast any Salzburg performances to Germany, he told Austrian officials, and he would leave the festival for good. The scheme was dead. Naturally, the Nazis retaliated. They declined to let certain German singers appear in Salzburg, and there were last-minute problems.

In his orchestral performances Toscanini had taken pains to include music by Mendelssohn, which was under Nazi ban in Germany. This, too, had been no accident.

It followed then as the day followed night that Toscanini would turn his back on Salzburg the moment the Nazis moved on Austria. On the day Hitler's troops and armor rolled into Vienna—Toscanini was then in New York at the head of the N.B.C. Symphony—the maestro was scheduled to conduct a rehearsal. He took his place on the podium in Studio 8H in Radio City wearing an agonized look. He conducted for a few moments and then ostensibly took offense at something that happened in the orchestra. He turned and fled into his dressing room. There he barred the door to family and friends. He threw scores on the floor, turned over chairs, kicked the table, tore at his clothes, and wept. For hours he went through this solitary lamentation. It was not the rehearsal that had upset him but the blow to free men in the loss of Austria to Hitler.

There was no doubt in his mind that he was finished with Salzburg. This would be a personal loss, for he had come to love the work there and to relish the free time spent in his retreat in the mountains outside of Salzburg. Members of his family and friends were wont to spend holidays with him, and he would purchase tickets for the Salzburg programs for them. He would even buy tickets for himself for events in charge of other conductors. When the National Broadcasting Company paid him twenty-five hundred dollars for conducting a concert on August 29th broadcast from Salzburg, he turned the money over to the festival for its fund to rebuild the theater. He had given thought to new productions for the 1938 festival. Though there were reports in the press that he was considering *Iphigénie en Aulide, Boris Godunov,* and *The Barber of Seville,* he was actually planning to do *Tannhäuser.* This was the opera he had done in his Bayreuth debut, and certainly it was designed as a further manifestation against the Hitlerism rampant there.

But the personal loss was small compared to the world tragedy. As a matter of course he had a formal announcement issued that he was abandoning plans to return to Salzburg. This stand was taken on February 16, 1938, even before the date of the *Anschluss.* He had planned a concert for the benefit of the Salzburg theater at Carnegie Hall on March 4th, and he announced that he had changed the beneficiary. He wanted seventy-five per cent of the proceeds to go to unemployed musicians in New York and the remainder to the Verdi Home for Aged Musicians in Milan. He was careful to tell those people who had bought tickets for the benefit concert on the assumption that they would be helping Salzburg that they could have their money refunded if they did not like the change in beneficiaries.

Again there was pressure on him to change his position. He received a cable from Bruno Walter and other pillars of the festival, pleading with him to come to Salzburg to show that art stood above politics. Toscanini's reply was, "If you want my advice, get out of Austria yourself."

A newspaper in Bologna took the trouble to run an article reminding Toscanini that he had been slapped before for mixing politics and music and warning him that he was going too far. But that did not disturb the maestro. He spent part of that summer and the next in Italy.

When the war ended, officials at Salzburg immediately appealed to him to return.

"I said no," he remarked recently. "I would not mingle with Furtwängler, Karajan, and others who had worked for Hitler and the Nazis."

20

Other Lands

IN THE thirties, Toscanini began increasingly to accept engagements to serve as guest conductor for a relatively short span in different countries. Being relieved of the duty of managing a big opera house, he evidently found that he would like more to do. When he began to cut down the number of his concerts with the New York Philharmonic, he had still more free time. Traveling about to conduct in friendly cities became a habit.

London, in the period before the outbreak of the war, became a regular port of call. The British had long sought Toscanini, and after his visit with the Philharmonic in 1930, they pressed hard to induce him to conduct one of their own orchestras. In the spring of 1935 he finally managed it. He conducted four concerts with the B.B.C. Symphony Orchestra, and until 1939 a spring series with this ensemble became a regular commitment. The concerts were increased to six and in 1939 there were seven devoted to a Beethoven cycle that encompassed the nine symphonies as well as the overtures.

The Toscanini concerts were treated very much like a festival. There were always many more who wanted to attend than there were seats in the hall. For the 1939 Beethoven festival there were advance requests for seventy-five thousand tickets and only a small percentage of these people could be accommodated.

The cream of London's social and intellectual worlds

turned out for the Toscanini concerts, which made no difference to him so long as he and the orchestra gave performances
that satisfied him. King George VI and Queen Elizabeth were
at one of the 1939 concerts and sent the maestro an invitation
to visit the royal box during the intermission. The reply came
back that Mr. Toscanini appreciated the honor but regretted
that he could not accept, since a royal presentation in the middle of a concert would break into his concentration on the
music.

Several years before, in Vienna, ex-King Ferdinand of Bulgaria had wished to offer his personal congratulations to Toscanini and had been told that the maestro saw no one during
a concert. Ferdinand had assumed that Toscanini had not
quite grasped his identity and had sent the messenger backstage again. The messenger had returned with word that the
conductor was sorry but could not break a lifetime rule even
for a king.

The English made a warmhearted, enthusiastic, and devoted audience, but one would guess that Toscanini drew the
greatest pleasure from the good will and application of the
players of the B.B.C. Symphony. He liked this ensemble; he
consented to make a number of recordings with it. It is almost
unnecessary to add that the mutual admiration of players and
conductor was occasionally disturbed by blow-ups. Toscanini
might be a guest, but once he took his place before an orchestra he expected perfect results. He shouted, cajoled, walked
out, returned, walked out, and returned again. But the English players, though they might be taken aback by the violence
of his outbursts, understood from the outset that Toscanini
was intent on only one thing—the music.

In his book, *The Orchestra Speaks*, Bernard Shore, principal
violist of the B.B.C. Symphony, spoke of the high privilege he
and his fellow-musicians felt it to be to make music with Toscanini. As one who had worked under many conductors, Shore

testified to the inspiration the men drew from Toscanini's rehearsals and performances. He noted that every moment of preparation was employed constructively and that it was rare for the maestro to use the full time of the final rehearsal. At the very first rehearsal in 1935, Toscanini surprised the men with the pains he took in preparing a detail of an English piece —as well as with his knowledge of the music. "The care he took with the sustained harmonies of the lower strings accompanying the opening of the 'Enigma Variations,'" Shore wrote, "is still vividly remembered." And Shore quoted the maestro's words: "It is only 'armony, yes, but it is lovely music and it must be alive. For me it is too dead."

There was one rehearsal where Toscanini, using his mixture of English, German, French, and Italian, thought he was not making himself clear, and that is something that always gets him frantic. He asked the players to return to letter "G" in a score. Somebody, very likely a man from the North country, muttered, "Ay." Toscanini thought the man was arguing that the orchestra should start at the letter "I." He began to shout in Italian, which the orchestra had learned was a bad sign.

"If you were an Italian," he cried, fighting hard to remember that he was a guest in a foreign country, "I would send you out of the orchestra. If you want to argue, come outside. If not, then I go."

And out he walked. That was the end of that rehearsal.

In the end, of course, the rehearsals were held and the concerts were played. Between performances, when he had the time, Toscanini traveled about the countryside. He went down to Glyndebourne once because he was attracted by the idea of a small theater in the country and because he was curious to see a production of Verdi's *Macbeth*. Years later he recalled that Fritz Busch, the conductor, had done a good job, and that Carl Ebert had staged the piece admirably. After the performance he had suggested to Ebert that the first act needed more movement, and Ebert, agreeing, proceeded to rework it.

Toscanini also visited France from time to time. In the spring of 1936 he contributed his services to a program to raise funds for a monument to Saint-Saëns, and stayed to conduct another concert at the Salle Pleyel. In December of the same year he was back in Paris for several concerts with the Orchestra Straram, an ensemble which he had conducted before and had taken once to Brussels. His choice of programs was attacked, particularly his inclusion of pieces by Sonzogno and Busoni. His taste in contemporary music was frequently under fire in his later years.

In 1937 he returned to Stockholm, but because of illness conducted only one of the two promised concerts. That year the Viennese made a special occasion of his seventieth birthday and got him to come and conduct the Vienna Philharmonic in a gala concert. Then he conducted in Budapest.

Of all his travels the two trips to Palestine touched his emotions most profoundly. Early in 1936, Bronislaw Hubermann, a violinist of stature and a man of deep human compassion, had come to Toscanini to invite him to conduct an orchestra he was organizing in Palestine. Most of the players were to be men who had fled from Nazi persecution, and William Steinberg, formerly a conductor in Germany, would do the preliminary work of assembling and rehearsing the ensemble. Toscanini was so pleased with Steinberg's work that he sent a letter to a New York Philharmonic official recommending him for a chance to conduct that orchestra. Toscanini had accepted Hubermann's invitation at once, remarking, "It is the duty of everyone to fight and help in this sort of cause according to one's means."

In December the maestro reached Palestine and conducted the first concerts of this orchestra, in Tel-Aviv, Jerusalem, and Haifa, and then took it to Cairo in Egypt. For him these were more than concerts; they were an affirmation of his political and human faith. His heart went out to the musicians who had been victimized by Hitlerism, and yet when it came to making music, he did not spare them. They, for their part, played for him not only with the devotion of good musicians but with a feeling of personal gratitude and love.

Toscanini was eager to see how Palestine was being rebuilt. He went out to visit the colonists in their remote settlements and to watch them at work. At Ramot Hashavim one day he was presented with the title and deed to an orange grove. When he arrived for the ceremony, a chorus of school children greeted him with a Hebrew song composed for the occasion. After the presentation of the deed, the maestro and Hubermann each planted a tree. A small boy and a small girl came forward with baskets of oranges, grapefruits, honey, and eggs—produce of the settlement—as gifts for the visitors. Then the maestro went to the home of the mayor and, over a glass of local wine, listened to the history of the three-year-old settlement which sheltered sixty German families. "There are seven pianos in this small settlement of ours," the mayor said proudly, and the maestro nodded, deeply touched.

He was taken back to see his orange grove upon his return to Palestine in the spring of 1938, and when they brought him oranges picked in his own grove, he held them in his hands and wept.

During this second trip the tension between Arabs and Jews had deepened, and the maestro was under constant military protection. Once Toscanini and his wife narrowly escaped a bomb thrown at a car in which they were riding. Nevertheless, he insisted on traveling about the country and giving his full schedule of concerts. Wherever he went there were immense crowds. Even though houses were sold out, and the people knew it, they came by the thousands in the hope that they might see him pass.

When he realized how many were disappointed at their

inability to obtain tickets, he suggested that a full house be invited to rehearsal at a small admission charge for charity. Later, when he was annoyed by latecomers, he would expostulate, "Why should they be late? I'm always there; the orchestra is always there. Why not the audience?" and then tell about this audience in Palestine. He arrived at the hall a half hour ahead of time and was astonished to note that there was no crowd at the doors. Could it be, he wondered, that there was no interest in the rehearsal after all? He entered the hall and found that it was jammed. The audience had arrived hours in advance of the starting time. As he walked out on the stage, he could see that there were children in the arms of parents. The quiet and attention of this audience was something incredible. As he raised his baton, he felt like weeping again.

Some of the concerts took place in an exposition hall. When the maestro arrived for the first rehearsal, one of his traveling companions was horrified to find that there were a lot of songbirds in the hall. "This won't do," he told the local manager. "You'll have to take them out or shut them up, or the maestro will blow up." The birds were left in the hall. Toscanini began to rehearse, and as the orchestra played the birds sought to match the instrumental song with their own fine, careless raptures. The local manager and Toscanini's friend glared at the birds and thought about strangling and poison, but the maestro appeared not to notice. Suddenly he brought his baton down sharply, signaling for a halt. "Please," he said to the musicians, "please, why can't you sing like those birds?"

During this visit Toscanini insisted on conducting an all-Wagner program. Wagner's music had not been played in Palestine since Hitler's terrorization of the Jews, but Toscanini told the musicians and the people of the country, "Nothing should interfere with music."

The maestro was interested in the people around him. His

226

sturdy young chauffeur was despondent one day, and Toscanini asked what the trouble was. His wife was unhappy, the young man said, because she could not attend his concerts. "Why not?" Toscanini wanted to know. "Because she is expecting a baby," the chauffeur answered. Toscanini and his wife offered to visit the young woman, and they went to the chauffeur's house for tea.

The maestro and his wife wandered about the streets of Tel-Aviv. They looked into the shops, and they paused to watch the children at play on the streets.

"I like to go into Jewish homes, eat Jewish food, and feel the pulse of Jewish life," Toscanini said.

Perhaps he told some of his new friends in Palestine what he had said often to friends in Italy and New York—that he believed firmly that he was partly of Jewish origin. He would laugh at the silly Nazi propaganda that his real name was Arturo Tosenstein and that this proved he was non-Aryan. But more seriously he would point out that Jews in Italy had traditionally worn the names of cities and provinces. His own name undoubtedly had been Toscano or Toscani to start with, he would point out, and this meant Tuscan or Tuscans. Toscanini, in turn, meant the little Tuscans. Could anything be more convincing?

Toscanini refused to accept payment for any of his concerts in both Palestinian visits. It was a privilege to him to contribute his services and to reveal publicly his solidarity with the persecuted. In the same way he grasped quickly at another opportunity to make music that would be an unmistakable demonstration of opposition to Nazism.

In 1938, Adolf Busch phoned him in London from Geneva inviting him to join in a festival to be arranged in Lucerne that summer. Since Toscanini had declined to appear first at Bayreuth and then at Salzburg, his appearance in Lucerne, which was not too far from Germany, would have its inevitable moral effect. The idea appealed to him. Busch undertook to recruit the string section of the orchestra, and Ernest Ansermet the winds. The city of Lucerne put at Toscanini's disposal a villa at Kastanienbaum, not far from Triebschen, where Wagner and Cosima had lived.

There were fine musicians in the orchestra, with Adolf Busch as concertmaster and Enrico Polo, the maestro's brother-in-law and old comrade-at-arms, in the string section. Bruno Walter and Fritz Busch also conducted, and the concerts attracted the international set. Once again Toscanini helped to give a festival worldwide attention. Another series of concerts took place in 1939. In 1940 Toscanini planned to do a Brahms cycle, but the outbreak of war ended Lucerne's interval of festival glory. In 1946 he went back to Lucerne for a couple of concerts, but at seventy-nine he felt too old for a rigorous festival schedule.

For Toscanini the proximity to the Wagner tradition was one of the treasurable aspects of his work at Lucerne. In 1938 he conducted a concert at Triebschen attended by Daniela Thode, one of Wagner's daughters, and by Friede-lind Wagner, his granddaughter. The Swiss took unlimited pains to make the conditions perfect. Steamers on Lake Lucerne were detoured, cars were rerouted, church bells were hushed, and even the cows in the near-by fields were stripped of their little bells. The high point of the program was the "Siegfried Idyl," which Wagner had written, and directed on the stairway of the villa, as a surprise birthday offering for Cosima on Christmas morning, 1870.

In 1939 Toscanini prepared fifteen string players in the "Siegfried Idyl," played this time as a surprise for Wagner's two surviving daughters, Daniela Thode and Eva Chamber-lain, at the villa in Triebschen. The audience was a small group of friends and relatives. There was no applause. When the music ended, the two old ladies kissed the maestro, and he turned silently and went to his car.

On the chance that Hitler and his friends at Bayreuth knew what was going on, Toscanini was telling them that Wagner belonged to the world and that this time, should war come, the world would not let them take exclusive possession of his music.

21

N.B.C. Symphony

WHEN Toscanini left the Philharmonic-Symphony Orchestra and New York in the spring of 1936, he took it for granted that this was truly his farewell to America. He had Salzburg and guest appearances here and there, but he had no desire for a full-time position and its responsibilities. But America did not forget him. It bought his records, and many made pilgrimages to Europe just to hear his performances at Salzburg. And Toscanini, though he was in Europe, was eager for news and gossip of the United States.

Some Americans wondered how they could induce Toscanini to return to America for a while. Even before he had left the United States, Philharmonic officials had suggested to the Radio Corporation of America that its subsidiary, RCA-Victor, should stand sponsor for a tour by the Philharmonic the following year with Toscanini conducting. There had been evidence that the maestro might be persuaded to return for such a tour. In December, 1936, a proposal was cabled to the maestro, and he turned it down. In the same month another offer was cabled to him to return for recording sessions with the Philharmonic. Again he declined. David Sarnoff, then president and now chairman of the board of the Radio Corporation of America, then thought of a plan that might be more enticing. N.B.C. would organize an orchestra especially for Toscanini if he would come to the United States to conduct it. In January, 1937, he asked Samuel

Chotzinoff, his friend and Toscanini's, whether he would go abroad and place the idea before the maestro personally. Chotzinoff agreed to try and sent a cable to Toscanini asking whether he might come to visit him in Italy. "Of course you may come," Toscanini replied.

Chotzinoff arrived on the little island in Lago Maggiore and spent some days with the maestro. They talked about music and mutual friends, and finally Chotzinoff broached the object of his trip. The idea of an orchestra built to his specifications and subject to his musical wishes appealed to Toscanini; the fee, four thousand dollars a concert net, with taxes paid, was one of the largest he had ever received. But he hesitated.

"I am too old," he said, "to start something new."

Chotzinoff disagreed.

Toscanini insisted that he wished to be let alone. This was too big a venture to have launched just for him. No, he could not do it. However, he would think about it; he would not make this a final no.

As he thought about it, he was increasingly attracted to the plan, particularly because the concerts were not to be designed for an audience limited by the walls of a hall but were to be specifically for the millions who listened to the radio. Very well, he would take his courage in his hands and do it. Chotzinoff left jubilantly.

Having committed himself, Toscanini began to fret. Had he done right? It was still months before he was to return to the United States for the opening concert, but he did not sleep a wink the night after giving his word to return. When his wife asked why, he said, "I was worrying about the first program."

When the news was announced, a friend in New York, whose affections were with the Philharmonic, sent Toscanini a message saying that his new affiliation looked like a comedown. The maestro's reply was, "It does not matter whether the preacher is in St. Peter's in Rome or in a little church in the most obscure village in Italy so long as he preaches the true faith."

The first program took place on Christmas night, 1937. Studio 8H in Radio City was filled with an invited audience, and for years N.B.C. has had a long waiting list of applicants from all over the country who have wished to see the maestro as well as hear him. The studio was outfitted to give the best results on the air. There were criticisms that its acoustics were not favorable, but Toscanini was assured that the sound of his orchestra was reproduced faithfully on receiving sets, and that was what counted with him.

The orchestra had been assembled and auditioned by Artur Rodzinski, whom Toscanini had got to know in Salzburg, and when Toscanini came to rehearse it he was not displeased. Over the years there were changes in personnel, but many who were there at the start remained.

The opening program consisted of Vivaldi's Concerto Grosso in D minor, Mozart's G minor Symphony, and Brahms' First. Though he was seventy, the old gentleman had not lost his touch. The performances were incandescent, as they are now. Nor has he lost his capacity for making a rehearsal an affair of consuming intensity.

The men of the N.B.C. Symphony will tell you that in recent years Toscanini seemed to grow mellow. Yet at eighty-three he could erupt loudly and violently, hurling furious invective at a player who had crossed him. If this was mellowness, what could it have been like when he had not become gentle and soft? The players will tell you that at times it was frightening and frightful. He threw watches to the floor and stamped on them until they were ground to bits. He took a valuable score and with what seemed like maniacal deliberation ripped out page after page until they lay like ravaged leaves around him. He kicked at the music stand near him so often that it was finally set in an iron brace to keep him from demolishing it. He would then pull and haul at the stand until it came loose, when he would pick it up and hurl it off the stage. And he walked out and locked himself in his dressing room while frantic radio executives, who thought that they had seen all there was to see of tempers and temperament, sought to placate him.

Mind you, this was not an orchestra made up of green musicians. N.B.C. had spared neither effort nor money to bring together men who had held leading positions in other orchestras of the country. First-desk players in other ensembles were hired to sit in the rear sections of this orchestra. That made no difference to Toscanini. Performance, not reputation, counted. He wanted a homogeneous, subtly responsive ensemble, and in his relentless drive for work and more work he succeeded in transforming this orchestra into a musical instrument built in his own image.

It was an orchestra that learned to know his every mood and gesture on the podium, and it got so that it reacted in his way even when another conductor stood before it and Toscanini was in the audience. There was the time when an eminent conductor prepared a Mozart symphony in the style that he thought was right. His approach was light and graceful, whereas Toscanini had demanded more bite, weight, and drive in this symphony. The guest conductor spent a good deal of rehearsal time struggling to get the piece done his way and finally he succeeded. At concert time the men in the orchestra caught sight of Toscanini taking a seat in the studio and when the guest conductor gave the signal for the start of the symphony, the men played it not as he had trained them but exactly as Toscanini always did it. Was it hypnosis or just fear of the old man?

Toscanini might make scenes in rehearsal, but his satisfaction with the orchestra grew steadily. The fact that he was eager to lead a tour to South America with it in 1940 was proof of his readiness and desire to show it off. He came to feel a sense of ownership in this orchestra, and this feeling of personal identification led to a temporary break with N.B.C.

Since the N.B.C. Symphony was the company's staff orchestra, its members were required from time to time to play on programs other than those conducted by Toscanini. And these extra programs had commercial sponsors as a rule. It was important to N.B.C. that rehearsal and performance schedules of Toscanini's programs and the others should not clash, and every effort was made to arrange plenty of leeway between a Toscanini rehearsal and a commercial program. But the maestro could be indifferent to other commitments. One afternoon he kept rehearsing long after the fixed quitting time, and some of the men began to fidget because they were due to go on the air in another show within a few minutes. Finally, a temerarious executive gave the players permission to leave, and they started to slip out. Toscanini was enraged. This was his orchestra; what right had it to be at anybody else's disposal?

He did not feel otherwise when he happened to be taking time off and guest conductors were in charge of the orchestra. If he was in town, he would appear in Studio 8H and sit in on rehearsals and performances. His motives might be of the purest. He might be there only because he wanted to keep an affectionate eye on his orchestra or hear an unfamiliar score. Thus when Ernest Ansermet was rehearsing a new piece by Frank Martin, a Swiss composer, Toscanini listened with careful attention and then, finding the score interesting, borrowed it to take home and study further.

But other conductors might be pardoned if they felt uneasy or resentful when the maestro turned up. Toscanini's presence, in fact, was upsetting to other conductors, and it had its effect on the players, who could scarcely forget who was their real boss. Even if Toscanini sat as quietly as a mouse at such rehearsals, he imposed a strain on the guest conductors.

But he did not always sit and he did not always keep quiet.

Once a conductor, a devoted admirer of Toscanini, was the guest leader. Toscanini, of course, came to his rehearsals, and the poor fellow was nervous. At one point the guest's pacing of a composition disturbed Toscanini, who began to beat time as he felt the piece. The men in the orchestra saw what the maestro was doing and began to follow him. The guest conductor did not turn around, but he understood what was going on.

On other occasions Toscanini made scenes while other conductors were rehearsing. He stood up and walked out ostentatiously after ten minutes of a session because he was annoyed by the manner in which the guest conductor was fussing with a Mozart concerto. He objected audibly when the rehearsal methods of another conductor, a man of considerable eminence, disturbed him.

Put in the best possible light, such behavior indicated that where music and his orchestra were concerned, Toscanini forgot normal, human impulses of kindness. It is probable that Toscanini could not restrain himself in such a situation. But the guest conductors might well ask: Did he have to attend their rehearsals?

The big explosion came in the summer of 1941. N.B.C. had adopted a policy of broadcasting concerts of a popular nature during the warm months, and it invited guest conductors to run them. That summer Toscanini was not traveling, and he looked in on his orchestra frequently. One day he walked in on a rehearsal of a Brahms symphony. What he heard outraged him. He went roaring through the halls of the building and collared a company executive.

"That is not my orchestra," he roared. "I do not recognize my orchestra! What has that man done to it?"

The executive tried to say something, but Toscanini was scarcely listening.

"That is not my orchestra!" he cried again, with the agony of a man who had been afflicted suddenly by some unspeakable personal tragedy. "That is not my orchestra!"

"He's guest conductor for only another week," the executive offered by way of appeasement.

"He is a disgrace!" Toscanini shouted. "He has ruined my orchestra. Why didn't you ask me to conduct? I would conduct summer concerts for you."

"It is only one concert," the executive said defensively.

Toscanini glared at the man and shouted, "That is not my orchestra!" once more and stormed out. He went home and raged. He sent word that he would not conduct the N.B.C. Symphony again. He refused to answer the phone when N.B.C. people phoned, and when they came to his house, he would not leave his room to see them.

The chances are a thousand to one that he would have left the United States and rushed off to brood in Italy if the war had not been raging at this time. The chances are better than fair that if he had done so he would not have returned to the N.B.C. Symphony. As it was, he sat and fed on his grievances for months. He even accepted an invitation to lunch with William Paley, head of the competing Columbia Broadcasting System, and if an attractive offer had been forthcoming, perhaps he might have gone over to this organization. He did not appear on the regular N.B.C. Symphony series during the 1941-42 season.

But the war was on, and he cared passionately about its outcome. As the months went by, he became restless for activity. He was particularly eager to make some contribution to the war effort. When N.B.C. proposed, through intermediaries whom Toscanini would see, that he conduct its orchestra in a series of benefits in behalf of the United States Treasury's bond drives, he acquiesced. He did five such concerts between December 6, 1941, and April 4, 1942. He found, of course, that his orchestra had not had its quality and character ruined after all. By the fall of 1942 he had agreed to resume his role as its principal conductor and to direct the major part of its winter series. And in the summers of 1943 and 1944, just to show that he had not forgotten, he took the trouble to conduct concerts of gay, light, popular pieces to prove his point that such music could be played without injury to the standards of his treasured orchestra.

His programs with the N.B.C. Symphony over the years relied predominantly on the music and the composers he loved. There were a couple of Beethoven cycles, a Brahms cycle, performances of Beethoven's Ninth and *Missa Solemnis*, Verdi's Requiem, and Berlioz's "Romeo and Juliet." There were Wagner, Debussy, Mozart, Mendelssohn, Sibelius, Bizet, Verdi, and Tchaikovsky programs, with the "Pathetic" Symphony at last returning to his repertory. To show off the remarkable ensemble and homogeneity of his string sections, Toscanini conducted movements of Beethoven's last quartet and all of Verdi's only quartet. He found American works to play—pieces by Samuel Barber, George Templeton Strong, Roy Harris, Aaron Copland, Paul Creston, Morton Gould, George Gershwin, Elie Siegmeister, Don Gillis, Kent Kennan, Charles M. Loeffler, Henry F. Gilbert, Charles T. Griffes, and Ferde Grofé. He conducted music by living composers of other lands—Oscar Lorenzo Fernandez and Francisco Mignone of Brazil, Kurt Atterburg of Sweden, Vittorio Rieti and Castelnuovo-Tedesco of Italy, Vaughan Williams of England, and Kabalevsky, Kalinnikov, and Shostakovich of Russia.

He was so stirred by the Russian fight against the Germans that he went out of his way to make sure he would conduct the American *première* of Shostakovich's Seventh Symphony, the one that had been composed in large part during the siege of Leningrad. There was a delicate bit of sparring between him and Leopold Stokowski over this *première*. The two exchanged letters arguing their claims with gentlemanly tact. Stokowski pointed out that he had conducted the American *première* of other Shostakovich works in the past and that, by birth, he had a Slavic background. Toscanini replied that for twenty years he had fought Fascism and Nazism, sometimes at close range. There was no question, of course, with N.B.C. that Toscanini could have the *première* if he wanted it, and he did.

Though he no longer worked in the theater, opera remained in Toscanini's blood, and he began to do an opera or two each season in concert form. Over the radio, after all, acting and stage sets made no difference, and these were programs for the radio audiences. In the summer of 1943 he did the third act of *Rigoletto* with a group of soloists, and used Gertrude Ribla, a dramatic soprano, to do Gilda. To those who were surprised that the customary coloratura soprano did not fill the role, Toscanini pointed out that the use of a coloratura was another arrant and almost universal violation of Verdi's requirements. He pointed to the score, showing that the florid decorations added to Gilda's part were not written by Verdi.

In February, 1946, fifty years after the *première* he had conducted in Italy, Toscanini did *La Bohème* in two broadcasts. In following seasons he conducted *Fidelio, La Traviata, Otello, Aïda,* and *Falstaff,* stripping away the impurities that had gathered around these operas and letting them sing forth with incredible power and pathos. Even the singers who worked with him for months to bring these performances into being were later amazed to find what they had done. Herva Nelli, who sang Desdemona in *Otello,* listened two years later to a recording taken from the performance and exclaimed, "How did I do it? He must have hypnotized me."

During the war years Toscanini conducted concerts for the sale of war bonds—more than ten million dollars in bonds were sold for one concert—and for various charities, and after the war he continued to do these special programs. It delighted him on two occasions to take a small orchestra and give wonderful, intimate concerts in Ridgefield, Connecticut, in the high-school auditorium for a local cause, because he had enjoyed pleasant visits in the area as guest at the Chotzinoff summer place.

At some of his war benefits he not only contributed his services but insisted on paying for a box for his family. In December, 1942, after conducting a Red Cross benefit with the New York Philharmonic-Symphony, to which he had returned as a guest a little earlier in honor of its centennial, he sent a signed blank check to the orchestra management to make sure that the beneficiary would net twenty thousand dollars. His added gift turned out to be about one thousand dollars.

On May 25, 1944, Toscanini directed a concert at Madison Square Garden that netted more than one hundred thousand dollars for the Red Cross. The N.B.C. and Philharmonic-Symphony Orchestras joined to make a huge ensemble for this event, and there were soloists and a chorus of six hundred. Nearly eighteen thousand persons packed the Garden to hear the Wagner-Verdi program.

Toscanini conducted several benefits for the National Foundation for Infantile Paralysis. After one in 1943 he received a personal letter from President Roosevelt, which said in part:

The magnificent contributions you have made to the world of music have always been highlighted by your humanitarian and unyielding devotion to the cause of liberty. Like all true artists, you have recognized throughout your life that art can flourish only where men are free. Once again your baton has spoken with unmatched eloquence on behalf of the afflicted and the oppressed.

Toscanini's reply was heartfelt. One can imagine how much thought and time he gave to composing it.

As for myself [he wrote in part], I assure you, my dear Mr. President, that I shall continue unabated on the same path that

I have trod all my life for the cause of liberty, liberty that, in my opinion, is the only orthodoxy within the limits of which art may express itself and flourish freely—liberty that is the best of all things in the life of man, if it is all one with wisdom and virtue.

The boldness of his convictions had not been tamed by age, and he remained ready to embark on new adventures. In March, 1948, at eighty-one, he cheerfully assented to having his broadcast televised, even though the hot lights placed an inordinate strain on him. Several times later he agreed to a telecast.

And in 1950, at eighty-three, he set out on a tour of America from coast to coast with the N.B.C. Symphony, covering areas of the country—the Southwest and the Northwest—where he had never visited and conducted before. It was suggested that he take along two different programs; he prepared six.

He traveled in a private car, and every thought was given to his comfort. Nevertheless, there were long hauls and many days and nights to be passed trying to rest and sleep on a speeding train. There were also new halls, some with difficult acoustics. But he had always loved trouping, and he bore up under all hazards with fortitude and, save for one or two outbursts, with remarkably good cheer.

He was an avid sightseer. He was touched by the unstinted admiration people all over America seemed to have for his music. He could relax and have fun, going up in a ski-tow lift at Sun Valley and conducting his boys making merry with pans and pots and other singular musical instruments. He was a happy man on this tour, and he worked hard, as always.

There was the evening in Houston. It was hot and humid, and the hall was not air conditioned. The audience sat in shirt sleeves, but Toscanini conducted in full-dress regalia. During the intermission an effort was made to dry out his dress coat by holding it aloft in front of a blower. The big work of the evening was the "Eroica," and during the slow movement the

men in front of him thought that the old man would faint. There was a glazed look in his eye as though he were far, far away. Suddenly he seemed to pull himself together with a jerk. The eyes blazed and the body became alert and concentrated. His beat became vigorous, and his control of the performance more gripping than ever. The trouper of iron will had caught himself and he had driven forward with revived intensity.

The acoustics in Pasadena were poor, and this upset him. He refused to eat after the brief rehearsal and would not order any food for his usual light bite before the concert. A few minutes before 8 P.M. he said he was hungry, but it was too late to get food for him. He was in a dark mood throughout the concert, and at the very end he missed a cue. The men finished correctly, on their own, but he stumbled off the stage, muttering, "*Scusa.*" When he was changing his clothes in his dressing room, he had trouble fastening his collar. This precipitated an explosion. He pulled the shirt off and ripped it to shreds. He swore at himself and then bit deeply into his wrist.

The next day, sitting at lunch on a terrace overlooking a swimming pool, he seemed subdued. He showed the gash on his wrist to a friend and said contritely, "I was bad last night."

The friend replied with a smile, "You are a savage."

Toscanini nodded his head. "Yes," he said sadly, "I am."

In St. Louis the concert took place in a movie house and here, too, the acoustics were bad. The "Eroica" faced him once more. This time he was like a battler whom nothing could defeat. He fought the hall, the audience, and the orchestra, and out of this struggle came a performance of incredible tautness and spiritual depth. In the intermission he strode into his dressing room, throwing the baton ahead of him angrily. Then he stood there, talking to himself. "Have patience, Toscanini," he kept muttering, "have patience!"

In Cleveland bright spotlights were turned on overhead unexpectedly, and they cast shadows of himself directly in front of him as he conducted. He began cursing at the start of the program and did not seem to care what was happening. Some of the men observed that his cues almost misled them. At the intermission he walked into his dressing room, snapped his baton in two, and said, "I can go home now." And he meant that he was going—at once. It took some eloquent persuading to keep him in the hall. The spotlights were turned off, and the rest of the evening went well.

In Pittsburgh when he entered the hall and saw that the background for the orchestra was a circle of drapes, he said quietly that he would not conduct unless there was some sort of band shell. Tour officials said that they thought they could borrow the Pittsburgh Symphony shell. "If it's here at 5 P.M. for rehearsal," Toscanini said, "we shall have a concert." It was there.

At the end of the tour, at a party he gave to his orchestra, Toscanini remarked, "It is a miracle. When I agreed to this tour, I was afraid. Now that it is over, I can hardly believe it."

It was a miracle. Barnstorming at eighty-three, he had conducted performances that had all the refinement of detail and over-all sweep one would expect from Toscanini. These performances had something deeper, too, a ripeness and spirituality that turned the heart to water. It was not only the music that moved the audiences and even the men in the orchestra, but the indomitable will and passionate heart of the old maestro.

PART TWO

22

Conducting—A Way of Life

IT HAD BEEN a remarkable rehearsal. Almost nothing had gone wrong, and nearly every note, phrase, rhythm, and color had fallen into place. The music had come very close to Toscanini's ideal of it. He relaxed and permitted himself a rare moment of self-satisfaction. With disarming candor he said to his men, "I am not beautiful. I am not a genius. I am not a composer. But I am a conductor."

To be a conductor, in the full and true sense of the word, has been the objective of the greater part of his energies for the greater part of his life. It has been a calling that has imposed obligations on him as severe as any undertaken by the most devout servant of God. There could be no end to the service of music, no limits to make himself better fitted and worthier to carry out his work.

A conductor, he has often said, must be born, not made, and he has scoffed at the temerity of men who have sought to teach conducting by giving courses and holding master classes. By that he surely means that the gift for musical leadership must be innate; he does not mean that it does not require constant cultivation, study, and enrichment. He himself has never ceased to study and to seek fresh illumination of music he has done for half a century and more. But he despairs of being able to teach others who have not the irreplaceable gift—the capacity to study and hear and grow. Several years ago he received a manifesto from Rome, calling

245

upon him to come and conduct in the Italian capital and to show a new generation of musicians the proper way to do the operatic repertory. "Ridiculous!" he exclaimed. "They do not listen, learn, or remember."

To be a conductor, he has learned, is a stern, exacting, unending task. "This *porco* of a stick," he once said wrathfully, holding out his baton contemptuously, "I cannot make it express what I feel here."

A musician can never say: This performance is good and I shall leave it this way. The miracle and challenge of music are that it must be made anew with each performance. The composer's dream is sketched in black marks on white paper, and the musician who would share this dream with the public must try to capture the essence of this dream in sound. As soon as the air ceases to vibrate, the sound is gone. It cannot be precisely the same each time, and the good musician does not try to recapture what he did yesterday. He seeks to come closer each time to his conception of what the composer has tried to say.

For the conductor the task is more difficult than for the musician who depends only on his own brain, heart, throat, lips, and fingers. He must fuse the efforts of other men and women of different backgrounds and tastes; he must dominate and magnetize them so that they respond to his subtlest wishes. His instrument, be it symphony orchestra or opera company, is a complex of diverse instruments and personalities. It is hard enough to play on it so that it sounds well; it is infinitely harder to play on it so that the sounds probe deeply into the composer's heart.

In the beginning, for the conductor and all other musicians, there must be the music. Toscanini once told a young colleague, "You must not conduct a piece of music until the notes have marched off the paper and come alive in your head and heart." You get the feeling, after watching Toscanini over the years, that he is possessed by the music. In him there seems to sing an ideal version of every voice and every instrument, and his unremitting purpose as a conductor is to make the living sound correspond to the song that surges in his brain.

To a young conductor seeking advice, Toscanini once said, "I shall tell you my secret; all my life I have been studying scores." And that is the whole truth. The man who has conducted Beethoven's "Eroica" countless times over a span of more than five decades feels that he has to examine it afresh at the age of eighty-three. And at eighty-three he seeks to improve his performances. Recently he decided to take the grace notes in the slow movement on the downbeat. Before he acted on this decision, he gave it much study and reflection. His only aim was to seek out a juster and finer version of the "Eroica."

He once told a friend that he was weary of hearing of this conductor's "Eroica" and that conductor's *Aïda*. It should be enough, he said, to be the means of projecting Beethoven's "Eroica" and Verdi's *Aïda*.

To get at Beethoven's "Eroica" and Verdi's *Aïda* means thinking and studying, searching always for some new secret, trying a new approach and then studying and thinking once more. In the course of his recent tour with the N.B.C. Symphony, Toscanini played several times some symphonies that had been in his repertory for many years. Yet in the hours preceding a concert he took out these scores and perused them, beating time, as though they were something he was to conduct for the first time.

Sometimes he feels intolerable anguish at the thought that a detail has gone amiss even though the performance as a whole has been magical in its sweep and insight. Listening to the play-back of a recording of the magnificent performance of *Otello* he led for broadcast several years ago, he dashed to the phonograph and stopped the record. "At this point," he shouted, "I was betrayed."

In the ideal version he hears in his head there is no betrayal.

247

Speaking of *Otello*, he once observed to a young friend, "The soprano goes one way"—the long square index finger pointed to the right—"the tenor goes that"—the finger waved to the left—"the orchestra goes there"—an upward sweep and a sigh. "I am only the conductor. I cannot keep them all in the center of the road, where they belong. Soon there is no Verdi. I like *Otello* best in my study when I read the score. Then it is perfect."

In his study it may be perfect. In the concert hall and opera he is never satisfied that perfection has been attained. And he does not hesitate to blame himself and to admit shortcomings. A musician who had collaborated with him in several performances of Beethoven's Ninth remarked that the latest had been better than the others. "Yes," Toscanini said, "but the Ninth is difficult. Sometimes the chorus is not good. The soloists are seldom good. Sometimes the orchestra is not good. Sometimes I am no good. You know, I still don't understand the first movement."

Milton Katims, a young conductor, directed Mendelssohn's "Scotch" Symphony, and Toscanini listened to the rehearsal. Afterward he said to Katims, "The Scherzo is difficult but it went all right. It will really come in about ten years. The last movement of this symphony is a little weak, and it needs to go faster or it falls apart." The conductor had studied Toscanini's recording of this symphony made some years before and had followed his tempos. He decided to be brash and to say so. Toscanini did not take offense. "I was stupid then," he cried, "but I have thought about it and now I think it should go faster."

Another conductor, a man of some eminence, met a friend of Toscanini's and confided aggrievedly that he was hurt by something Toscanini had said about him. "What do you think of it?" the bitter conductor observed. "I thought we were friends and he said I conducted like an idiot." The mutual friend doubted, he said, that Toscanini had said any such

248

thing but would make inquiries. Later he put the question to Toscanini. "I did say it," the maestro said. "Tell him sometimes I conduct like an idiot, too."

Toscanini is the first to concede when something has gone wrong. During a performance of Elgar's "Enigma Variations" he forgot to cue the orchestra for a repeat but the men played it anyhow. Even Toscanini could nod; it did not diminish the respect of the men. Another time he failed to give the signal for the contrabassoon in "The Sorcerer's Apprentice," but the player came in on time. But Toscanini did not forgive himself. When Mischa Mischakoff, N.B.C. Symphony concertmaster, entered the maestro's dressing room to observe that the Elgar had been a fine performance, Toscanini shouted, "Not true, it wasn't!"

Toscanini does not pretend that he knows if there is any doubt in his mind. In preparing a recent broadcast performance of *Falstaff*, he was dissatisfied with an effect made by the singing of the off-stage chorus. He paused and reflected. "Something is not right," he said. "I'm not quite sure what." Speaking to the assistant conductor, he said, "Maestro, try again. We shall work it out."

Another time he remarked that he played a certain composition badly, like a pig. His friends replied immediately that it wasn't so. "So you think I don't know music?" he shouted. "The trouble with all of you is you have been poisoned by me."

The drive for perfection is relentless, and it does not matter whether he himself or anybody else gets hurt en route. On three different occasions he attempted to record Debussy's "La Mer" with the N.B.C. Symphony, and each time he rejected the final product. He had spent his own time and energy without compensation, and the cost to the recording company was about $6,000 a session. But Debussy had not been sufficiently well served, and there was nothing more to be said. In 1950 he undertook to try again. A friend said, "I'm sure it will go well this time," and Toscanini replied softly and humbly, "I hope."

Some years ago he agreed to make a new recording of Beethoven's Seventh Symphony with the N.B.C. Symphony Orchestra, and the session was set to start at 8 P.M. The players took the wrong rhythm in the opening phrases of the first movement, a passage he had slaved over in past rehearsals and performances. He turned his back on them, threw his baton to the rear of the studio, marched off the stage in a rage, and locked himself in his dressing room. At 8:05 P.M. he was through with the session. Nothing would persuade him to return to the podium. An effort was made to save something of the session by having an assistant conductor record a few light pieces, but it did not work out. James B. Dolan, who had just joined the orchestra as its librarian, slipped to the rear of the studio, picked up the baton, and took it home. He kept it as a memento. "The six-thousand-dollar baton," he calls it.

Toscanini may lash out at the musicians who work with him, but he is most demanding of himself. "Look at me," he shouts in rehearsal, "look at the old man." And he punches himself on the chest. "I give everything—all of myself." And this is no idle boast. He holds nothing back on the podium—not concentration of mind, not temper, not energy. Music absorbs all of him and he cannot abide collaborators who do not give in the same way. For those who do he has unlimited affection. He pointed one day to a man in his orchestra and said proudly, "Look at him, he sweats more than me."

Toscanini's performances, no matter what he conducts, bulk infinitely larger to him than a job. He brings the same intensity to all kinds of music and all kinds of appearances; he never stops to think about the nature of the audience or the size of the fee. Once he begins to work with a group of performers, it is the music in which he is all wrapped up.

His absorption in the music begins long before he reaches the podium. The notes have long since left the page and come alive for him, and yet he returns again and again to the printed page to see whether the flesh and bones are in the right places and whether the blood courses warmly enough. The score, new or old, has become as familiar and vibrant as a close friend, but a friend whom he does not take for granted.

Toscanini's capacity to study and learn an intricate score by heart in a few days has been hailed as an extraordinary feat of memory, and it amounts to that. Yet he does not attach any great importance to it. That is how his mind happens to work. Since his eyesight is weak, it is a kindness that he does not have to rely too heavily on it. But the memorizing is not a process engaged in for itself. It is his road to mastering a score.

If he happens to be learning a new composition, he takes it to bed with him and, propped up against a cushion, he reads through it. The next morning he takes it to the piano. He does not bother to sit down. Rocking to and fro, with his weight shifting from heels to toes, he pounds away until he knows it. Then he goes through it again, without the aid of the piano, fixing in his mind this new face in all its subtleties of planes and lineaments. Then he reads the score away from the piano, and his hands begin to beat time. The music is now sounding in his head with all its voices clearly defined, and he is calculating the manner in which he will call them forth when he meets with the performers.

Towering masterpieces or delightful little genre pieces, old scores or new, they are broken down and synthesized by Toscanini in his laboratory as a chemist might work with his elements.

He considers first the problem of tempo; he once called it "the all-important subject." Music lives and breathes in time and the pace at which it moves may make all the difference between eloquence and stuffiness. For Toscanini the study of tempo has been a primary, lifelong concern. He has read everything on the subject, not only the music but books dealing with the composer and his times. He is mindful of the fact that conditions change with every place and epoch, that an allegro in Italy in the second half of the nineteenth century might be something subtly different from an allegro in Austria in the eighteenth century. He relies on the internal evidence of the music and then, almost as heavily, on his instinct.

"As a student," he told a friend one day, "I always had the right tempo. I felt the music naturally. Then I began to think. There was trouble. Slowly I worked my way into the right path. Now that I was doing it by thinking, I had to think constantly about tempo."

A score like "The Sorcerer's Apprentice," which might not give another conductor much pause, troubled him for years. When he played it for the first time decades ago, he was disturbed because in one place the composer's indication was 176, which means 176 beats to the minute. He met Paul Dukas, the composer, in Paris and told him that much as he liked to follow the author's instructions, it was impossible to take the passage that fast, especially since it called for a number of accelerandi. Dukas agreed with Toscanini, and in a later edition the tempo mark was changed to a slower beat. When Toscanini saw the new edition, he began to mutter, "I can't play it that slow." In his own score, he has marked the tempo here as 168. In fact, in many places in this piece his tempo marks differ from the printed editions. He plays it the way he feels it. At one point the score marking is 126. Toscanini has scrawled the word *"Pourquoi?"* near the mark, and has changed it to 116.

Once he has fixed on a tempo he insists that it must be sustained. "Why must they speed up the tempo for a crescendo?" he once exclaimed about some of his colleagues. "Why must they slow it down for a diminuendo? Why can't they hold it?"

He holds his tempos. Officials connected with orchestras he has conducted have clocked him in certain standard symphonies, and the time he has taken to go through a composition has not varied by more than a second or two in performances years apart.

But holding the tempo firmly does not mean being as rigid as a metronome. There is ample opportunity for flexibility within the measure. Here Toscanini functions with the subtlety of an artist. He has a way of letting air into the spaces between notes. He uses rubato, which is a shortening of one note in a bar to lengthen another within the measure, without loss of the fundamental rhythm or tempo. A sensitive young virtuoso, listening to Toscanini conduct the "Eroica," said, "There is no rigidity within the measure, but the rhythm is steady, like a great heartbeat."

When he was young as a conductor, it was complained of Toscanini that he held the tempo and rhythm of the music firmly to its course and that it had the mechanical exactitude of a metronome. Possibly the charge was sometimes justified. Before you can achieve flexibility you must have accuracy, and in the opera houses of Italy when he was a new conductor the habits of singers and orchestral players were slovenly. The prima donna ruled the roost, and any liberties she might take to show off were rarely opposed. From the start Toscanini fought against these violations of the composer's intentions. Perhaps in his struggle for precision he was willing to overlook nuance. But in time he demanded both and would not compromise for less. Precision was the foundation on which nuance must be built.

In later years when he has conducted an orchestra that has understood his every move and that could be depended upon to follow him, he has made subtle changes of expression in the midst of a performance that have surprised even the most perceptive musicians. Playing Schubert's "Unfinished" Symphony recently, he made little alterations that had not been intimated in rehearsal or previous performance. In the heat of the performance, he relied on his feeling and instinct. As one of the men said afterward, "The old man would be hard put to explain the changes himself."

Gifted musicians who have given years of study to the question of tempo have listened to performances Toscanini has conducted and have declared that here at last was the right approach. Ernest Bloch, the composer, spent two years analyzing the "Eroica," reaching to its core, and then he listened to countless performances led by many conductors. When he heard a performance directed by Toscanini, he wrote the maestro that this was the first time he had found a conductor who understood the symphony. Carlos Chavez, a conductor and composer, once observed that only Toscanini grasped fully the proper tempo procedure in Beethoven.

Once he fixes on the tempo, Toscanini proceeds to other matters. He seeks for the proper balance of instruments. All harmonies and counterpoints are clearly filled in so that no strand of tone is lacking its proper and defined place in the fabric. The notes of a chord, though they are sounded by instruments of different choirs, are freighted so sensitively that they emerge like perfect mates. His ear can pick out unerringly the voice that needs to be softened or strengthened even in a vast tumult of sound.

His aim is everlastingly to make each detail of the music achieve its just value, and to have every note sound. Just before a concert in Austin, Texas, he asked the third and fourth horns to play a phrase of Rossini's *William Tell* Overture an octave lower, and after the performance he beamed. "I heard those notes tonight," he said. For a passage in *La Traviata*, he had the second violins doubling the first violins and he divided the violas so that half of them would play the music allotted to the second violins while the remainder did their own music. He could have asked the first violins to play more strongly, but evidently he felt that this might rob their tone of some of its delicacy. The solution he chose gave him the balance and tone quality he wanted.

Robert Shaw, who was preparing the chorus for a Toscanini performance of Beethoven's Ninth, once proposed hesitantly that he would like to rearrange the voice distribution for a contrapuntal passage, assigning some of the tenors to the soprano part and some of the baritones to the tenor part. "Will it make the music sound?" Toscanini wanted to know. "I think so," Shaw replied. "Good. Anything that makes the music sound is good," Toscanini said.

A single brick in a great symphonic edifice can give Toscanini endless concern. For years he fretted about a measure in the final pages of the last movement, Bars No. 434 and No. 438, of Brahms' First Symphony, and one evening a few minutes before concert time he hit upon an idea. It was a measure in which the violas had one long note followed by three short ones. The other instruments save the timpani in that measure were through with their share of the measure while the violas went on with the last two short notes. Toscanini decided that those two notes should be eliminated. When he made his decision the scores were on the stands and the musicians were in their seats on the stage. Nevertheless he sent out Dolan, the librarian, to mark the change. Before Dolan could get through with all the parts, Toscanini came out to start the concert, and the poor librarian had to crouch behind a couple of players, marooned on the stage until the symphony was finished.

Attention to trifling details is what in sum gives special character to Toscanini-led performances. They are not trivia to him because he has the capacity to fit them into the overall design of the music. Of this he does not lose sight, come what may. If he plays a piece at all, he respects it and its composer. He conducted the *première* of a work by Samuel Barber, then a rising young composer. Toscanini decided that a note sounded by a solo trumpet did not make its effect and he wished to add another trumpet. Since the composer was alive and near by, he tried to reach him for approval of the slight change. Unable to get hold of Barber, he made the change, anyhow. But after the concert when the young composer came backstage to express his gratitude, Toscanini apologized to him for presuming to add the trumpet without consulting him.

The grand conception and the details are both worked out in Toscanini's private studies, and alterations come as a result of experience and his own maturity. Relentless study and hard work are some of the ingredients that have gone into the final product of the performance. But let us not underestimate the intangible things that each man brings to an elusive art like music. Work and study are not enough; other men are capable of devotion and energy. The qualities that have helped make Toscanini what he has been are his taste and imagination. These have not remained static. They were developed and shaped by the years and events of his life, but, at bottom, they were there from the start, waiting to be shaped.

In that sense, of course, a musician is born, and Toscanini was unmistakably born to be a musician. Since he had the gift of projecting the fruit of his work, study, taste, and imagination to other men and women, he was obviously destined to be a conductor. His baton technique does not have the neatness of other conductors; it was not worked out by rote in a school for conductors. But musicians who have played with him will tell you that it is clear, expressive, and very much to the point. What he does on the podium, some of the men say, is almost intuitive, a direct communication to the players of how music must move and take form. There is no waste motion, no gesture for effect, certainly not the slightest playing to the gallery. Every move is functional—the hands, fingers, arms, eyes, mouth, and body are all involved in the task.

He carries the performers with him, and they have often felt that he has lifted them to new heights. Samuel Antek, an intelligent and perceptive violinist in the N.B.C. Symphony, put it admirably in a piece he wrote for the *Saturday Review of Literature* some time ago.

"Playing with him," he wrote, "makes you particularly proud of being a musician; it brings a special dignity and nobility to your work. You are not only a skillful violinist, flutist, or trumpeter. You feel yourself an artist, an integral part of the performance. It is this uncanny ability, the talent he has for making musicians unlock the secret door of their personal emotions, the hidden reservoirs of their resourcefulness and ability, that is, in my experience, one of his exceptional characteristics. There is no question that every musician who plays with Toscanini gives up some special part of himself *only* to the Old Man."

After conducting for decades Toscanini is sure of himself and his ability, and yet he takes no performance for granted. Each concert is like a debut. He is always nervous and tense before the start. His son Walter, who is in the habit of embracing him and kissing him on the cheek before he goes on stage, says that he can always feel his father's muscles quivering.

Toscanini's mind and heart are immersed in the music as a performance approaches. I remember the sight of him in New Orleans recently a few minutes before concert time. He had not put on his dress coat yet, but, too tense to sit in his dressing room, he walked up and down in a corridor, a little, gray-haired man in white tie, white vest, dress trousers, and pumps. People passed him, and he did not seem to see them. His head was bent, his hands behind his back. Only Brahms was on his mind. I remember another occasion when a recording he had just made was being played back to him in Studio 8H. Some of the men of the orchestra were seated on the stage; others were lolling on chairs where the audience normally sits. Many were chatting. Toscanini was oblivious to movement and voices around him. As the music came forth from the loud-speaker, he stood on the podium in his black alpaca rehearsal jacket, waving his baton, giving cues, still hearing the ideal version in his head and shaping the sounds that emerged from the record.

His absorption in any performance is so intense that applause can be like a shocking interruption. In Italy once, before going on to conduct *Pelléas et Mélisande,* he spent all day soaking himself in the score. As he walked out into the pit, he was at one with the world of Debussy. There was a burst of applause, and he felt as though a spell had been snapped. He was annoyed and disturbed. He could not will himself back into the mood. He conducted mechanically, he recalled later, for a couple of acts; he did not feel that he was there at all.

Applause has always disturbed him. After a recent performance of the "Eroica," the audience thundered its approval, and he kept coming back for bows, feeling more uncomfortable with each return to the stage. Later he said exasperatedly, "What did they want me to do?" A friend replied, "What did you do when you were moved by a performance?" Toscanini did not unbend. "At nineteen," he said, "I heard *Lohengrin* and I was moved, but I didn't applaud; I cried."

One day the singers who had appeared with him in an opera performance with the N.B.C. Symphony began to applaud as he came out on the stage for a curtain call. He caught sight of them, and glared. When he went off the stage, he would not return, though the audience shouted and pounded its hands. "Shame on them!" he muttered. "Applauding me, too!"

His reaction to applause is not, however, a sign that he holds the public in contempt. Far from it; he respects its judgments. Talking about first reactions to new works, he defends the public taste, insisting that it has always been right. He makes a careful distinction between the ordinary listeners and the experts and critics who might come to a new work with preconceived notions. He points out that where enduring operas and symphonies have failed with the public at the start the cause has been poor performances or miscalculation on the part of the composer. "Take *Madame Butterfly*," he says. "It was a fiasco on opening night. But was the public wrong? No, it was Puccini who was wrong."

He thinks of the public in making his symphonic programs, remembering that in a gathering of thousands tastes might differ. He seeks to balance the towering masterpieces of the repertory, from which he draws the profoundest personal satisfaction, with smaller works of perhaps wider appeal. When he went on tour with the N.B.C. Symphony he arranged long programs, feeling that people who went to great expense for one concert were entitled to a full evening of music. His friends told him that his programs were too long, but he did not bother to argue.

He is aware of the regard innumerable strangers have for him, and he is touched by it. When a cigar salesman passing through a small town in California saw that the special Toscanini train was standing in the station and came down to leave a gift of cigars for the maestro, Toscanini, who does not smoke, was touched. When he heard that a man in Dallas had closed his office and had followed him to California, calling it his "Toscanini vacation," the maestro was moved. He may forget listeners in his concern with the music in the course of a performance, but he does not pretend that he is indifferent to their affection for him.

He remembers faces in the audience, a child, a handsome woman, an attentive old man. His memory seems to retain everything, not only audiences but halls, orchestras he has heard, history, literature. One day he happened to be talking about acoustics and he rattled off some of the theaters of the world that had pleased him, recalling their physical and acoustical properties in detail. When he entered the Lyric Theater in Baltimore for a rehearsal recently, someone offered to show him the way to his dressing room. "Never mind," he said, "I know the way. I conducted here as long ago as 1911. It was *Gioconda*." With a smile, he added, "And Taft was President."

The Boston Symphony entered into the conversation one evening, and he proceeded to name all its conductors since the founding of the orchestra in 1880—and in the correct order of their appearance.

On May 5, 1950, he conducted the "Eroica" in Pasadena, and observed to a friend that it was a good day to play the symphony since it was the anniversary of Napoleon's death. "How do you know?" his friend asked. Toscanini's glance seemed to say that any schoolboy should know that, and then he proceeded to quote from a recent book on Napoleon.

The maestro's chauffeur, who listened regularly to a quiz program on an Italian-language station in New York, reported to him that a question that had been baffling people for days concerned the date of the *première* of an opera in Italy and the people who had been in the cast. As soon as Toscanini heard that the opera was *Cristoforo Colombo,* he placed the *première* in 1892 in Genoa and gave the names of all the singers. He remembered it accurately, too.

The maestro was chatting about Rossini one day and mentioned *La Cenerentola,* an opera that is seldom produced. To illustrate a point he began to sing a passage from the opera— words and music. Even his son Walter was surprised. "How did you know that?" he asked. "Did you ever conduct it?" Toscanini shook his head. "Only the Overture," he said, "but I have read the score."

Very probably he had read it ages ago. Talking one day about Mendelssohn's "Songs Without Words," a group of piano pieces, he sat down at the piano and played many of them through. It turned out he had not looked at the music since his student days forty years before.

The man's memory for music has come to be taken almost for granted by his friends and associates. They know how thoroughly his blood stream and very nerve ends are soaked in the stuff. Music, in essence, is his life. To him it seems the most natural thing in the world to remember it all. And yet even those who take his formidable, encyclopedic knowledge and memory in stride may be left breathless at times.

He was preparing the Overture to Boito's *Mefistofele* for performance with the N.B.C. Symphony and declared that he wanted to incorporate the off-stage band called for in the original score but rarely used. But the available scores did not include the off-stage band's music, and the parts could not be obtained. The evening before rehearsals he sat down and wrote out the missing music from memory in his bold hand, using his favorite red ink. The off-stage band included flügel-horns and other uncommon instruments with their strange staff notations, and he scored them in modern notation, making the necessary transpositions as he went along. Copyists prepared the parts by working all night, and at rehearsal time in the afternoon the extra players had not only been rounded up but had had time to familiarize themselves with their music.

On another occasion Toscanini thought that he would like to have the string section of the N.B.C. Symphony play the slow movement of Joachim Raff's Quartet No. 5. Now, the music of Raff, which had a vogue in the latter part of the nine-teenth century, is rarely played these days; a symphonic piece shows up on a program once in a long while but the chamber music almost never. New York was scoured for a copy of the quartet, but it could not be found. Toscanini, who had prob-ably not played the music since his student days and very likely had not seen a copy of the score for decades, wrote out the entire slow movement from memory, complete with mark-ings. As things turned out, he did not conduct the music, but his manuscript in its bold red writing was filed away in the N.B.C. music library. Some months later Edwin Bachmann, leader of the N.B.C. Symphony's second-violin section, who makes a hobby of rare editions, dug up a copy of the Raff score. Toscanini's version of the slow movement was checked; it had only one error in it.

Orchestral players have found that Toscanini will close his eyes and sing accurately bar after bar of an inner voice or of background harmonies played by supporting instruments like a second clarinet or a third horn. He remembers accompanying figures separately and in their entirety. Once a troubled trombone player approached him just before an opera performance and said that one of the low notes on his instrument would not sound. There was no time to get the trombone repaired or to borrow another. "What shall I do, Maestro?" the player said nervously. Toscanini shut his eyes and seemed lost in deep thought. Then his eyes flashed open, and he smiled. "Don't worry," he said. "That note is not in tonight's opera."

23

Rehearsals

THE REHEARSAL is the place where the conductor translates his knowledge, taste, and perception into the shape the performance will take. In the heat of the performance there may be slight changes and an intensification of feeling, but essentially what the public hears is what the conductor has hewed out in the practice sessions. And in the privacy of the rehearsal chamber it is easiest to measure the musicianship of the conductor as well as his powers of leadership and communication.

"Rehearsals have meaning," Arturo Toscanini said quietly one day. His rehearsals, even to those who have made music under his direction for years, are endlessly exciting and exacting experiences, and to the visitor lucky enough to gain admittance they are a revelation. Whenever and wherever he has worked, the story has been the same. For more than sixty years his rehearsals have been an advanced seminar, a battleground, and a place of consecrated service to music. Even more than the performances in opera house and concert hall, the rehearsals have given rise to the tales that have helped to create the legend of Arturo Toscanini. I have talked to hundreds of men and women who have rehearsed under Toscanini, and there has not been one without some vivid memory, some scar, or some flash of illumination to recall.

Yes, rehearsals have meaning, and if they have failed of this requirement, Toscanini has been unaccountable for his behavior. And he has meant the rehearsals of other conductors,

too. If he happens to walk in on a rehearsal without meaning,
he acts with ruthless incivility. He visited the Scala some years
ago and looked in on a rehearsal of *Tosca* under the direction
of a young conductor. He felt that the young man was beating
time flabbily. He noticed that the singers and orchestra were
being told nothing, though they needed guidance. He could
not restrain himself. He marched up to the young conductor
and began to make suggestions. The young man listened attentively and gratefully. "But it was futile," Toscanini recalled. "The performance turned out a poor thing."

Toscanini has always known the value of a rehearsal. The
basic reason has been that he has always known in advance
how he has wanted a piece of music to go. When he enters
the rehearsal hall, he is thoroughly prepared. There is no uncertainty or improvisation in his approach. No one can predict
how he will react if things do not go as he wishes them to go,
but the explosions do not stem from any lack of preparation
or prevision on his part.

Where he has worked with a group of musicians before and
knows their abilities, he comes to rehearsal expecting that
they have taken as much trouble to prepare themselves as he
has. If a new work is to be rehearsed, he assumes that the
performers have studied their parts at home. If it is an old,
familiar piece, he hopes that they have done some private
preparation. Often he gives his collaborators credit for being
as conscientious as he is, and he erupts in shocked outrage
when it becomes clear that they have been no such thing.

Musicians of several generations who have worked with
him agree that he is a master psychologist. They wonder
whether the temper tantrums that have shaken him and his
rehearsals have not often been turned on deliberately. They
admit that once he gets steam up, his rages may follow an unpredictable course, but they feel that in many cases Toscanini's outbursts are nicely calculated to arouse the performers

to the pitch of intensity and concentration he wants all rehearsals to have.

Players have noticed that when an orchestra is lackadaisical
he worries it like a tenacious dog with a bone. He causes the
men to repeat a single measure, remonstrating each time at
shortcomings. This goes on until he senses that the men are
keyed up. They may be resentful, too, but in rehearsal he
cares only how the music sounds. He does not hesitate to
bring musicians to the cracking point, but the moment he
sees and hears them digging in with spirit, he relents. Then he
is capable of going through a rehearsal without pausing once
for correction or comment.

Toscanini rehearses, of course, only for results. He will stop
a rehearsal long before its scheduled end and dismiss the men
because he is satisfied. "There is no need to rehearse," he said
one day, "when the orchestra knows the music." He will also
rehearse for hours beyond the fixed close, oblivious of time,
other commitments, extra charges. Everything depends on
how the rehearsal has gone. When he returned as a guest
leader of the New York Philharmonic-Symphony in 1942, he
told the men that they would have to go through a Brahms
symphony twice, since they were probably rusty. He would
have gone through the symphony three or four times if he
had thought it necessary, but he was also goading the players
in advance. They rose to the challenge, and after they had
gone through the symphony once, he smiled, said, "Not bad,"
and went on to another composition.

Toscanini has even been satisfied without any rehearsal at
all under his personal direction. Robert Shaw prepared his
Collegiate Chorale for a performance of Beethoven's Ninth
with the maestro, and Toscanini arrived one evening after the
chorus had been rehearsing for six hours under Shaw's direction. Presumably Toscanini was to take over the rehearsal.
"You go ahead, Maestro," the old man said to his young col-

league. Shaw stood up before the chorus and gave the signal to start. Toscanini slowly walked up and down the room behind him, and Shaw could see that the eyes of his singers followed the old man's steps back and forth as though they were watching an exchange of shots on a tennis court. At a crucial change in tempo, Shaw could see Toscanini pause and listen intently. When Shaw finished, Toscanini patted him on the back and prepared to leave. "Aren't you going to conduct?" Shaw asked. Toscanini shook his head. "But they are used to my conducting," Shaw protested. "Don't you want them to familiarize themselves with yours?" Toscanini shook his head again. "They will know what to do," he said.

The maestro is rarely satisfied that easily. Often he enters a rehearsal expecting the worst. If the piece in hand is something that did not go to his satisfaction the previous time, he is primed for trouble. He may say to the musicians, "The last time we did this work you were not good, and I was not good." Or if it is something the men may take as a matter of course, he will be doubly alert for the slightest complacency. He quickly stops them and shouts, "You think this is easy. You have played it too much."

The recurrent mistakes in the oft-repeated compositions drive him frantic. They haunt him even when he is not rehearsing with the players. There is a story of something that happened on tour with the New York Philharmonic that sheds a bright light on the way his mind works. During a short train hop, he was seated in a corner of a parlor car going over a score he was to conduct that night. The men could watch him waving his arms, beating time and giving cues to an invisible orchestra. At one point he gave a signal straight ahead of him —obviously to the wind section—and suddenly shouted, "No! No!"

A rehearsal is all business for Toscanini. The performers must be in their places at the appointed hour, all tuned up and ready to go, and he reaches the podium on the dot. He mentions the work he wishes to start with, raises his baton, and proceeds. Unlike some other conductors, he does not exchange pleasantries; these are reserved for off-hours. Nor does he deliver a long dissertation on life or art or the piece about to be played; he hates "talking" conductors.

If something goes awry, he tries to illustrate the right tempo, phrasing, or expression in a musical way, either by his gestures or by singing the passage. His hoarse, cracked voice breaks out into song, and it is strangely effective in telling players or singers exactly what he means despite the fact that its range is limited and its quality negligible. He breaks into illustrative song without even stopping the flow of the rehearsal, letting his raucous tones do the correcting as the music goes on. Or he stops the music, and sings a snatch of it. Once during an opera rehearsal he stopped the singers and went through a whole scene with the orchestra, singing every part and every word and note himself.

When singing and gestures do not turn the trick, then he breaks out into spoken comment. His remarks are brief and ejaculatory as a rule. They may pierce through the sound of the music or they may bring the music to a halt. They may be pleading, sympathetic, hurt, sorrowful, angry, abusive, piquant, funny, tortured, and apocalyptically outraged. They are always directed at the point in question; their purpose is always musical. And yet, if you add them up, they are a revelation of the breadth of his frame of reference, of his familiarity not only with music but with all the concerns of the minds and hearts of human beings. He has this vast background and store of knowledge at his finger tips and tongue's end. He does not prepare words or illustrative action in advance. He does the graphic thing almost by instinct.

Remo Bolognini, a violinist, who has played under Toscanini in the New York Philharmonic and the N.B.C. Symphony for two decades, formed the habit of jotting down the maestro's comments and instructions. He accumulated thousands of them, and they were amazingly varied and at the same time amazingly consistent in musical point of view. Toscanini might have noticed that Bolognini was always making notes, but he did not mind. It probably pleased him that the violinist was so attentive.

Let us look at a sampling of the maestro's rehearsal adjurations, culled from many sources and covering all sorts and conditions of performers and performances.

Instead of technical directions, he may say, "Be happy," "Understand," "Enjoy," "Realize this sorrow, this anxiety, this fever." To a singer, "Sing like an angel," or "Please let your face express that you feel this music. That will bring out the words and music, too." To the B.B.C. Symphony during the "Preislied" section of the *Meistersinger* Prelude, he said, "First violins, play *sotto voce*, but with intense feeling, as if you said"—and here his voice became a hoarse whisper—" 'I love you, I love you'—but whispered, under your breath."

Still in a reasonable, calm mood, he may say:

"I do not know who taught me, but I have always remembered that in pianissimo each player must not hear himself, but in fortissimo each player must hear the other players."

Or: "Each note must come out separately yet knitted to the next. The air must circulate between them. Put a dot over and a round pause between each note and then let it go."

Or: "The contrabasses must not exaggerate. There is crescendo, yes, but if you color immediately there is nothing left to grow. Piano, piano. There is time. There is time."

Or: "This does not go. This does not go. Make it legato as much as you wish, but each phrase must have its cesura which distinguishes it from the next. Surely you have never heard a person who arrives at the end of a sentence without taking a breath. These are things one cannot write in music. They must be understood of themselves."

Or—and this or an equivalent appeal has ever been on his lips: "Sing, please sing. *Cantando, sempre cantando.* You must sing every note, even through your rests. Music, unless you sing, is nothing."

All is well if the rehearsing musicians show good will, concentration, and energy. But let there be some sign of stupidity or indifference, and the conductor's gorge begins to rise, his language turns more colorful, and his words break off in the middle of sentences and phrases.

"Look at me! Look me!" he exhorts. "Sing, make it sing! Piano! Piano!" The voice becomes loud and piercing. "PIANO!"

He could not get a soft effect once and suddenly he shouted thunderously, "*Tranquillo* here!"

Another time the tempo went wrong. "My tempo," he screamed, "not yours!"

Or the rhythm: "*Ritmo! Ritmo!* Take care! Take CARE! Don't sleep. Wake up. Is morning."

Or the volume: "Roar! Roar!," singing at the top of his voice during a passage in *Die Götterdämmerung*. "Roar like a lion!" And another time to the trumpets: "This must sound far away, but not too far—Brooklyn."

Perhaps he knew that this would get a laugh. It did, and it relieved the tension. He does not mind laughter if his patience is not yet strained to the breaking point, and the musicians know when it is safe or dangerous to laugh.

Comments may be specifically about the music:

Of "La Mer": "Fortissimo—the waves are rough!"

Of Strauss's "Don Juan," when it did not have enough fire: "Here, here!," pointing to his viscera. "This is love, love!"

Of French music: "Here you caress, not assault!"

Of German music: "Assault, not caress. Look at how much rhythm I have in me. Maybe one of my ancestors was a German!"

Of "Iberia," to the wind players: "I understand your discomfort in that passage. I have always been uncomfortable in it."

Of a Rossini overture: "This is an Italian piano, not Beethoven piano. Sing, sing! Sing naturally, without accent!"

Of a Beethoven symphony: "Fortissimo! It is not I who wants it, but Beethoven!"

There was a passage in which he wanted the violins to play together near the bottoms of their bows but could not get the effect he wanted. In Italian he said, "I wish I had the restraining gear they use to train trotters at the race track. Then I would keep you all tied down and confined."

A little later he burst out: "You play correctly. Maybe it's better you play not so correctly. Be freer!"

Points are made by suggestion and implication:

"You play all music as if it were written by Wagner."

Or: "All orchestras claim to be the first orchestras in the world. I would like to conduct for a change the second orchestra of the world."

Or: "This music is played badly all over the world—in London, in Paris, in Berlin, in Milan. Also here. Yes, also here."

He turns gently sarcastic. To an American orchestra rehearsing an American score, he said, "This is not Italian music; this is not German music. This is American music."

An accent in a symphony did not get proper stress. "I think there is an accent here," and he shrugged with an air of defeated indifference. "But I am only Toscanini, and I am probably wrong." Then there was a roar. "Let us see!" The score was brought out, he examined it, holding it close to his face, and he seemed to be flabbergasted. "Imagine, my dears, I am right. The composer has written an accent here!"

Another time his voice became appealing: "I know it is difficult to be intelligent—but try, please try!"

Suddenly he loses control of himself. He begins to shout epithets in a fine mélange of languages and extensive vocabulary. He cries out, *"Pagliacci!" "Imbecilli!" "Vergogna! Shame!"*

To an oboe player: "I could kill you, because you kill me!"

To a violinist of Italian extraction: "I cannot believe you are an Italian."

To the contrabasses: "Letter 'N,' like Napoleon. If he were a contrabass, he'd be an imbecile, too!"

To the whole orchestra: "Damnation on Guido d'Arezzo for his invention of notation!"

Or: "After I die, I shall return to earth as a gatekeeper of a bordello and I won't let any of you—not a one of you—enter!"

Or, at the age of eighty to men half his age: "You play like a bunch of old men! Shame on you!"

Singers have received a rough going-over. To a young baritone singing Germont in *La Traviata* he once said, "Ever been a father?" The young man said he hadn't. "It sounds it," Toscanini said. "You don't sing as if you understood what a father would feel."

Another unfortunate baritone, asked to repeat a passage at the end of a long rehearsal, murmured something about being tired. Toscanini went red in the face and began to scream wildly. "I just want to say—" the baritone began an explanation. "Don't speak!" Toscanini shouted. "Don't say anything! If you want speaking, I'll fill the hall with thunder! Look at me." He tugged at his perspiration-drenched clothes. "I'm tired, too."

A well-upholstered soprano could not get anything straight. He looked at her commiseratingly and said, "If you had as much here," pointing to her head, "as you have there," pointing to her full bosom, "you'd be a great artist."

If his breaking point is reached, he barges out of rehearsals, breaking batons, tearing scores, hurling watches as he goes. Sometimes he returns; sometimes he does not. Once in Studio 8H he decided to leave the rehearsal by going past the men straight to the back of the stage, glaring at them as he went. When he reached the rear he tried a door and found it was locked. He turned to the right and tried another door; it was also locked. He walked to the left and pulled at a third door, and it did not budge. He let his hands fall to his sides, looked around with the air of an animal at bay, shrugged his shoulders, walked downstage again, picked up his baton, and resumed the rehearsal.

Two things are certain: no Toscanini rehearsal is ever dull and no two rehearsals are ever alike. He may blow a pleased kiss at a player for his handling of a solo passage, or he may make a gesture that he feels like cutting his throat. At eighty he stamped his feet and jumped up and down like a child in the midst of a tantrum. He will try delicate tactics like holding aloft a silk handkerchief and letting it fall to the ground; see, this is the kind of delicate pianissimo effect he wants.

Recurrently there is a phrase beginning with "I am seeking." It is hardly necessary for him to use this introductory phrase. Every one of his rehearsals is a quest for the last word in projecting the composer's thought. He does not fuss with obvious things. In rehearsal he gives musicians only the most important entrances and cues; in performance there are fewer. He wants the players to be alert.

"Put something! Put some blood in it!" That is his ever-present battle call, and his musical forces are stirred to fresh effort. His own blood is in every note, and his mind and muscles control the ebb and flow of tone with the discipline and power of a master sculptor. Out of these passionate, dedicated labors in rehearsal come performances that seek, in a never-ending search, the heart and spirit of the music.

24

It Is Mutual

THERE IS no harsher critic of a conductor than the musicians who work with him. The conductor, after all, is the musical boss, and it is an ancient and honorable practice to take pot shots at the boss when his back is turned. Orchestra players and singers who fancy themselves authorities in their own right do not, as a rule, examine the musicianship, character, and foibles of the conductor in an indulgent spirit. They dwell on his mistakes in judgment, they laugh at his pretensions, and they ape his mannerisms. No conductor is immune from searching, often malicious, analysis by the people he directs. If you listen to musicians in their private conversations, you will find that there are precious few conductors who emerge unflayed.

Toscanini has been one of these, especially when it has come to an evaluation of his stature as a musician. It would be futile to pretend that there have not been orchestral players, singers, choristers, chorus masters, stage directors, ballet dancers, scene designers, other conductors, and members of boards of directors who have found him to be God's angry little man and have loathed him for it. But rarely have they withheld their respect for him as an artist.

Toscanini has seared people's feelings; in the heat of making music with them he has been ruthless and cruel. A few who have felt themselves injured have carried the resentment through the years. But the great majority have felt that they have gained by the experience of working with him. Singers have said that they have not only learned roles more thoroughly than ever before under his tutelage but that they have come away with a new approach to their studies and with fresh inspiration. Orchestra players have felt that it has been a rare privilege to take part in performances of incomparable incandescence.

A member of the N.B.C. Symphony Orchestra said one day, "When the old man picks up the stick, there is a tremendous sense of excitement." Another player observed, "He makes us feel like playing till we drop." A third man said, "After playing 'La Mer' twenty times, there is a sense of discovery and freshness in preparing it the twenty-first time with him." A violinist who had turned down an offer to become concertmaster and associate conductor of another orchestra explained, "I wouldn't leave as long as the maestro is around. I learn something at every rehearsal." An emotional fellow said in all sincerity, "I would give my life for him."

There have been players in this orchestra and in others he has directed who have professed no such devotion. To be plain about it, they have hated Toscanini. They have said that his language in rehearsal is coarse and vulgar. They have felt that his relentless pounding made nervous wrecks of them and gave them ulcers. They would not, in their bitterness, even concede that his performances were superior to those of other conductors.

The position of these dissidents and nay-sayers is scarcely surprising. It has been inevitable that Toscanini has made enemies of colleagues whose abilities he has criticized. What has been more surprising is that there have been relatively few musicians who have clung to lasting resentments. Most of the men may complain about the maestro, but their fundamental feeling is affection and pride. They realize that when he curses them, he does so, as a rule, impersonally. Even when a musician has given proof after proof that he is not first class, Toscanini may not bring himself to have him fired. He struggles with him, yowls at him, abuses him savagely, but he may not take steps to deprive him of his job. There was one fellow in the N.B.C. Symphony whose playing was a constant source of anguish to Toscanini, but he kept him for ten years, and then the man left of his own accord. There were players in the New York Philharmonic who were growing old and should have been pensioned, but Toscanini could not bring himself to force their retirement. But even in this respect he has not been consistent; his only consistency is his devotion to the music. Once in a European capital, meeting an orchestra for the first time, he went through the first two movements of the "Eroica" without a word. During the Scherzo there was a violent explosion. He stormed off the stage and would not return until half a dozen replacements had been made in the orchestra.

Yes, he can be savage. Those who have felt his wrath in rehearsal know it well. Yet one man who had played with Toscanini in the Scala orchestra and then joined him in the N.B.C. Symphony said, "My head is bloody from some of the things he has said to me over the years, but I know in my heart that he is a good man."

Away from rehearsals and performances, most of his associates have found him a delightful and amiable man. They have considered it a privilege to chat with him, to get his ideas on musical matters, and to trade gossip with him. In later years they have complained that he was being kept away from them. And they have been right. There have been officious people who, in their zeal to protect Toscanini from all disturbances, have thought that he should not be bothered even by the men who play with him.

On the trip to South America in 1940, Toscanini was seated on the deck and saw a stranger in a knot of musicians. "Who is he?" he asked a neighbor, and he was told, "Our librarian." He sent for the man, and for several hours held an animated conversation with him. An N.B.C. official was furious with the librarian. "What right has he," the official demanded, "to talk to the maestro?"

This official did not realize that Toscanini was fond of being with his musical associates. They were his boys, and he was proud of them. When the N.B.C. Symphony had a guest conductor whom Toscanini regarded as a poor musician, he bellowed, "It is an insult to the men to put a conductor like that before them. There are dozens of men in the orchestra," and he proceeded to name them, "who know more about music than that imbecile."

He has been helpful and encouraging to the men who have had aspirations to become conductors. He looked upon Alfred Wallenstein, who was his first cellist with the New York Philharmonic, as his friend and protégé long after the younger man had established himself as a conductor in his own right. When he was rehearsing the Philharmonic once, Toscanini wanted to hear a passage from the back of the hall and called for a volunteer to take the baton. A number of the men had had conducting experience, but they were loath to conduct in the maestro's presence. Toscanini handed the stick to Leon Barzin, first viola player, and said, "Here, Leon, you do it. I'm sure you can." Barzin took the baton and went through the passage capably. When Toscanini returned to the podium, he patted Barzin on the back and said, "You are going to be a conductor." And when Barzin left the orchestra to become a conductor, Toscanini carefully followed his career.

Milton Katims, first-desk violinist with the N.B.C. Symphony, is another man whom Toscanini has encouraged to become a conductor, and he was instrumental in getting him a chance to lead the N.B.C. Symphony. He invited the young musician to call on him for advice, and Katims visited the maestro at his home in Riverdale. The first time Katims went his object was to discuss his initial program, and he planned to stay a short while. But Toscanini enjoyed talking music with him. His conversation was punctuated by running to his shelves to pull out scores and books for exact quotation of relevant comments. At one point Katims alluded to the lightness and transparency of Mendelssohn's orchestrations. Toscanini got out a book of letters by Mendelssohn and read, with amused relish, a passage in which the composer said that he felt like washing his hands after looking at the richly orchestrated pages of a Berlioz score. For two hours Toscanini chatted with Katims, and the latter rose nervously to leave. "Stay," said the maestro, "I have nothing to do." He invited him down for tea. He continued his lively talk, and he was still holding forth on music to his young friend when he escorted him to the door.

During the 1950 tour across the United States, Toscanini, then eighty-three, was sheltered from intrusion because it was felt that his energies needed to be husbanded. From time to time, however, he would leave his private car to go down the length of the long train for visits with his players. Nearly every musician had a camera, and each one wanted his own shots of the old man. Whenever there was a stop en route and Toscanini would get out to stroll down the platform, they had their cameras focused on him. Though he disliked being photographed, he did not object to their endless shooting of him. At one fairly long stop these amateur photographers had a field day. Toscanini noticed that Carleton Cooley, the first violist, whom he knew to be a camera fan, had not been in the group taking shots. He sent for Cooley and said, "Where were you? You've been wanting pictures of me." Cooley regretted he had missed the chance. "Well, take them now," said Toscanini. As Cooley got out his camera and began to prepare it, the maestro put on his dark blue beret which he had been wearing when the others had made pictures of him. "Now," he said, smiling, "you will be equal with the others."

After the Detroit concert, while the special train was on its way to Cleveland, the men invited the maestro to be their guest at supper. Obviously he could not sit at the same table with more than a hundred men. But he wanted to spend a little time with each. He was seated at a table for four, and the men took turns sitting and chatting with him. For hours they came and went in relays of three, and he kept on talking with a vivacity that belied the fact that he had just conducted a strenuous concert or that he was eighty-three.

On the tour to South America there was an overnight jump on a train that had few sleeping accommodations. Toscanini was provided with a compartment, but most of the men were obliged to sit up all night in coach chairs. The maestro abandoned his compartment and spent the night in the coaches, sitting up with his men.

He can put his players at ease in emergencies. Some of the trunks did not arrive at the hall in time for the first concert in Rio de Janeiro, and Karl Glassman, timpanist of the N.B.C. Symphony, found that he would have to wear a green suit that night. Troubled about going on the stage without a full-dress suit, he went to Toscanini with his problem. "Don't worry," the maestro said. "It isn't the suit that plays, it's Glassman."

He also shares their sorrows. Just before the return from South America, one of the viola players was killed in an automobile accident in Rio. The maestro did not notice the man's absence in the final concert, and the musicians conspired to keep the news of the tragedy from him until the last days of the home voyage. When Toscanini heard about it, he burst into tears and would not come out of his suite. He heard later that the men had contributed twenty dollars each to raise a widow's mite, since they knew the dead man's insurance would have to go for payment of a recently purchased house, and he contributed a thousand dollars to the fund.

Toscanini can be considerate of his men even where music is concerned. Winthrop Sergeant, who once played the fiddle in the New York Philharmonic under him, told this story some years ago in an article in *Life:*

A few years ago Wagner's *Tannhäuser* "Bacchanale" was to be played in Carnegie Hall. Toward the end of the operatic excerpt, in its concert version, there is a passage where four solo violins delicately echo the music of the Venusberg maidens. The passage is an exposed and ticklish one, and is usually assigned to the concertmaster and his assistants of the first two desks of violins. Toscanini, with the idea of intensifying the off-stage effect of this passage (which in the opera is sung by a chorus in the wings), directed that it should be played by the *last* two desks of the first violins. Now, violins in the rear ranks of a section, however competent they may be, are not used to playing solo passages, and are likely to shudder with apprehension at such a prospect. But Toscanini was determined to have it so, and so it was. Rehearsals turned out to be fairly satisfactory. At the performance, however, everyone was apprehensive. The chaotic, orgiastic surge of the music unwound itself in the usual manner and subsided at the end into its customary, and on this occasion somewhat frightening, calm. The place for the entrance of the four lone violinists finally arrived. The violinists, jittery with fright, launched into their solos like reluctant waders in an ice-cold brook. Their bows began to wobble and stagger down their strings. Before a note had passed it was obvious that the whole thing was likely to end in a catastrophe. At this point Toscanini stopped conducting altogether, and, pulling out his handkerchief, started coughing violently into it. The effect was instantaneous. Seeing the "old man" himself in difficulties, the four violinists suddenly realized that it was up to them to save the show on their own heroic initiative. All trace of nervousness immediately disappeared in the face of the overwhelming emergency. Their performance was magnificent. Many of the men thought the coughing fit was genuine. But, by a strange coincidence, similar coughing fits had a way of cropping up in similar emergencies. The foxy old maestro had probably used the recipe on many a jittery soprano during his long years in the opera house.

Toscanini can be as proud of a man for playing one note properly as if the fellow had gone through a difficult concerto. One evening after a recent concert he kept reiterating his delight at the accomplishment of his tuba player. "In one of the chords of the *Meistersinger* Prelude," he told all his friends, "I heard, for the first time, the low F of the tuba." And even when he does not hear a note, he is inclined to give the players the benefit of the doubt if he knows that they are capable. After a concert in Houston, he was annoyed because he had not heard the French horns in a passage of Tchaikovsky's "Romeo and Juliet." He reflected on it for a while and said, "They are good boys; they probably played it. It must have been the peculiar acoustics of that hall."

He decided once to rearrange the scoring for the cellos of the opening passage of the *William Tell* Overture, and his changed scoring imposed new responsibilities on each member of the section. Before a rehearsal one day, Frank Miller, the first cellist, assembled his section and led it through a separate practice period. The maestro walked out on the stage and stood to one side, his hands behind his back, watching and listening attentively. A pleased smile played around the corners of his mouth. It was not only the way the passage sounded that gratified him but the *esprit de corps* of his players.

In pauses during rehearsals Toscanini often remains on his feet on the podium, discussing fine points in a score with players who congregate around him. He even exchanges banter with them. One day, when he was with the New York Philharmonic, the men were teasing a colleague who was reputed to be very strong physically. Toscanini turned to him and said, "Let's see how strong you are." The challenged musician approached the maestro and picked him high off the ground and held him aloft, while the orchestra cheered and the maestro chuckled.

Remo Bolognini's friends in the N.B.C. Symphony know

that he is an amateur wrestler of some talent and when they told Toscanini the maestro was enchanted. He is fond of watching wrestling on television, and on different occasions Bolognini has brought Primo Carnera and Antonino Rocca, a couple of the most distinguished practitioners of the sport, to the maestro's dressing room. And the maestro has talked wrestling with them, not music.

Toscanini enjoys hugely the antics of some of his boys away from the stage. During the recent American tour, Toscanini sat one day in the upper section of a vista-dome car. The train stopped in a Nebraska town and workmen set up ladders and began to clean the windows of the car. Bolognini clambered up one of the ladders with a pail and brush in hand and began to polish the window near the maestro. Toscanini pointed a finger at him and laughed. "Look at him," he said, "*il lottatore*, the wrestler."

The men always remember the maestro's birthday, and even though he forbade celebrations after he was eighty, they have invariably chipped in and sent him a gift. Once, when he was not conducting, they called him by phone and played and sang "Happy Birthday" to him. Another time they made a recording of the greeting for him. They also remember him at Christmas time. He, too, thinks of them. For Christmas of 1949 he sent each man of the N.B.C. Symphony a copy of a book he had enjoyed reading, Adam Carse's *The Orchestra from Beethoven to Berlioz*. After the recent American tour, he took the trouble to autograph more than a hundred photographs of himself on a ski-tow chair in Sun Valley, writing in red ink the name of each recipient on each picture and the inscription, "In sweet remembrance of our unforgettable tour, Arturo Toscanini."

He seldom forgets old comrades-at-arms. If you mention a singer who sang with him four or five decades ago, he will describe the person's voice, bearing, and handling of roles with the particularity of one who has not forgotten a detail. And if it is a musician he respected, there is an added warmth in his voice.

In New Orleans recently a shy, diffident man named Gino Alessandri, who had played the cello with Toscanini at La Scala more than forty years before and then at the Metropolitan, had tried to reach Toscanini at his hotel by phone. He could not get through, and he came to the hotel several times, hoping to meet the maestro. He was too reticent to leave a message and decided to give up the idea of seeing him. A short while before the concert, however, he came to the hotel again and stood in the lobby. Toscanini emerged from an elevator and, with his mind on the music to be played shortly, he walked toward the street, looking neither left nor right. Alessandri called out, "Maestro!" There was an annoyed look on Toscanini's face as he stopped and turned around. Then a broad smile broke out. "Alessandri!" he said. "What are you doing here?" When Alessandri told him that he was in town to play some concerts in the local orchestra's pop season, the maestro said, "You will come to hear the concert tonight." Alessandri was embarrassed. "I am not rich these days," he murmured. Toscanini took him by the arm and led him to his car. As they rode to the hall, Toscanini recalled the old days of music-making together. In the hall, just before he went out to conduct, Toscanini led Alessandri to a place in the wings and told him to stay there through the concert. That evening Toscanini conducted not only with his usual concentration but with a rare ebullience. One of the players said to him, "Maestro, you are happy tonight." Toscanini smiled gently. "Yes," he said, "I have an old friend here tonight."

25

Musical Values

TOSCANINI could not always conduct the music he loved. When he was young and had the responsibility for an entire opera season, he was bound to undertake a diversified repertory which included pieces that did not enlist his most ardent admiration. When he was older and was in charge of the greater part of an orchestra season, he had to be mindful once more of the need to make balanced programs, and the music he liked best had to be mingled with music he liked a little less. But throughout his long career, he has rarely concerned himself with compositions he detests. More than most conductors, he has insisted upon and won the right to do the things that have pleased him.

His lifelong musical activity provides the best index to his personal tastes. Verdi and Wagner are the composers he has conducted most frequently in the opera house. Mozart, Haydn, Beethoven, Schubert, Brahms, Debussy, and Wagner are the composers he has conducted most often in the concert hall. There have been many other names on his opera and concert programs, some appearing more often than others. In sum, his taste has been wide, and his curiosity wider.

"Music," he once said, "may be written by a German, an Italian, a Frenchman, an American, or a Russian, but to me it is unimportant. It is either good music or bad music. Music is not like wine; it does not improve with age. Nor is it like an egg that spoils when it is kept too long. There is good old music and there is bad old music, just as there is good or bad new music."

His love of Wagner and Verdi, Beethoven and Brahms, Haydn and Debussy has not been something he has accepted as a matter of course the way one accepts one's family. It has been an ardor that has refreshed itself by constant re-examination of the face of the beloved. It has been a love tested by time and by repeated restudy and revaluation. Despite the charge laid against the maestro that he has been interested only in his tried and true repertory, the facts have been otherwise. His interest and curiosity have been far-ranging. He has kept abreast of contemporary currents, listening to new scores and studying them. When he has not been preparing his own programs, he has read through scores that he might never conduct and tried them at the piano. He has listened to performances on the radio and on recordings. He has gone to rehearsals. He has had an insatiable appetite for music.

His values, especially where they concern the towering figures, might be fixed, but they have not been frozen. "Fifty years," he once said, "is but a tiny incident in history," and he has been conscious of the fact that even his vast span of activity has covered a small fragment of musical development. He has spoken disparagingly at times of the men who have hunted for new musical vocabularies and of the music that has resulted from their researches, but he has had the curiosity to keep alert to their output. His opinions have stemmed from experience, not ignorant prejudice.

His favorite subject of conversation is music in all its manifestations. All through his life he has read not only scores but everything pertinent to music, and when he speaks it is out of a deep knowledge not only of the original sources but of an amazingly varied body of commentaries. By listening to his performances over the years, you could form a reliable idea of where his deepest allegiances lay, but only those who have known him well have had any idea of how keen and adventurous his mind has been.

When he speaks of Beethoven, there is awe in his voice and words. He loves not only the music but the flaming tenacity of the man who relentlessly hacked away at his own innards to arrive at his ultimate expression. When he speaks of Wagner, his admiration is unstinted for the enormous industry and encompassing knowledge of the man.

"Yes," he once said, "Wagner used the ideas of others, but he made them his own. Take the Prelude to *Lohengrin*. Everything in it had been there before, but he put it all together in this new way for the first time."

Verdi! "Ah, Verdi!" he once said. "There was a man! From *Nabucco* on, we have a new voice. It is brutal, savage, but clear and personal. No one can be a genius twenty-four hours a day every day of the year. But look at the way his music fits words and action. Every single opera has touches of genius." At this point the maestro sang snatches from the best- and least-known of Verdi's operas, and his eyes glowed.

"Look at *Falstaff*," he went on. "Study the original manuscript. Notice how many places there are where Verdi's own first version was commonplace and where he turned, with small touches, these ordinary passages into moments of genius."

Brahms, he feels, was a composer who had the character to grow. And so was Mozart. Yet Mozart's perfection sometimes troubles Toscanini. "He was too perfect," he once said. "Everything is just where it should be. Some of this music I find cold. But he was a unique genius."

It is clear that Toscanini has sought to find the warm, human, passionate voice in Mozart. He has read his letters and knows the sufferings the composer lived through. Some music he could not bring himself to play until he found the key to its deepest humanity. The G minor Symphony, while he could recognize that it was a masterpiece, gave him pause, and in his earliest symphonic programs he held off from conducting it. He had heard the opening theme played lightly and delicately, and that had always alienated him.

"Tweet, tweet, that's what it sounded like," he recalls. "Then Puccini went to Berlin and came back with a report of how Hans von Bülow conducted it. There was bite in the strings. The first theme was strong and passionate. At last I understood. That was the way for me."

Toscanini seems to have a closer personal identification with Haydn. "Look at this flute part," he once said, pointing to a symphony. "It is in the low register. Not perfect, but how human!" For a concert with small orchestra in Ridgefield, Connecticut, he once planned to do a Haydn symphony and then changed his mind. "There is no time," he said, "to prepare it properly. In Haydn there is no hiding or covering anything."

I once mentioned Liszt and the way he befriended composers who needed help, and Toscanini replied, "Yes, but he was too agreeable. He was the friend of bad and good alike. He was a poseur. They talk about the originality of his harmonies. No, not Liszt. Do you want to see true originality of harmonies? Look at Chopin."

Debussy fascinates him. "*Pelléas* is a perfect opera," he says. "Debussy told me he was planning another. He said it would be something different. But he never got anywhere. He had only the one opera in him." Works like "La Mer" and "Iberia" are a repeated challenge to Toscanini. After doing "La Mer" a number of times on tour in 1950, he prepared for a performance in San Francisco by rehearsing it from beginning to end, and when someone suggested that he might want to go on and rehearse another piece for an encore, he said, "It is enough to do 'La Mer' well." When he rehearsed "Iberia," he said to the orchestra, "This rehearsal is for me, not for you."

He admires the simplicity of means Rossini used in *The*

Barber of Seville. "Just tonic and dominant," he says, "but for genius that is enough. *William Tell,* however, is full of original ideas. It is a masterpiece. What a tremendous career the man had in about fifteen years of writing activity. Then he stopped, discouraged, I think, by the success Meyerbeer was having with his superficial effects."

Rossini's works, like so many others, are engraved in his memory. One day on tour he decided to rewrite the bass-drum part of the *William Tell* Overture, and he did so from memory. He tore up the fourth trombone part provided by the publisher, crying, "*Casa Ricordi!* Stupid as always! Just like German editions of Italian music. Rossini did not ask for a fourth trombone."

When the rented parts were sent back to Ricordi, the music for fourth trombone was found to be missing, and the publisher's representative demanded its return. He was told that the maestro had torn it up, and he was not satisfied to have the set without a fourth trombone part until he was shown the fragments.

When Toscanini talks of opera, you can see that the field in which he did his first conducting still holds a powerful attraction for him. He says longingly, "I would like to do opera," and, shrugging his shoulders, "but it is impossible with these people—these singers." Because of "these people," he has failed to do operas, such as *Norma,* which he admires.

His eyes light up when he discusses Bellini. A photographer who had managed to obtain admittance to the maestro's home to make a set of pictures was having trouble getting him to unbend. A mutual friend, who had arranged the appointment, saw that things were not working out and said casually to Toscanini, "Isn't it wonderful, Maestro, how Bellini influenced Chopin?" Toscanini went to the piano and began to play Bellini arias, singing as he played. Two hours later Toscanini was still talking about Bellini and illustrating his points, and the photographer had a couple of hundred shots.

Many opera composers have been Toscanini's friends. He has conducted the *premières* of their works, but that does not affect his judgment of them. "Puccini," he once said, "was very clever, but only clever. Look at Cio-Cio-San. The poor woman has been waiting for years. She thinks he is returning at last. Listen to the music. Sugary. Look at Verdi in *Traviata*. Listen to the agitation of the music, the passion, the truthfulness."

Toscanini likes music whose pulse and heart he can feel. Mussorgsky, to him, is such a composer, but Tchaikovsky only rarely. The "Pathetic" he can do, he has said, because he feels that it is honest music. Before doing the "Pathetic" some years ago, he took home all the parts and spent hours editing every one of them in his own hand, carefully marking tempos, expression, bowings. He wanted the men to study their parts beforehand, and to learn them as he conceived the music. This was an enterprise of high seriousness to him. The Fifth Symphony, he declares flatly, is impossible for him; it is too banal. The Fourth has its points, he admits, but he does not feel it. "Manfred," despite its weakness, affects him differently, as does "Romeo and Juliet" with its youthful vigor. Do most conductors understand, he wants to know, that "Manfred" is really an opera without human voices? And if they have not conducted opera and do not grasp this point, they will never do "Manfred" properly, he insists.

Mahler and Bruckner? He knows all their symphonies. He has studied them, but he cannot conduct them. He tried a couple of Bruckner's, but has not returned to them in late years. He has found Mahler's too long and thinks the best of his big works is *Das Lied von der Erde*. He cannot react to Rachmaninoff either, although he has some respect for "The Bells," which he regards as the best of the big scores.

What about the music of the last generation or two? Toscanini cannot abide the efforts of some groups to coin new composing techniques. Talking to Busoni, an advocate of new ideas, the maestro once said, "Modern vocabularies are nonsense. Look at the wonders Beethoven managed with a simple tonic and dominant."

On another occasion he launched into a tirade against young composers who showed how learned they could be by writing fugues. "Even Bach wrote too many," he declared, "but he had a heart. A man with a lot of technique covers up his lack of heart with a fugue. Give me a melody, a phrase with feeling, something from the heart."

When he speaks of contemporary trends, he reveals that he has made a conscientious effort to study the leading composers. When Dimitri Mitropoulos and Joseph Szigeti joined with the N.B.C. Symphony to do Alban Berg's violin concerto, Toscanini went to rehearsals and followed them with a score. Try as he would, he could not respond to the music. On another occasion he encountered Artur Rodzinski, who had made a recording of a Berg score, and insisted on a direct answer to the question, "Did you like the music? Yes or no." He chuckled at the recollection that Rodzinski seemed to evade a flat answer.

Toscanini makes no secret of the fact that he hates Arnold Schönberg's theories and music, as well as the influence he has had on his followers and disciples.

Some of Prokofieff's and Shostakovich's early efforts he can feel, but most of their later ones leave him cold. When you ask him how it happens that he conducted Shostakovich's Seventh Symphony, he replies that in the emotion of wartime he had some feeling for it. Later on he obtained a recording and followed it with the score. "I asked myself," he said, "did I conduct that? Did I work two weeks memorizing that symphony? Impossible! I was stupid!"

He acknowledges that Béla Bartók was a good musician and he says that he admires the diligence with which his young Italian friend Guido Cantelli prepares and directs his music. "But it is not for me," he says. "It does not get under my skin."

Whenever he hears of new figures among the composers,

he hurries to obtain their music. He read through a score of Gottfried von Einem's *Danton's Tod* and found it interesting, and he recommended it as a possible novelty for La Scala.

He listened to Benjamin Britten's *Peter Grimes* in a broadcast performance and said he did not care to express an opinion, since an opera needed to be seen as well as heard. He has looked into some of Britten's other scores, and has found "Les Illuminations," which he also heard on a recording, worthy of attention.

He knows the music of Heitor Villa-Lobos and respects the man's talent, while regretting his lack of proper study.

Gian-Carlo Menotti, he thinks, is a clever man of the theater, and he feels that *The Medium* and *The Consul* are stage works of merit. Menotti's earlier operas do not attract him.

He has conducted some of Stravinsky's pieces but has no high regard for him. In the course of a sea voyage, Stravinsky remarked to Toscanini that Beethoven was a bluff, and the maestro turned his back on the composer and would not talk to him the rest of the trip. "Look at Cherubini," he once said. "He has instrumental effects one hundred years ahead of Stravinsky. Effects alone? Bah!"

He watches the activity of American composers, observing, "When I first came to the United States, composers had no technique. Now they have technique, but there is no heart." But he is not despondent about the future of the United States or any other country. "There will be composers in time," he says.

He can be harsh when he hears contemporary pieces that are annoyingly vapid. After listening to a program of music of new trends at an international festival in Venice in 1935, he observed to a friend, "Now they should close the theater and disinfect it."

His eye and ear are always measuring the validity of the musical expression. If a composer attempts to set words to music, he holds him to strict account on the way he handles his assignment. "If the composer knows his business, like Verdi, Wagner, and Mussorgsky," he says, "he sets words for their meaning. Even if I didn't know the language, I would know from the music what the correct verbal sounds should be. The music tells all, if the composer is greatly gifted. In many Puccini operas, the words and the notes are not inextricable. You could change the words, and any other set would do."

Not only the way words are set but the very handwriting of the composer is revealing to Toscanini. A friend once showed him a rare Debussy score and said that it was an original manuscript. The maestro peered at it closely. "No," he said, "that is a copyist's hand. There is no feeling in the writing." And he turned out to be right.

Toscanini's evaluations and procedures may be in conformity with established traditions, but he takes his position after examining the tradition thoroughly in the light of his own judgment. He likes the old-fashioned way of seating an orchestra, with the first-violin section to his left and the second violins to his right. "The first and second violins," he says, "are like a pair of shoulders, and like shoulders they must be strong and equal." He rails at conductors who fool around with the seating of the orchestra, insisting that they are throwing out the balance sought by the composer. When he saw a younger conductor's reseating of an orchestra, Toscanini muttered, "The trouble with some conductors is they conduct by eye instead of by ear."

And yet he does not hesitate to be inconsistent. He, too, makes slight rearrangements in seating if he thinks they will benefit the balance of a composition. In "La Mer" he moves the harps close to the woodwinds because he wants to clarify and blend the texture of the music more effectively.

His sense of musical values is revealed in the way he works over the scores he conducts. When he prepares to do an unfamiliar composition, he wants all editings of previous conductors removed. He noticed once that Mengelberg had added a fourth trombone in Beethoven's Fifth and struck it out, muttering, "These Germans, are they conductors?"

The N.B.C. music library has a large collection of music, and some of the Italian compositions are in German editions. Toscanini refuses to use these, insisting that the editors have thickened and coarsened the instrumentation. N.B.C., therefore, must go to the added expense of renting Italian editions for his performances.

He is happiest if he gets a clean score. Occasionally he finds mistakes in printed copies made by an early editor and followed by generations of editors and publishers. He has found and corrected such errors in Beethoven's Seventh and Ninth Symphonies and the "Leonore" Overture No. 3, in the Prelude and first act of *Tristan,* and in the second act of *Die Meistersinger.*

He writes his corrections and editings into the scores, sometimes even into the parts, in a large, bold hand. Once the violinists complained that his notes were so big that they could not tell whether they were on the lines or in the spaces between the lines, and he retorted indignantly, "They call themselves musicians!"

Toscanini denounces other musicians who make alterations in scores—in the Mussorgsky-Ravel "Pictures at an Exhibition" another conductor had marked a ritard and Toscanini wrote near it, "*Perchè? Vergogna!*"—and yet he fusses with many compositions. On a work like Schumann's "Rhenish" Symphony he does a substantial amount of rescoring. In some pieces he uses muted horns to back up clarinets and bassoons, or a muted trumpet to help out an oboe. These doublings blend so neatly that you scarcely know they are being made, and the voice that he has felt needed assistance achieves the saliency he seeks. Thus at the very opening of Tchaikovsky's "Manfred" Symphony he wrote in four bars for the clarinet doubling the bass clarinet's first four measures to give aid to the lower instrument.

After much soul-searching, he decided that a passage in the Ravel orchestration of Mussorgsky's "Pictures at an Exhibition" had not been orchestrated by Ravel. The reason? It was not well orchestrated. He rearranged this passage—it is the seventeen measures from Nos. 107 to 109 in the score—filling it out and giving the woodwinds and strings more to do and greater salience.

Is all this contradictory? Of course. Toscanini says in his own defense that he has never tampered with the music of men who knew exactly what they were about. And it is true that while he is freest with insertion of nuances in the works of composers of the eighteenth century and earlier, whose scores bear few markings, he intervenes less frequently in the case of nineteenth- and twentieth-century composers, who provided fuller instructions. And yet in the "Pastoral" Symphony, he begins the long crescendo in the first movement with a pianissimo instead of Beethoven's piano; the purpose and result are to add power and stature to the climax.

There is no doubt whatever that Toscanini's motive in making changes is not to magnify himself as an interpreter but to give more eloquent expression to the composer's thought. In the end, he must be judged by the sensitivity of his taste and intuition, and on these he can rarely, if ever, be faulted.

Far from seeking to "improve" and "interpret" works, he has an abhorrence of "interpreters." He once wrote these sentences for the son of a friend: "Blessed are those works that don't need interpreters. They cannot be vitriolized by histrionic mountebanks as it happens very often to the divine art of music."

The maestro's scores are treasures revealing his musical perceptions and points of view. Young conductors have gone to great lengths to lay their hands on them in the hope of culling Toscanini's secrets, just as they have listened to his performances and have sought to copy them. To Toscanini the effort to imitate him is both amusing and irritating. To young conductors he might say: Study, yes; ape another man, no. You must feel the music independently; you cannot wear another man's style.

Toscanini's alertness extends to all sorts of musicians as well as to music. He is especially curious about conductors, past and present. He watches the young fellows coming up, insisting that their principal shortcoming is that they do not study hard enough. "I conducted more than a dozen operas at the start," he once said, "but I didn't puff up with my importance as a conductor. I kept on studying, and I thought of myself as a cellist, not a conductor." A friend remarked of a new conductor that one ought to reserve judgment since he was only thirty-five, and Toscanini responded, "When I was twenty I was young, but at thirty-five a conductor should know something."

To be truthful, Toscanini does not have many kind words to say of other conductors. He assumes that Hermann Levi, to whom Wagner entrusted the first *Parsifal,* must have been a talented man, otherwise the composer would not have turned over such an important assignment to him. Hans Richter, he observes, was all right in German opera, but his tempos in Italian operas were impossible. Toscanini never heard Anton Seidl, but he has a low opinion of him because he consented to conduct Wagner with excessive cuts. Artur Nikisch, he feels, was a born conductor, but he does not admire some of the things he did in his last years. The fact that Nikisch heard Toscanini as a young man in Italy and hailed him as the comer among Italian conductors does not cause Toscanini to trim his opinion of him. Of German conductors like Mottl and Muck he does not think much; they were heavy and slow, he says, and "you sleep." He went to hear Bodanzky at the Metropolitan Opera in 1921 and later recalled that he was a good musician, precise and cold. "No blood," he said succinctly. He was introduced to Emil Cooper in an N.B.C.

office several years ago, and stared at him. "I remember hearing you conduct in 1901," he said. "It was terrible."

Toscanini can be almost childish in his desire to keep tabs on some conductors. He was curious to watch Koussevitzky rehearse, and he contrived to have himself slipped into the gallery of Carnegie Hall one morning when Koussevitzky was working with the New York Philharmonic-Symphony. Years later he could do quite an act imitating Koussevitzky's mannerisms.

He puts on the recordings conducted by some of his contemporaries and, score in hand, heaps invective on their absent heads. Or he listens to them on the radio and shouts to the empty room, "*Asino, pagliaccio, stupido*, why do you ignore the composer's tempo markings?" He listens avidly to reports of what and how they rehearse, and he broods about them. I remember that we were strolling one fine afternoon in a lovely park outside of Seattle. The Japanese cherry trees were in full bloom, and in the distance Mount Rainier seemed to float in the sky like a gigantic, snow-covered valhalla. The scene seemed too beautiful for words. Toscanini was quiet, apparently intent on it. Suddenly he turned and said angrily, "Will you please tell me why it is necessary to rehearse the Tchaikovsky Fourth over and over each season when you play it all the time with the same orchestra?" I could guess whom he was talking about, but said nothing. "If the orchestra knows it and you know it and you play it every season, why? Once, yes. *Basta!*"

On another occasion he confided that he had made a recording of Mozart's *Divertimento* for strings and two horns for the benefit of his colleagues, the conductors, not particularly for the public. Fed up with wrong tempos, he wanted to show them what the right pacing should be. In the slow movement, he had always felt something lacking and decided that what was needed was a cadenza for the first violin. After he had

295

made this addition, Toscanini found a letter from Mozart to his wife which confirmed his hunch.

Toscanini can be misled in his judgment of a conductor. Once he listened to a recording led by a man whose name he had not encountered before. Astonished by the brilliance and precision of the performance, he rushed to Chotzinoff and suggested that this man be engaged by the N.B.C. Symphony. The conductor was hired, and turned out to be a failure. No one could explain how he had managed to make such a fine recording. When reminded of the incident, Toscanini smiled and said, "See, I've always said it: any fool can conduct."

He can be sharp with some of his friends among the young conductors. He found one sitting on a high stool while rehearsing and said acidly, "You sit when you eat lunch." Another conductor said one day, "I've been reading the critics on my Beethoven, and . . . ," when Toscanini broke in, "Never mind the critics. Read Beethoven."

26

Away from Music

"Blessed be simplicity."

This phrase is often on Arturo Toscanini's tongue. He admires simplicity and honesty in others, and all his life he has tried to live simply and honestly. His basic attitudes, toward music and toward his personal life, are all of a piece. He hates cant and sham in his art, and he cannot tolerate them around him.

He does not have to wage a struggle to achieve simplicity and honesty for himself. They are fundamental aspects of his character; even as a lad he saw through fraud and pretension. But as he grew older he was able to give conscious formulation to standards which remained unchanging through a life filled with unsurpassed triumphs and acclaim.

To be a good musician, he believes, is also to be a good man. He was revolted by Richard Strauss's worldly side, and in a stormy encounter he said to the composer, "I take my hat off to you as a composer," and with a disgusted gesture added, "I put back ten hats as a man." Though Toscanini is not a churchgoer, his ethical precepts are high and firm. But he has no need to parade them, and has no desire to do so. They are part of him, and he assumes that they are part of his friends and family.

In some ways this leads to a disarming naïveté. He thinks he is above flattery, but there are people in his orbit who apply it so skillfully and with such an air of sincerity that he is fooled occasionally. He believes that he has never conducted a symphonic concert for less than a sold-out house. Since he has no way of checking the facts, he must trust the assurances of those who supposedly know. And it is true that he has rarely failed to play to a capacity house, although there was a period during the depression years when Carnegie Hall was not always sold out for his New York Philharmonic-Symphony concerts.

People who come to his dressing room or to his home to gush indiscriminately over his performances irritate him, but some who have been sensitive enough or good enough musicians to know what his own reaction to a performance might be have been able to win their way into his good opinion by saying the right thing at the right time. Many men and women have said the right things because they truly felt them, but some have been particularly careful to do so because they have wanted his friendship and help. He has given both freely, but he has not been so naïve as to be unaware that efforts have been made to impose upon him. There was the time when the wife of a conductor who was an old friend wrote to complain that another man had been engaged to be guest conductor of the N.B.C. orchestra when her husband should have received the invitation. The maestro returned the letter, with these words scrawled across it, "Sent to the wrong address."

He is impatient with vanity. He has even criticized Verdi for preserving some of his letters for posterity. He is glad to have those letters; he can quote from them extensively, but he has observed that it was a sign of weakness that Verdi knowingly saved them for reproduction after his death. He is watchful for signs of vanity in himself and deals roughly with them. And yet there have been times when he has not noticed a touch of frailty in himself. Some devilish friends thought up a gag one day. He had presented them with many autographed photographs over the years, and once when he was coming to dinner, they got out the pictures and placed them on display all over their apartment. When he entered, he looked at them without surprise. He paused and examined several of the photographs, and recalled when he had given them to his friends and what he had been doing at the time. If he realized he was being baited, he gave no sign.

Another time he was shown a copy of a magazine that carried a series of pictures of himself. In one he had been caught with his coat off, his suspenders showing. When he glanced at this picture, he pushed the magazine away in distaste.

He can also see himself objectively, with a sense of humor. He was once discussing a score with a young friend and automatically began waving his arms, beating time and giving cues. Suddenly he stopped, his arms still in mid-air, and smiled gently. "It's silly, isn't it," he said, "for a grown man to be throwing his arms around like that."

There have been times when his own weakness has made him petulant. He was illustrating at the piano the tempo of a piece of music for a young musician. "This must go like a metronome," he said, "*molto preciso.*" He set his electric metronome and started to play. After a few measures a certain freedom crept into his playing. His friend said nothing, but both he and the maestro knew that it was not "*molto preciso.*" Toscanini paused and glared. "After all," he exclaimed angrily, "man isn't a machine."

With his friends he can be by turns sweet and considerate, unreasonable and deflating. He had lunch at Geraldine Farrar's house in Ridgefield, Connecticut, several years ago. During the meal he began to scowl. When he left Farrar's house with another friend, he was still annoyed. "Darn that woman," he muttered. "We were friends for seven years at the Metropolitan and she has forgotten that I hate caviar!"

He was visiting the home of another former colleague at the Metropolitan, and this soprano boastfully referred to her age in passing. "*Senti, cara,*" Toscanini chided, "you are getting younger." The lady went to her bookshelves and pulled

out a copy of *Who's Who in America.* "Look," she said proudly, "I was born in 1885." Toscanini nodded, apparently convinced. Some weeks later she was visiting at Toscanini's house,
and he was ready for her. He opened a much older edition of
Who's Who in America, and with a mischievous gleam in his
eye, pointed to the year of her birth. "*Eh, cara,*" he said, "what
do you say to this? It says 1881."

When Toscanini was at the Metropolitan, he had a devoted
admirer who quietly put together a scrapbook of all the newspaper stories that had been written about him and one fine
day presented it ceremoniously. Toscanini leafed through the
book without relish and said to his friend, "What will I do
with it?"

In the later years of his life, Toscanini has been surrounded
by a coterie of friends and representatives of the musical organizations he has worked for. He has been shielded from
intruders and interruptions, for though his energy has been
amazing, it does have to be husbanded. He has no use for
autograph hounds and hero-worshipers of that ilk, and is
diffident about meeting strangers. But there have been times
when the protections thrown around him have gone beyond
sensible bounds. Occasionally, the iron in the old gentleman
causes him to break through the walls put up around him, and
he takes off cunningly on his own sweet way.

One day several years ago he had his chauffeur drive him
downtown from his Riverdale home to the N.B.C. studios.
Before he had left his house he had carefully changed a ten-
dollar bill. At N.B.C. he asked for a score and scooted out of
the building before it was brought to him. He had told his
chauffeur to wait in Rockefeller Plaza, and he slipped out of a
side door and hopped into a taxi. He was gone from 3 to 7 P.M.
No one knew where he had gone, and when he did not appear
his friends began to make worried calls all over town. He
returned in a taxi to the N.B.C. studios, got into his limousine,

and was driven home. Had he been to see an old or new friend? A man or a woman? He wore a pleased smile, and his mission remained his secret.

At times he has been approachable and at others he has sealed himself up in a shell. Some years ago Gian-Carlo Menotti and Samuel Barber, young composers just out of their teens, were spending the summer in a small northern Italian town not far from Toscanini's island. They both admired the maestro and wondered whether they could get to meet him. Menotti's mother knew Mrs. Toscanini and gave him a letter of introduction to her. One day the boys got up enough courage to appear at the Toscanini door, and Menotti was resolved to ask for the maestro. But when a servant appeared, his nerve failed him and he asked for Mrs. Toscanini. The servant, asking them to wait, went inside. After a while she returned and said, "The Signora is out, but come in. Maestro has nothing to do; he can see you." It turned out to be the beginning of a long friendship. The maestro liked the young musicians. They chatted about music. Toscanini went to the piano and played Monteverdi's *Orfeo,* and Barber, who has a good baritone, sang the role of Orfeo while the maestro, in his hoarse voice, did Euridice. He would not let them leave; he insisted that they stay for tea and then for dinner.

When he does not feel like being sociable, he can be infuriating to his friends. During his South American tour with the N.B.C. Symphony, he was inveigled into going to a party at the home of the American Ambassador in Buenos Aires. He had been assured that it would be a small gathering, but there were several hundred guests. He sat silently, glum and brooding, in the characteristic posture of discontent: chin on hand, brows knitted, eyes remote and cold. His neighbors talked to him but he did not respond. The soup was served and he did not touch it. Then the soup was taken away. Suddenly he let out a yell: "Where is my soup?"

But given an intimate circle, he can relax and be gay. He once went to the home of friends in Chicago where there were young and active children at large. A four-year-old stepped on his feet and he did not seem to mind. A big rubber ball was bounced off his head, but he did not miss a beat in his conversation. Someone mentioned Scarlatti and he went to the piano and, standing over it, proceeded to play many of the composer's pieces from memory.

There was a mad scene on the special train after the final concert of the recent tour. Toscanini was entertaining V.I.Ps. in his private car, but his daughter Wanda and her friends were holding an informal and lively party in one of the drawing rooms. Toscanini got wind of it, excused himself, and joined the crowd in the drawing room, which was so jammed that it looked like a scene in a Marx Brothers film. He pushed his way in and sat there, squeezed in among friends, laughing with immense relish.

He is inordinately fond of practical jokes. A friend showed him a trick, collapsible knife and he borrowed it and gleefully put it beside his wife's plate. Then he waited and watched. But his wife that evening chose to cut her meat with the edge of her fork. He kept prodding her to use her knife and she persisted in using the fork. Thoroughly annoyed, he exploded, "Imagine, eating meat without a knife!"

He takes delight in simple pleasures. He went to the Zoo in New Orleans and a peacock with tail and wings outspread caught his fancy. He tried talking to the bird. "Yuh, yuh!" he called. The bird paid no attention. "Yuh, yuh, yuh!" Toscanini called. Still there was no reaction. Toscanini turned away in disgust. "Stupid," he said, "like a musician."

When I joined the special train on tour recently, I brought a gift of a bottle of rare brandy for him from his friend Ray Vir Den, husband of Frances Alda. Vir Den had enclosed a note, saying "Don't give any to the bearer; it's too good for him." Toscanini carried the letter with him and insisted on reading it aloud to me. When the bottle was opened, of course, he handed me the first drink.

On the N.B.C. orchestra trip to South America, one of the men in the party spent hours playing a slot machine aboard the ship. The fellow was losing a half dollar at every throw, and since the machine was not rigged to give a sucker a break, he was gambling away all his money. His friends, failing to entice him away from the machine, appealed to the maestro, who trotted off obediently to try his powers of persuasion. Minutes later he was found at the slot machine relentlessly inserting coin after coin, while the man he had been sent to reform pleaded for a chance to try his luck.

Toscanini can show his friendship in delicate ways. The N.B.C. Symphony was in Montevideo on July 4th, and he called a rehearsal for eleven in the morning. The men, thinking that this was to be a holiday, arrived at the hall full of grumbling. Toscanini marched out on the podium and led the orchestra through a performance of "The Star-Spangled Banner." "It is your national holiday," he said, dismissing them, "and furthermore, it is the birthday of two of our party." And he pointed to Chotzinoff and John F. Royal, N.B.C. vice-president, as the objects of this birthday remembrance.

Wherever he travels, hotel managers, restaurant owners, and chefs put themselves out to do something special for him, and he receives the attentions, which are sometimes obtrusive, with graciousness. In Salzburg he once went to a little café with a friend, and the owner took ceremonious charge of the honored guest himself. Toscanini was in fine, good humor and asked for a large glass of wine. "A large glass," he said, smiling, "the largest glass in the house." The owner scurried off and brought back an enormous beakerful of wine. Then he took up a permanent post near the maestro, watching him lift the glass to his mouth. Toscanini did not like the wine. He whispered to his companion that it was vile stuff, and the latter suggested that it be changed. Toscanini glanced at the café owner and continued to sip the wine. The friend made as if to call the owner, but Toscanini stopped him. "No, no," the maestro whispered, "it'll hurt the poor man's feelings."

When he was on tour recently, the two Negro girls who took care of his rooms in a New Orleans hotel told him that they would like to go to his concert but could afford no more than three dollars for a ticket and these tickets were gone. He arranged for them to be his guests backstage.

Early in the tour one of the porters led him into his bedroom and pointed to a button near the bed. "Any time in the middle of the night you want something, Mr. Toscanini," he said, "you push that button." Toscanini protested, "But I'll wake you." The porter explained patiently, "That's what I'm here for." Toscanini did not ring, even though he was awake most of the night. Each evening the porter made the same speech, but Toscanini never rang for him in the middle of the night.

His generosity to people in trouble is warm and quick. A friend received a letter from Europe that a singer who had appeared with the maestro was sick and impoverished. He told Toscanini about it, and that very day a sizable check was on its way. When the Teatro dei Piccoli, a marionette theater group run by a man named Podrecca, whom the maestro admired, ran into trouble in the course of an American tour and needed help to get home, Toscanini quietly sent a check for one thousand dollars.

He is well aware that in his rages during rehearsals he behaves like a madman, and he has said that there are two Toscaninis—one an autocrat in music and the other a democrat. The latter Toscanini is the one his friends know when he is away from music, but there have been times when the irritations of the day have continued to gnaw at him and the grumpy, noncommunicative Toscanini has appeared at a party. Realizing that his manners have been bad, he apologizes, murmuring, "I have a bad character." When I was touring with Toscanini and the N.B.C. Symphony recently, I planned to leave the special train in St. Louis and then because of a railroad strike in the Midwest decided to stay on until Chicago. I remarked to Toscanini, teasingly, that I had been ordered to remain and keep an eye on him. "Yes," he said, "watch Toscanini. He is crazy."

If he was partly in earnest then, he can also jest with the appearance of being serious. He was making a recording once and an engineer came up to warn him that his outbursts of song were audible on the disks. "Don't worry," said Toscanini, with a straight face. "Tell the public it's the Toscanini tenor and you'll sell more records." He was walking in a festival town in Europe once and an excited lady rushed up to him and exclaimed, "Aren't you Maestro Toscanini?" He looked at her gravely and shook his head. "Oh, I'm so sorry," she said, and hurried off in confusion.

He can be patient and impatient as the mood strikes him. He does not like plane travel because he cannot abide waiting if the weather happens to be bad. He has flown the Atlantic several times, and it has seemed to him wholly unreasonable that a plane should be held up twenty-four hours in Gander, Newfoundland, while the weather cleared. He moves about like a caged animal when he has to wait. Once he has started on a journey or an enterprise of any kind, he wants to be forging ahead steadily.

And yet he can take infinite pains to do the right thing. He paid a visit to the Science Museum in Chicago, and when he was leaving he was offered a tiny guest book to sign. He saw that the signatures were all virtually microscopic, and he took a sheet of paper and practiced signing his name in minute letters. He did not want to spoil the book with a clumsy signature.

In the midst of anger, he may suddenly take a philosophic view of a situation. One day he strolled out on the terrace of his Riverdale home and noticed that many of the tulips in the garden had been cut and carried off during the night. "And they say," he told a friend, "that Italians are always thieves. But an American took those flowers. What a shame!" He paused and his anger seemed to melt into sorrow. "But how do I know," he went on dolefully, "that it wasn't an Italian?"

A man of mercurial moods, he reacts to similar situations in violently contrasting ways. The white light of publicity that has beaten on him has been a frequent nuisance, especially since it impinges on his cherished privacy. Yet he can be tolerant of newspapermen and photographers, and even wistful with them. On the special train recently he passed a room in which the N.B.C. staff photographer was developing pictures of him. The photographer held up a roll and said that it contained thirty-six shots. "Isn't that enough for the trip?" the maestro inquired. When his son, Walter, traded blows with a photographer at a Los Angeles airport over a flash bulb, Toscanini was hurried away into a car. He didn't want to leave. "Let's go back," he said to Walter, "and finish that fellow." He recalled proudly that he had taken a poke or two at an obnoxious cameraman on several occasions.

Another time, on returning to America by boat, he barricaded himself in his stateroom and declined to come out for nine hours until the press departed. Walter Toscanini and Chotzinoff stood guard during the entire period, relieving each other long enough to attend to personal affairs at intervals.

To the people who write him from all over the world, he gives attentive ear. He reads nearly all the letters himself and occasionally answers some of them personally. He rarely writes to his close friends and family while traveling, but he may compose a long and thoughtful letter to a stranger who happens to stir him up with a provocative comment about music.

Though he has lived most of his life in cities, he feels a close kinship to nature. At Sun Valley in Idaho recently, when the sun was warm and the air rare, he lay down and rolled in the grass out of sheer exuberance. At Mount Shasta in California he looked silently at the fourteen-thousand-foot, snow-covered peak and then unaffectedly applauded it.

Music has been the essence of his life, but his culture is wider than his own art. He is well versed in the best of the world's literature. He knows Shakespeare so well that once, when he met an actress who had just played *A Midsummer Night's Dream* in German and who began to speak some of the lines in that language, he took up the recital, recalling the next passage from memory in English and in Italian. A young female admirer once sent him a book as a going-away present with this inscription on the flyleaf: "Farewell, thou art too dear for my possessing." He knew at once that this was a line from a Shakespeare sonnet. His reply had one sentence: "Farewell, thou are too young for my possessing." Shakespeare, he observed once, must be read in English. Victor Hugo's French translation, however, is not bad, he said, and Boito worked from it when he made his librettos of *Otello* and *Falstaff* for Verdi.

He read Walt Whitman before his first trip to America. He admires the writings of Washington Irving; he said once that he had read every word Irving wrote, including his letters. He can quote Heine and Goethe. Once I heard him speak with special warmth of Lincoln, comparing him with Goethe and concluding that he was purer, humbler, and nobler. He adores Poe, remarking, "What music in his poems!" After he left Richmond, Virginia, recently, he turned to his son with a horrified expression. "Walter," he said, slapping himself on the forehead, "we forgot!" Walter looked worried. "Forgot what?" he wanted to know. "We forgot," said Toscanini in a hollow voice, "to visit Poe's birthplace in Richmond."

CHAPTER

27

At Home

THE tradition of the family is strong in Toscanini. Possibly it is stronger in him than in most Italians of his generation because when he was young he had less intimate home life than most boys his age. He spent half his boyhood behind the walls of the Conservatory, and after receiving his diploma he went to work. Later he achieved a normal home life only at intervals, for his engagements kept him hopping from city to city and from country to country. It was not until he grew older and began to limit his commitments that he had all the time he wanted to devote to his family circle, and then his children were grown and were living their own lives. The Toscaninis remain a close-knit family even when they are apart on different continents; and when they reside near each other, the maestro expects frequent reunions.

He is not a modern parent in our sense of the word; he did not deviate from the pattern of fathers of his time. His children were watched over by a faithful nurse; they had good schooling and comforts that he had not known as a child. There were moments of warm intimacy, but one gathers that they were rare. Toscanini usually had too much on his mind. It was not until the grandchildren came along that he found the time and inner tranquillity to unbend.

When his career was in full tide, Toscanini worked day and night. He might rage and let off steam in the theater, but his problems burrowed under his skin and remained with him

308

when he was at home. His children remember that when they were young their mother was constantly shooing them out of Papa's way. They learned to tread gingerly when he was around, and he did not make things easier for them with his frequent seizures of silence and brooding. At home he did not rant and scream; he just sat and stared. Everyone sensed that he was tormented by private concerns, but no one dared to ask him to unburden himself.

The children remember long periods when Papa was grim and uncommunicative. At meals he would munch at scraps of food or would sit at the table without eating at all. No one knew what demons possessed him—mostly, of course, they were musical demons—but his heavy, intense silence was like a somber cloak covering all of them and suppressing normal childish gaiety.

At times the family table churned up in spirited disputation. When the children had become adults, they were less hesitant about speaking up. The whole family then might toss animated darts at one another. The arguments in Italian might rise to a high pitch of excitement. The outsider might think that they were about to attack each other, and then would find that the difference of opinion might be over something trivial. Presently they might be laughing in relish over a mutual recollection, and a few moments later they might be in violent disagreement again.

Occasionally the Toscaninis might become so riled at one another that a special system of communication had to be worked out. Wanda recalls that once when she wished to say something to her father, she spoke to her brother, who spoke to Wally, who spoke to Mrs. Toscanini, who spoke to the maestro. And when this system was stretched to the breaking point, Toscanini would cut through the intricate pattern of communication and address his reply directly to Wanda.

Disagreements have not lasted long, and they have not impaired the fundamental relationship of parent and child.

Toscanini likes to tell his friends that he has given his children complete freedom, and it is true that in the end they have gone their own ways, marrying whom they wished and leading the lives they chose to lead. Nevertheless, his son and daughters feel that there have been unwritten rules of behavior for them. Their father, they know, expects them to share his life. No one has ever told them that they must attend rehearsals and performances, but they believe that they must. If they cannot be present, they find themselves apologizing. They know that he wants them at his house for dinner every evening and if he chooses to spend an evening watching television they have to do likewise, even if the stuff on the screen happens to bore them.

When Wally has come from Italy for a winter visit to America in recent years, her father has seemed to think that she should spend every evening with her parents. One night she decided to stay at her sister's house, and he kept going to her room all night to see whether she had returned. "I'm old enough to be a grandmother," Wally exclaimed, "and he treats me like a little girl."

The autocrat of the concert hall and opera house, for all the mildness of his manner, tends to be tyrannical at home. If his children do things that seem silly to him, he dismisses their preferences as incredible. When Wally announced that she was going to marry Count Castelbarco, who happened to be blond, Toscanini protested, "Who ever heard of such an idiotic thing, marrying a blond-haired man?" When his children or his friends pass the time in card games, he exclaims, "Who ever heard of such a silly thing as card-playing?" Some time ago Wally spent almost a month in the comparative isolation of the maestro's island off Pallanza and took to diverting herself by fishing. He did not like fishing and it struck him as a fruitless occupation. "Who ever heard of such an idiotic thing as fishing?" he protested.

He may complain about details, but in sum he is devoted to

his children and grandchildren and proud of them. In his wallet he carries photographs of all of them, and on his wrist he wears a gold identification bracelet with a little heart for each member of his family. When his grandson, Walfredo, failed to make the ascent in the ski-tow lift at Sun Valley some time ago and someone remarked that the young man was nervous about heights, Toscanini declared firmly, "No Toscanini is afraid!" When Wanda was a child, he forced her to go up in a Ferris wheel that terrified her. Throughout the ride she lay on the floor of the car and cried in fear, but he reported that she took the ride bravely. His granddaughter, Sonia Horowitz, showed talent for the piano and he would make special trips to his daughter's home just to sit quietly and listen to the little girl. Occasionally he would play duets with the child, and when the girl once told him he was not so hot as a pianist, he delightedly repeated the comment to his friends. When Sonia began to paint, he came and listened to her explanations of the pictures and bought one, taking it to Italy and hanging it in a prominent place in his home there. Some time ago Wanda noticed that a New York critic had slept through one of her father's broadcasts and she confronted the critic with what she had seen. Toscanini was pleased by her boldness. "I envy you," he told her. "I wish I had the nerve to do such a thing."

Toscanini's views are old-fashioned in some respects. He is against divorce, believing that one wife should be for life. He takes this position on moral, not religious, grounds. In more than fifty years of marriage there have been inevitable tensions between him and his wife, and yet, despite his eye for good-looking women, it has been a firm and lasting relationship.

Preoccupied with his music, Toscanini does not concern himself with the management of the money he has earned. He leaves nearly all of this to his wife. His property is in her name, and if she happens to make errors of judgment in business matters, he does not seem to notice. In the 1940's, when the war brought about high income taxes, N.B.C. was obliged to suggest a change in contract; it had become too costly to be responsible for his taxes. The maestro made no objections. He said to his wife, "I didn't see how they could keep it up."

His daily routine in recent years has been simple and unhurried. He arises early—probably he has slept fitfully and has killed time reading books and scores, for he calls night his enemy—and rings for breakfast, which may consist of orange juice, a poached egg, Italian breadsticks, and strong Italian coffee. Then he patters into his studio to bid good morning to his canaries. He removes the covers from the cages and puts on a record of a canary in song. Then he stands at the piano and plays, while the birds sing. He matches their trills, and they try, to his joy, to compete with his music.

If he has no rehearsal, he remains in his study, reading through scores and playing the piano. Then he dresses. He has always been fastidious about his personal appearance. He shaves himself, and since he never goes to a barber, his wife or daughters trim his hair. He likes good, conservative clothes, and he carefully matches shirt, tie, socks, and suit. His womenfolk occasionally darn his socks, but he does not like patched things and throws them away. And yet with apparent forgetfulness he has sat with companions of an evening and observed wistfully that his old friend Martucci had a wonderful wife who sat in his dressing room before concerts and mended his socks.

The midday meal is the main one. Not that he ever eats much. He likes a good thick soup, which he eats with relish. The rest—meat, vegetables, salad, dessert—he nibbles on. His family has observed that if he is not closely watched he may eat a reasonable amount of food; if too much attention is paid to him, he may not eat at all. If he does not eat substantially at mealtimes, he manages to get enough nourishment in the course of the day. He has a bowl of fruit in his bedroom and studio. Occasionally he swallows a bit of cheese or a piece of chocolate. Those who know him best say that he eats more than he appears to be eating and that it has become a fetish with him to pretend—and perhaps to believe—that he hardly ever takes food. They say that it is the same way with his sleeping habits. He insists that he sleeps only a few hours each night, but his family occasionally accuses him of napping through a radio or television program, and he makes an indignant denial.

There may be water on the Toscanini table, but it is there for decorative purposes. The maestro, like a good European, drinks wine—most often fine red wine—with every meal. After a concert he invariably slakes his thirst with a glass or two of champagne. In the intermission he takes some milk and sliced bits of melon which are stored in a refrigerator provided in his dressing room. In breaks between rehearsals he is fond of oranges. From time to time he chews on rock candy before going out on the podium.

In the afternoon, if there is no rehearsal or performance, he studies some more or takes a drive into the country. In years gone by he was fond of walking for exercise, but recently he has been content to sit on the terrace of his pleasant home and let the sun warm him. Save for mountain climbing in his youth, he has rarely bothered with sport. He cannot swim; in the water, he says, he is like a stone. He does not go in for competitive sports. The truth is that he needs no physical outlet other than his conducting. He stands on the podium in rehearsal or performance and waves his arms and body vigorously for hours, and he comes away soaked in perspiration. Even for a young man the exertions of conducting can be sufficient exercise; for a man in his eighties it is inordinately strenuous physical activity.

In the afternoons he may take time to work with his paintings. He has an extensive collection and likes, as he puts it,

313

"to change their landscapes." He may spend hours taking a painting out of one frame and placing it in another. Then, with the help of his chauffeur, Luigi Gaddoni, he rehangs them all. In his Riverdale home he has almost forty oils and water colors, nearly all by Italians of the nineteenth and twentieth centuries. There are about ten by Crubici, a friend, whom Toscanini admired as a man and artist. A painting by Fontanesi hangs in the maestro's bedroom, and the works of Previati, Basini, Gayda, Alfred Geast, Boldini, Monticelli, Trecourt, Israel, Sernese, Spagnolini, and Pokitnow are scattered through the house.

The evenings are available for family and friends. Toscanini watches television programs for hours on end, from broadcasts for children through comedy shows and murder mysteries to sports events. He laughs like a child at the antics of Milton Berle. When some gag pleases him, he points a finger at the screen and his cracked voice calls out, "Look at him!" He is fond of wrestling and boxing and becomes so aroused during a match that he stands up, shouts, flails his arms, ducks, feints, and attacks, and calls out dire threats to the gladiator he happens not to like. "Give it to him!" he calls. On the night of the second Joe Louis-Joe Walcott fight, he invited so many friends that two television sets had to be put into use.

He never attends a wrestling match or a fight, but he has learned the fine points of each sport. A friend once sent him a book on the art of prize fighting, and he studied it like a significant new score, and then for days he discanted on the subtleties of the ring like an expert.

His house in Riverdale is a fine, spacious one, with lawns and garden and a view of the Hudson and the New Jersey Palisades. In the living room there is a magnificent phonograph with loud-speakers in the four corners. An entire wall is devoted to records. These include not only his own recordings and test pressings of his broadcasts but the performances of many musicians. He listens frequently to records and broadcasts, not only the music of his own field but also jazz.

There is a grand piano at either end of the living room, and another one in his studio upstairs. On this instrument there are photographs of Verdi and Brahms and a cameo of Beethoven. On a bookcase there is a bust of Verdi.

The evening circle in Riverdale includes his family, a few musicians, and a handful of Italians who, the maestro has made sure, did not have any truck with Fascism. One of his closest and most loyal friends is a big, hearty, plain-spoken woman named Margherita De Vecchi. He met her in one of his early visits to New York, and she, out of devotion to his art, has put herself at the service of Toscanini and his family. She has influential friends in all walks of life and unhesitatingly calls on them whenever the Toscaninis need anything, whether it happens to be theater tickets, boat passage, servants, caterers, what you will. The maestro turns to her more frequently than to anyone else for advice, and when he was on tour, he telephoned her often to report on the trip's progress. Since she is an active woman with many interests, he occasionally finds her phone busy, and once he insisted on having her install a private telephone so that he could reach her when he wanted to.

Toscanini's health and vitality remain extraordinary. One doctor called him a biological phenomenon and another told him that his heart sounded like a young man's, to which Toscanini replied, in a moment of sad self-criticism, "I have never used it."

He still has his own teeth and is as reluctant as the rest of us about going to the dentist to have them attended to. He reacts to the fact of being an octogenarian variably, according to the mood of the moment. One day when he felt low, he told his family at dinner, "I looked into the mirror this morning and said to myself, 'You fool, you're old; you ought to be ashamed to show yourself in public.' " And he would not listen to arguments to the contrary.

More often, however, he seems to go on the assumption that he is ageless. For his eightieth birthday he was presented with a clock guaranteed to need no winding for fifty years. He held it out to the company around him, everyone younger than he, and said, "Just imagine, when this clock has to be wound everyone in this room will be dead but me." Another time one of his young friends started to leave a party at midnight, and Toscanini whispered, "Stay a while. Soon the old people will have gone, and we'll have fun." His friend Giuseppe De Luca, the baritone, kept on singing after he was seventy, and Toscanini, ten years his senior, bawled him out for persisting in a public career at his age.

Being fiercely proud, Toscanini refuses to accept assistance such as a helping hand when he steps out of a car or goes down a flight of stairs. He long ago formed the habit of counting the steps in the course of an ascent or descent, and he keeps it in mind so that he will not be surprised on the way back. There is a steep flight of steps in his house, and he sometimes rushes up and down with a speed that causes his friends to hold their breaths. He marches firmly up and down the steps from dressing room to podium without aid. Once, some years ago, he tumbled off the platform, and several horrified N.B.C. executives raced to pick him up. He glared at them, rejected their help, arose by himself, returned to the podium, and resumed conducting.

Toscanini's friends have speculated on the sources of his longevity and energy, and they have concluded that it is compounded of many factors. He had the luck to be born of sturdy, long-lived stock. He has kept his body healthy by using it but not abusing it. He has eaten moderately and sensibly, but he does not hold this a special merit, since he has not been tempted to do otherwise, just as his abstention from

smoking has been a matter of taste rather than choice. Of
great significance, his friends agree, is the fact that his emotional health has been sound. All his life he has let off steam
violently and drastically when he has been upset; his rages,
they hold, have been a form of catharsis that few other human
beings could afford or dare to indulge in. And most important
of all, he has had an abiding passion—music—that has kept his
interest and enthusiasm undimmed.

28

Italy

FROM 1939 to 1946 Toscanini did not see Italy. He felt at home in the United States, and when traveling was possible he sought stimulation in it. In 1940 he went to South America with the N.B.C. Symphony, and in 1941 he returned to Buenos Aires for guest conducting. In the United States he made guest appearances that helped give him the change of scenery he needed. He conducted in Philadelphia, Cincinnati, Chicago, and Los Angeles. But Italy was seldom far from his mind.

In the recurrent encounters with Mussolini and Fascism, Toscanini had never ceased to differentiate between the party in power and the country and people he loved. In the fall of 1938, he had been stopped by the police on his way out of Italy, his passport had been taken up, and it had required an appeal by his daughter Wally, wife of the Count Castelbarco, to Ciano, Mussolini's son-in-law, to get it restored, but in the summer of 1939 he went back for part of his holiday. In 1939 the Italian authorities detained him once again. This time the National Broadcasting Company and the United States Government had to swing their weight to obtain permission for him to leave Italy. He had made up his mind that he would not beg for his passport. He had also determined that he would not be held against his will. "I hired a plane," he said later, "and had it ready to fly me out without Fascist permission."

All through the thirties, though he no longer conducted in

Italy, he watched events there with pain and shame. He felt personally humiliated when La Scala played a joyous *Aïda* on the day Italy attacked Ethiopia. He suffered when his cherished theater put on this opera by his beloved Verdi, champion of liberty, to celebrate Hitler's visit to Italy to meet Mussolini. And in 1940, when Italy launched its jackal invasion of France, Toscanini, who was en route to South America, locked himself up in his cabin, and in a frenzy of grief tore at his clothes and wept, mourning as though he had lost someone precious to him.

He could not forget Italy. Its shame and sorrow were his shame and sorrow. His friends urged him in these dark years to apply for American citizenship. He declined, not because he did not value America and its hospitality but because he felt that to abandon his Italian tie when his compatriots were ruled by the Fascists would be like desertion of their cause. He followed events in Italy with special concentration. He read every scrap of news and sat up late in the night, listening to the radio. When it was ruled that Italians were not to be considered as enemy aliens, he rejoiced, knowing that this was true for himself and most other Italians in America. He was happy to have back his short-wave set—such receiving apparatus was temporarily forbidden to Italian nationals in the United States—because it enabled him to listen to broadcasts from Italy, seeking for the shreds of truth concealed in Fascist propaganda. The shedding of Italian blood in an unworthy cause sickened him, and defeat of Fascist arms gave him a somber pleasure. During the Civil War in Spain he had derived the same grim joy from the routing of Mussolini's legions by the Spanish Republicans, and at the same time he had grieved for the loss of Italian lives in a disgraceful intervention.

When he could, he made known his feelings directly. In preparing a performance of Verdi's "Hymn of the Nations" for broadcast early in 1943, he struck out the words *"Italia, patria mia,*" and replaced them with "*Italia tradita.*" On the day in August, 1943, when Mussolini's government fell, he hastened down to Radio City where his orchestra was waiting and began rehearsing a special concert. Italy did not surrender for five and a half weeks, and he waited in an agony of suspense, canceling plans to leave town. The day of Italy's liberation could not be far off, and he was determined to be on hand when the moment came, to signalize his hatred of tyranny and his joy at victory in the most eloquent way open to him—by making music.

A few days before he had written an open letter to the people of America pleading for understanding of his fellow-Italians. This letter, published in the magazine *Life*, bespoke help and understanding for the Italian people. They "have never been your enemies, people of America," he wrote. He hoped that a democratic Italy, rising from the ashes of Fascism, would receive "fair and equitable treatment as an equal member of the family of free nations."

This special program contained music that had assumed vast political significance for all free men—the opening movement of Beethoven's Fifth Symphony, with its imperious V-theme; the Overture to Rossini's *William Tell,* an opera which celebrates man's struggle against tyrants; the "Hymn of Garibaldi"; and "The Star-Spangled Banner," which he sang as he conducted. He led this program with a dedicated, exalted air, and he was delighted to hear that it would be short-waved to Italy.

He knew that the Italians would listen to his music. He had received word that through the darkest days of the war they like other Europeans, had tuned in on his short-waved N.B.C. broadcasts despite threats of punishment, just as they had listened surreptitiously to news broadcasts from Britain and America. He knew that countless Italian men and women had not followed the Fascist party line of antagonism to him personally. He remembered that in the thirties lesser Fascist officials had shown him little kindnesses, despite the fact that the higher echelons of the party frowned on him. His son Walter had found in the course of his trips from other European countries on his rare-book business that Fascist customs officials had let him pass without even looking into his baggage the moment they had discovered that his name was Toscanini.

Early in 1944, Toscanini finished making a film for the United States Government. He had volunteered his services, although in previous years he had rejected offers of hundreds of thousands of dollars to appear in a commercial movie. The picture was produced by the motion-picture bureau of the Office of War Information, and he knew that it was designed for distribution abroad, particularly, he hoped, in Italy. In it he conducted "The Hymn of the Nations," and he looked upon this film as a message from him to the people of Italy.

He must have smiled with ironic satisfaction when he heard late in 1944 that Mario Ghinelli, the Bologna Fascist who had organized the attack on him in 1931, was arrested in Naples and would be brought to justice. He had waited a long time for the moment of retribution.

When northern Italy was being liberated in April and May of 1945, the people of Milan thought of Toscanini even before the last Germans and Fascists had been driven out. American troops entering Milan found a large placard posted over the main entrance to La Scala; on it were printed the words *"Vogliamo Toscanini* [We Want Toscanini]."

The Italian Committee of Liberation sent an appeal to him to return to Italy and to help in the reconstruction of La Scala, which had suffered serious damages in an air raid. He was asked to continue "his noble work for Italian art." The appeal continued, "You will not hear this broadcast, but an echo will certainly reach you. . . . This appeal is addressed to you firstly by all members of La Scala orchestra, some of whom are here while I am talking."

He heard the appeal, and it echoed in his heart. He searched his conscience before sending this answer:

The echo of your message, although incomplete, moved me deeply. I have always been close to you in spirit during these dolorous years of struggle, grief, and despair. I have never doubted, even in the most sorrowful hours, of the generous contribution which the Italian patriots would make in the struggle for the freedom of the world in the hour of recovery against Nazi-Fascist tyranny.

But the scores of thousands of Italian patriots who died heroically in this war by the side of the Allied soldiers, the determination and the discipline of you Milanese demonstrated in the hour of the revolt, the swift, inexorable justice done to the principal Fascist criminals made me comply certain that the republican ideals of Cattaneo, Garibaldi, and Mazzini will be fulfilled by you and by the Italian people.

All the vestiges of a past of ignominy and treachery must disappear. Justice also demands that the one who gave to the Fascist tyranny all material and moral support, the arms and the legal power to deceive, subjugate, and oppress the Italian people for twenty sorrowful years, be now called upon to answer for his complicity in the crimes perpetrated by the Fascists in his name and for all the violations of the statute which made the Italian people the first victims of Nazi-Fascist terror.

You Milanese, who in 1848 began the revolt against German tyranny, have well deserved to conclude in 1945 this struggle of our Risorgimento.

I shall be happy to return among you as a citizen of a free Italy and not as a subject of the degenerate king and princess of the House of Savoy.

He did not return until the hated King Vittorio Emmanuele had abdicated, and he was not content until the Italian people had voted out the monarchy in favor of a republic. But he did not wait to show where he stood with respect to La Scala. A few days after sending his message to the people of

Milan and Italy, he cabled the management of La Scala, "With all my heart I authorize my daughter, Wally Castelbarco, to contribute in my name one million lire for the reconstruction of my beloved theater, La Scala. I hope to do more in the future."

His daughter Wally was flown to New York by American Military Government officials, who realized how much Toscanini's return would mean to Milan, for consultations with her father. Through her he sent back advice on how La Scala should be reconstituted. In the next few months he corresponded frequently with the Milanese in charge of rebuilding the shattered auditorium.

Toscanini returned to Italy in April, 1946. He was met at the border by relatives and close friends. He spent a few days resting at his villa near the town of Crema, where the people gathered to cheer him. It moved him to hear that Parma, shortly after the liberation, had named a street after him. In Milan he insisted on driving through the bombed areas. He consulted with Scala officials, and arranged to hold his first meeting with the men of the orchestra in a small reception room rather than in rehearsal. "I wanted to see you in an atmosphere of friendship," he told them, "as I remember all of you." The eyes of the seventy-nine-year-old maestro filled with tears.

But at the first rehearsal there was no sentimentality. The musicians who had last played with him seventeen years before found that he was still just as exacting. He shouted and stamped his foot at them. A painter was working in the rear of the auditorium, and Toscanini stopped to yell at him, "I admire your ear but please stop whistling."

He conducted a series of concerts at La Scala that were taken rightly to be more than music. On the very day that he resumed his place on the podium, King Vittorio Emmanuele landed in Alexandria, Egypt, to begin his exile. The insigne of the House of Savoy were stripped from the royal box, and old musicians from the Verdi Casa di Riposo sat, at Toscanini's invitation, in the place of honor. Outside the theater a vast throng overflowed into the Piazza di Duomo, where it listened to loud-speakers carrying the concert by radio. The Scala was one of the first Italian monuments to be restored after the war's end, and to the Italians it was an earnest of better days to come. Toscanini's return was turned into a national manifestation.

On June 2nd, Toscanini proudly took his place at the polling station to vote in the first free elections in Italy since the advent of Fascism. And late in June he conducted Beethoven's Ninth in the last of ten concerts at La Scala. The audience shouted the plea *"Ritorna, Maestro* [Come back, Maestro]" until it was hoarse. General Mark Clark, who had commanded the American troops in Italy during the war, came down from Vienna for the concert, and afterward Toscanini regretted that the General had to leave soon after the concert. "I wanted to discuss strategy with him," he told friends. "I wanted to ask him why they invaded Italy at Salerno instead of Genoa. But I guess I'd better stick to my music."

But a day or two later he used his music to protest against what he considered an injustice to Italy. He had agreed to conduct in Paris on June 30th and in London on July 3rd, but he canceled these engagements because of "profound bitterness" induced by the international agreement to revise the Franco-Italian frontier in favor of France.

He left Italy in August and did not conduct there again until 1948, when he returned to La Scala to direct a program of music by Arrigo Boito in observance of the thirtieth anniversary of his friend's death. That year he also opened the Venice music festival. In 1949 he again conducted in Milan and Venice. In 1950 he led the Verdi Requiem at La Scala and was making plans to conduct *Falstaff* at Busseto in the summer of 1951 in memory of the fiftieth anniversary of Verdi's death.

In America or in Italy, his heart has been with those of his people in need. In 1945 he conducted a special Carnegie Hall concert with part of the proceeds going to Italian war orphans. In 1947 he heard that the Verdi Casa di Riposo for aged musicians lacked heat and he quietly underwrote the bill for this service for that and succeeding years. In January, 1949, on the anniversary of Verdi's death, he sent six thousand dollars for distribution among needy musicians of Milan.

Private acts of beneficence, however, have not beclouded his idea of what his role in Italy should be. Late in 1949, Italy offered to make him a life senator, but he declined the honor. In a cable to Luigi Einaudi, President of Italy, he begged that his refusal should not be regarded as "a discourteous or arrogant act" but should be interpreted "in the spirit of simplicity and modesty that inspired it." Perhaps his dissatisfaction with some of the things that were happening under the government of Premier Alcide de Gasperi had something to do with his decision. It is more likely that his refusal, at bottom, was prompted by his conviction that he was a musician, not a politician. In the same spirit he declined a request that he accept the presidency of the Verdi Society of Busseto. "I am the president of nothing," he had said emphatically to friends. "I am a musician. Conduct *Falstaff?* Yes, but nothing else."

When he returns to rest on his little island off Pallanza, he does not see many old friends. Most of them are gone; that is a price to pay for living to old age. And some who still are around he refuses to see. He kept track of musicians who had served Mussolini and Fascism too eagerly, and now he will have nothing to do with them. One of them telephoned him in Milan one day and Toscanini answered. The voice identified itself, and Toscanini replied, "I am not here." He slammed down the phone. It rang again in a few moments, and the same voice identified itself as if the maestro had not understood. "Yes, I know who you are," Toscanini shouted, "and I am not here."

It does not matter that his Italian circle has shrunk. It is enough for the old maestro to sit in the sun watching the wind play on Lago Maggiore and the clouds move over the mountains. The sight and smell of his native land bring refreshment and peace to the little man who has voyaged far but whose heart has never left Italy.

29

Estimate

ARTURO TOSCANINI winces when he hears himself described as a "great conductor." He hates the word "great," whether it is applied to himself or any other conductor. He thinks that it should be used with the utmost care, and then only for the towering creative figures. Beethoven and Wagner and Verdi properly may be called great, in his judgment. But no interpreter deserves the adjective. If you are a conductor, you are either a good musician or not, and to be a good musician is accomplishment enough for any lifetime, even a generous one of more than eighty years.

Toscanini's persistent refusal to cut a public figure in ways other than music follows from the conviction that the business of a musician is to make music, of a conductor to conduct. He has taken public stands when the issues have been so weighty that he could not remain silent, but he has resisted constant pressure to sign manifestoes, make statements, give interviews, and air his opinions. The cities and states of the world have sought to heap honors on him, and if he has been asked for permission, he has rarely accepted. He was made an honorary citizen of Bayreuth, Salzburg, and Lucerne, but there was some reason for these gestures, since he had conducted festivals in these towns. In 1947 he accepted the One World Award for music. Italy not only has sought to make him a life senator, but at one time there was a movement to name him the first president of the new Italian Republic. He quickly scotched that idea. The universities of America and of other lands repeatedly have offered to confer honorary degrees on him. He accepted only once—in 1930, when Georgetown University honored him—and he must have been in a singularly agreeable mood in that period. When the question of other honorary doctorates has been posed, he has replied, "I'm no doctor. I can't operate."

He speaks with modesty and humility of his work as a musician. A friend phoned him after a concert out of town some months ago and asked how it had gone. "They say it was good," he replied. "The old man is doing the best he can." His daughter Wanda was a guest on a television program and was shown several kinescope shots of her father conducting and was asked to identify the music in each sequence just from his gestures and facial expression. One sequence stumped her, and she was urged, while she was on the air, to phone the maestro's house to ask him whether he could name the piece. He was watching the show on his television set and had seen the kinescope of himself conducting, and his answer was, "I don't know. I never watch myself conducting." He has never practiced in front of a mirror, as some other conductors are said to do, to perfect the most effective gestures. After his first telecast in 1948, he went backstage and asked his wife, who had been watching him on a television receiver in his dressing room, how she had liked it. Her surprising answer was, "You looked kind."

He may seem to want the opinion of others about his work and he may speak of himself with restraint, but he has a full awareness of his ability. Some of his friends say that he never reads criticisms, but I doubt that. I know he has read some. Once after a New York Philharmonic concert that someone else had conducted, he called the orchestra office to protest against two diametrically opposed reviews in the morning papers. "How can the public tell who's right?" he wanted to know. On another occasion he launched into a tirade against a critic who had disagreed with his tempos in a Schubert symphony. Obviously he reads some criticisms, just as he is acquainted with other written comments about himself.

I heard him say one day that there was one description of himself that pleased him most. He was talking of conductors and mentioned an article on conducting by Benjamin Grosbayne in the *International Cyclopedia of Music and Musicians*. The article briefly sums up the history of the art of conducting and mentions some of the outstanding conductors of the nineteenth century and of our own time. Of Toscanini it says that he "stands alone in a special niche both as man and as interpreter."

That accords with Toscanini's estimate of himself. He does not like to be compared with other conductors. He resents being described as greater than X, Y, or Z, or the greatest of all from A to Z. He wants to be considered as a man and musician apart.

Who can say that his judgment is inflated or erroneous? The consensus of informed opinion has been that he belongs in a class by himself. He is no genius, as he has been the first to insist; only the enduring creative figures deserve that appellation. Toscanini's merit is that he has served music, over the years, on a consistently lofty level.

If he has not created masterpieces himself, he has seen to it that the masterworks of others have been quickened into radiant life. He has illuminated whatever he has touched. The familiar has become new, and the new has become familiar and intimate. He has stripped away the dross and restored the freshness and magic of pieces that have fallen into the rut of routine. There has been no routine for him, no satisfaction with performances that have been good enough. He has rarely, if ever, been complacent that he has said the last word with a composition. After an incandescent perform-

ance, he once said to his men, "Not bad. We will try to do
better the next time." Once, following a noble traversal of
Beethoven's Ninth, he observed wearily, "That is the best I
can do." But in his heart he did not mean it; the next time
he did the Ninth he tried to do better. He would not agree to
recording this symphony because he did not feel he could do
justice to it.

Toscanini has never ceased to be ardent about his work as
a musician. He has approached the preparation of each performance as if it were a new trial of strength and a new
voyage of discovery. Music has been an ever-renewing adventure for him, and the excitement of the quest has inevitably
been communicated to his colleagues and to his listeners. In
his eighties he is still trying to learn and improve his understanding, and because of this drive he is younger than men
half his age. He has begged close friends to be sure to let
him know when he turns senile in his music. Before that
moment comes, he wants to quit. He is conscious that each
added day of activity is a precious gift to be prized and turned
to advantage. He says to his orchestra, "This may be the last
time we'll do this piece together; let's make it good," and an
icy hand is laid on the hearts of those men who venerate him.
But he is not dramatic about it. He has lived richly and looks
ahead calmly.

Toscanini's overwhelming contribution as a musician has
been that he has set standards for all other musicians to aim
at. He has accustomed audiences all over the world to hearing
performances that have been clear and pure, honest and passionate. Some of his most devoted admirers feel that he has
spoiled them for listening to other conductors, but most people are grateful that they have had the privilege of hearing
his evocations of the great musical voices of the Western
world.

Fortunately, the techniques of recording have been vastly

improved in the last two decades of Toscanini's career. While the tyranny of the recording studio has been a martyrdom to the maestro and while the recording engineers may not be able to imprison on their tapes and disks the last nuance of his conceptions, enough has come through to provide a true gauge of the maestro's distinctiveness. The tempos, the rhythmic verve, the clarity of texture are nearly all there. The only regret one may have is that all the great music Toscanini has performed in his lifetime of conducting has not been captured in permanent form. But there is enough for people who cannot hear him in the concert hall and opera house to get a just idea of his achievement. There is enough by which new generations of musicians and listeners may test the claims for Toscanini's ascendancy.

Toscanini's stature as a musician derives from his character as a man, and as a man he has set a shining example to hearten other men. He has been rough on collaborators and harsh with contemporaries, but he has been like a living conscience. Uncorrupted and incorruptible, he has been untouched by fame and *réclame*. Before Toscanini's first appearance in London, the playful Bernard Shaw innocently asked an American friend of the conductor's: "Tell me something about this man Toscanini. Is he sober, honest, and industrious?" He has been all these things—and much more. He has been sober and, at the same time, perpetually drunk on the spirits that effervesce through music. He has been industrious and, at the same time, daring and imaginative. Best of all, he has been honest. He has known no compromise with his own standards, and his incorruptibility has flamed like a gem through all the years of his stewardship of the music of his beloved masters.

As a man and a musician, he has been all of a piece. His principles were fixed early in life, and he has seen no reason to alter them. He listened with a pleased smile one day as a friend described admiringly how his daughter Wanda had relaxed and become less introvert in recent years, and suddenly he cried out, "In eighty-three years I have never changed."

Because he has not changed, Toscanini has been difficult at times for his family, friends, colleagues, employers, and boards of directors. At the core he has been a good man—good for music and good for mankind.

Index

Index

D

Dacci, Giusto, 13

Damnation of Faust, The (Berlioz), 105

Damrosch, Walter, 131-2, 167

D'Annunzio, Gabriele, 149

"Danse Macabre" (Saint-Saëns), 69

Danton's Tod (von Einem), 290

Darclée, Ericlea, 86

Debora e Jaele (Pizzetti), 155

Debussy, Claude, 108, 109, 151, 163, 197, 204, 237, 249, 258, 283, 284, 286, 291

Dejanice (Catalani), 32

Depanis, Giuseppe, 32, 34, 38

Destinn, Emmy, 121, 124

Didur, Adamo, 49, 122, 129

Dinorah (Meyerbeer), 104

Dippel, Andreas, 118

Divertimento (Mozart), 295

Dolan, James B., 250, 255

Dollfuss, Engelbert, 212

Don Carlos (Verdi), 61, 165

Donizetti, Gaetano, 71, 90, 171

Don Juan (Strauss), 269

Donne Curiose, Le (Wolf-Ferrari), 127

Don Pasquale (Donizetti), 129

Ducasse, Roger, 173

Dukas, Paul, 252

Dvořák, Antonín, 73

E

- Eames, Emma, 116, 121-2

Ebert, Carl, 223-4

Ebreo, L' (Apolloni), 78

Edmea (Catalani), 31, 32, 35, 39, 77

Einaudi, Luigi, 325

Elda (Catalani), 32

Eldy, Fanny, 108

Elgar, Sir Edward, 249

Elisir d'Amore, L' (Donizetti), 90-1, 94, 96

Elizabeth, Queen of England, 222

Emma Liona (Lozzi), 78

"Emperor" Concerto (Fifth Piano Concerto) (Beethoven), 199

"Enigma Variations" (Elgar), 223, 249

Ero e Leandro (Mancinelli), 78

"Eroica" (Beethoven), 177, 179, 240-1, 247, 253-4, 258, 260, 275

Eugene Onegin (Tchaikovsky), 87

Euryanthe (Weber), 99, 117, 130, 136

Overture, 162

F

Faccio, Franco, 31, 35, 44, 73, 80, 81

Falstaff (Verdi), 36, 58, 60, 61, 76, 78, 79, 82, 101, 123, 124, 136, 139, 145, 153, 154, 163, 164, 170-2, 198, 212-14, 238, 249, 285, 307, 324, 325

Farrar, Geraldine, 115, 122-3, 127, 131, 134, 299

Faust (Gounod), 17, 25, 29, 163

Faust (Wagner), 130

Overture, 130

Favorita, La (Donizetti), 29, 71, 77-8

Ferdinand, King of Bulgaria, 222

Fernandez, Oscar Lorenzo, 237

Ferrani, Cesira, 68

Fidelio (Beethoven), 165, 212-14, 238

Field, Marshall, 207

Fifth Symphony (Beethoven), 292, 320

Fifth Symphony (Tchaikovsky), 288

Figner, Nicola, 24, 31, 32

First Symphony (Beethoven), 73

First Symphony (Brahms), 73, 232, 255

First Symphony (Martucci), 187

First Symphony (Shostakovich), 185

Fischer, Franz von, 84

Flagler, Harry Harkness, 167

"Flirtations in a Chinese Garden" (Chasin), 186

335

ABOUT THE AUTHOR

As MUSIC EDITOR *of the New York* Times, *Mr. Taubman's work is probably as widely read and as influential as that of any music writer in the country. One of his recent assignments to receive particularly wide attention was the coverage of the transcontinental tour of the NBC Symphony during April and May of 1950. For his series of articles on this tour, he was awarded the 1950 prize of the Music Lovers League.*

It was during this tour that Mr. Taubman had the opportunity of bringing into focus the many years' research he had put in preparing to write the present book. His daily contacts and long talks with Arturo Toscanini enabled him to ask questions on every phase of the conductor's life and to note the very revealing answers.

Mr. Taubman's work has appeared in innumerable publications, such as the Saturday Evening Post, Collier's, *the* Atlantic Monthly, Reader's Digest, *and others; and he has also written three books on musical topics:* Opera Front and Back, Music as a Profession, *and* Music on My Beat. *In addition, he was the editor of* Memories of Opera, *by Giulio Gatti-Casazza, and of* The Roosevelt I Knew *by Frances Perkins.*

He lives in New York with Mrs. Taubman and their two sons.